*A second collection of articles from Extensions,
the Newsletter of the High/Scope Curriculum*

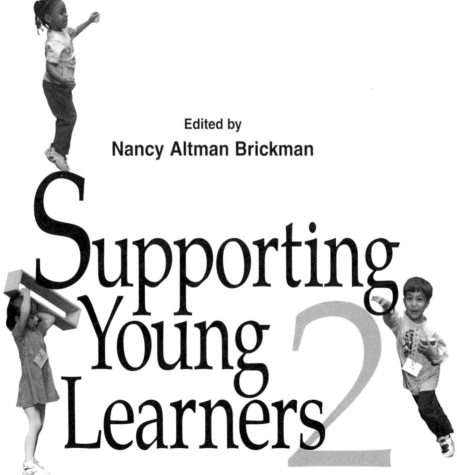

**Edited by
Nancy Altman Brickman**

Supporting Young Learners 2

IDEAS FOR CHILD CARE PROVIDERS AND TEACHERS

**High/Scope® Press
Ypsilanti, Michigan**

PUBLISHED BY

HIGH/SCOPE® PRESS
A division of the
HIGH/SCOPE EDUCATIONAL RESEARCH FOUNDATION
600 NORTH RIVER STREET
YPSILANTI, MICHIGAN 48198-2898
313/485-2000, FAX 313/485-0704

Editors: Marge Senninger, Lynn Taylor
Cover Design: Linda Eckel
Text Design: Linda Eckel, Lynn Taylor
Photography: Gregory Fox

Library of Congress Cataloging-in-Publication Data

Supporting young learners 2 : ideas for child care providers and
    teachers / edited by Nancy Altman Brickman.
        p.   cm.
    "A second collection of articles from Extensions, the newsletter
of the High/Scope curriculum."
    Includes bibliographical references and index.
    ISBN 1-57379-006-0
    1. Education, Preschool—Activity programs—United States. 2. Day
care centers—Activity programs—United States. 3. Active learning—
United States. 4. Children and adults—United States.
I. Brickman, Nancy Altman. II. Extensions (Ypsilanti, Mich.)
LB1140.35.C74S875 1996
372.21'0973—dc20   96-18555
                                                                CIP

Printed in the United States of America

10 9 8 7 6 5 4 3

Contents

Preface

The articles presented in *Supporting Young Learners 2* originally appeared in various issues of *Extensions: The Newsletter of the High/Scope Curriculum.* This book is High/Scope's second compilation of *Extensions* articles; the first, *Supporting Young Learners,* was published in 1991 and included articles appearing in *Extensions* from fall 1986 through spring 1991. The selections in this new collection span the period from summer 1991 through spring 1996.

Extensions is designed primarily as a professional development tool for early childhood program staff who are interested in the High/Scope Curriculum. The newsletter contains articles of interest to teachers, aides, staff of home or center-based child care programs, special educators, administrators, trainers, and curriculum specialists.

The High/Scope approach to early childhood education was originally developed in the 1960s by High/Scope President David P. Weikart and his colleagues, who at the time were working in the Ypsilanti Public School District in Michigan. Since 1970 the development of this approach has continued under the auspices of the High/Scope Educational Research Foundation, founded by Weikart.

While the preschool level (ages 2½ to 5 years) is the primary focus of *Extensions,* we have gradually added articles on working with infants and toddlers, since many programs serving preschoolers are now also serving this younger age group. *Extensions* also occasionally includes material aimed at early elementary school teachers.

The approach to early childhood education and care that is presented in the newsletter is continuously evolving. In recent years, High/Scope staff and field consultants have developed new strategies and practices in such areas as arts education, adult-child interaction, conflict resolution, and infant/toddler care. A major purpose of *Extensions,* which is published six times yearly, is to keep readers informed of such new developments. Because this evolutionary process continues even after the publication of new material in *Extensions,* the articles in this collection have been edited to reflect the latest developments in the approach.

As a collection of brief articles from an eight-page newsletter, this volume does not claim to present an in-depth picture of the High/Scope educational approach. For a more comprehensive treatment of preschool curriculum issues, we refer the reader to the High/Scope preschool manual *Educating Young Children: Active Learning Practices for Preschool and Child Care Programs* by Mary Hohmann and David P. Weikart and to other

High/Scope Press publications that are listed in the Appendix. In addition, for those with an interest in implementing High/Scope practices in their early childhood programs, High/Scope offers a range of training opportunities. High/Scope training and consulting take place at Foundation headquarters and at sites throughout the United States and overseas.

We would like to thank all those who have contributed over the years to the *Extensions* newsletter and the publication of this book. In addition to writing their own articles for *Extensions,* the authors—many of whom are past and present members of High/Scope's Program Division—have also been helpful in reviewing the content of the newsletter and have made many useful suggestions for improving it. High/Scope President David Weikart has also found time to carefully review each issue of *Extensions.* In addition, we appreciate the contributions of High/Scope practitioners from throughout the United States and overseas, including teachers, child care providers, field consultants, teacher-trainers, and administrators. These individuals have written articles for the newsletter or have suggested many of the ideas and strategies reported in it. Finally, we would like to acknowledge the efforts of Lynn Spencer Taylor and Marge Senninger, who helped to edit the newsletter and this collection, as well as those of our editorial assistant, Diana Knepp, who formatted each issue of the newsletter for the printer and helped to prepare the manuscript of this book for typesetting.

Supporting
Young
Learners
2

Chapter One

Adult-Child Interaction
· ·

*I*n the High/Scope approach, adults are committed to a "partnership" philosophy in their interactions with children. This philosophy guides adults as they converse with children, participate in their play, and assist them when they are frustrated or involved in a dispute. Instead of acting as supervisors or managers, High/Scope teachers and caregivers offer themselves as trustworthy companions. As children work and play, adults are readily available, offering assistance, support, and friendship as needed, but primarily enabling the children themselves to be the leaders in play and conversation.

High/Scope teacher-trainers have discovered that this partnership role is perhaps the most difficult curriculum component for teachers to master. In fact, to adopt this interaction style, adults must carefully analyze the ways in which they interact with children. In doing so, they are often surprised to discover that they frequently "talk at" rather than listen to children, that they tend to manage children's activities rather than participate in them, and that they frequently "take over" when children are upset or involved in a dispute with peers.

A systematic training process is often the best way for adults to change such behaviors, but the articles in this chapter can also be used to assist in this process. Each chapter defines specific, concrete steps teachers can take to make their interactions with children more supportive and more effective in promoting children's active construction of knowledge.

In the first article, "Let Them Speak! Conversing With Children," Mary Hohmann deals with a fundamental topic—how to carry on a conversation with a preschool child. Hohmann begins by describing how adults can look for natural opportunities for productive child-adult conversations. She illustrates types of conversation that are likely to arise during four typical kinds of preschool play: exploratory play, constructive play, pretend play, and games. Hohmann also provides specific strategies for opening a dialogue with children. In the rest of the article, and in the companion piece "Sharing Conversational Control," she defines the kinds of nondemanding adult comments and acknowledgments that make conversations with children flower, and she points out controlling conversational techniques that can dampen and limit an adult-child conversation.

The next selection, "In Praise of Praising Less" by Mark Tompkins, also focuses on the language adults use with children, specifically in relation to comments of praise, such as "Nice work," "Good job," or "I like the way Molly is sitting." Well-intentioned adults often assume that comments like these will help children feel good about themselves. However, Tompkins points out that such praise can actually undermine children's self-confidence and independence, making them anxious about their abilities, reluctant to take risks, and unsure of their ability to evaluate their own efforts. Instead of praising, Tompkins recommends, adults should acknowledge children's efforts and activities in other ways. Some of the strategies he suggests: encouraging children to describe and evaluate their own activities; making specific, nonjudgmental comments; and participating in children's self-chosen activities.

In the next selection, " 'Driving Master Brian': Supporting Children's Thinking," High/Scope President David Weikart describes his daily experiences driving his 3-year-old grandson, Brian, to the High/Scope Demonstration Preschool. Weikart illustrates how adults can use everyday situations to pose problems that stimulate a child's thinking. For example, during the 45-minute drive to preschool, he and Brian would often converse about the things they noticed along the way. Weikart describes how, through his casual comments, he was able to encourage Brian to notice and make predictions about a microwave transmission tower that was a regular landmark on the trip. The daily discussions about the state of the tower became an eagerly awaited game for Brian, who enjoyed guessing whether the beacon on the tower would be flashing. Brian also enjoyed offering various theories to explain his predictions. Weikart describes how Brian's abilities to make predictions, and then to verify them based on personal observations, were strengthened by these experiences. For Weikart, this game of predicting presented an opportunity to observe a preschooler's thinking processes and to look for ways to build on a child's spontaneous interest in the world around him.

"Conflict resolution" is a popular topic in education circles these days, as educators explore ways to reduce violence and promote constructive problem solving in our society. "Helping Children Resolve Disputes and Conflicts," by Betsy Evans, describes how children as young as 3 or 4 years of age can benefit from a systematic process of resolving disputes and conflicts. Evans explains how the conflict-resolution process is a natural outlet for the cognitive, social, and language abilities that children are developing in the preschool years. The conflict-resolution process that Evans recommends to High/Scope educators has been adapted from standard techniques presented in conflict-resolution literature. These techniques are used daily at the Giving Tree School in Gill, Massachusetts, which Evans directs, and her successful experiences with this process are the basis for training workshops she presents to High/Scope-oriented teachers. In keeping with High/Scope's emphasis on children solving problems as independently as possible, the six-step process outlined by Evans enables children to resolve their own conflicts with the assistance of adults trained to serve as mediators. In "Watch Your Language!" Evans presents language strategies adults can use to make the conflict-resolution process more effective.

Two more articles by Betsy Evans deal with the question of whether punishment is ever appropriate in dealing with children's conflicts and disruptive behavior. In "Punishment: What Does It Teach?" Evans explores why adults may have the urge to punish and what effect their punishment has on children's behavior. Having made a convincing case against its use, she then describes alternatives to punishment—prevention and interaction strategies that tie in with her earlier articles on conflict resolution. In "Language That Sets Limits," Evans recognizes that sometimes children and adults alike need ways to stop hurtful behavior **before** conflict resolution can take place. Evans suggests some ways that adults' limit-setting statements and "I" statements help to establish an atmosphere in which constructive problem solving can proceed.

Evans delves more deeply into conflict resolution and its relationship to aspects of preschoolers' development in the next article, "From Superheroes to Problem Solving." Evans looks at preschoolers' fascination with superhero play and explains how children express developmental needs for power and control by pretending to be superhero characters. She then explores how the process of conflict resolution can provide a more positive outlet for these same developmental needs, providing detailed examples of how this process can help children become more aware of both negative and positive ways to express power and gain a sense of control in difficult situations. Evans continues the superhero theme in the last article in this chapter, " 'Super-Strategies' for Superheroes," which provides suggestions for teachers and parents who wish to deal more effectively with the conflict and disruption that can result from superhero play in the preschool classroom and at home.

Let Them Speak!
Conversing With Children

By Mary Hohmann

. . . .

The more children put their own thoughts and experiences into words, the more involved they become in thinking about and interpreting their world. That's why *conversing with young children* is one of the most important things adults do as they work with and care for them. When adults are adept at recognizing and building on conversational opportunities, adult-child conversations will grow naturally out of children's work and play. Adults can use a variety of strategies to stimulate a dialogue in which children do most of the talking.

As a first step, it's important for adults to **look for natural opportunities for conversation.** The young child who is deeply involved in play may view as an intrusion an adult's attempt to strike up a conversation. Yet, during almost every kind of play, there are some moments when children pause or comment on what they are doing, thus creating an opening for conversation. Adults should watch and listen for these natural breaks in play. Children who are in transition—

Seizing the moment, this adult joins in a spirited discussion during work time.

who have completed what they were working on, who are changing their plans, or who are pausing in the midst of an activity—may welcome the chance to talk with an adult. At transition times like these, talking freely with an adult can help children to review what they have done or to clarify what they intend to do next.

Another key strategy for adults is to **consider the type of play in which children are engaged.** Here are some common types of play and some of the conversational opportunities they often offer:

Adults who position themselves at the children's physical level are likely to be invited to join an ongoing discussion. This adult has joined children who are lying on the floor and has become a member of the group.

• **Exploratory play.** Exploratory play, in which children explore the functions and properties of materials and tools, is a relatively simple kind of play that doesn't always lend itself to *play-related* conversation. If 3-year-old Kevin is cutting, pasting, swinging, or rolling clay with his hands, he may or may not feel the need to explain or comment on what he is doing. However, because of its repetitive quality, exploratory play frequently offers a relaxed occasion for the child to initiate a conversation about a topic of personal interest, such as a new pet or a recent visit with Grandma. The teacher who is pushing a child on a swing or rolling clay next to a child who is also rolling clay often receives a spontaneous update on the latest events in the child's life.

• **Constructive play.** In constructive play, the child makes or builds something. In contrast to exploratory play, this more goal-oriented play usually presents an opportunity for talk that is *related to the activity*. During constructive play, children may pause to take a look at what they have done, to consider how to solve a problem, or to simply seek acknowledgment of what they've done so far. A brief conversation with an adult can be helpful at these times. However, it's important for adults who want to converse with children during constructive play to *wait for the child to pause*—if the child is wholly engrossed in making something, an adult's comments may simply be disruptive.

- **Pretend play.** Role play, or pretending, usually stimulates role-related conversation among children. An adult who takes part in the pretend play—by assuming a role related to the ongoing play or taking on a role assigned by the players—will naturally be included in these conversations.

- **Games.** Playing games (including action games like tag, or quiet games like card games or board games) is another common kind of play for young children. Such games often involve verbal negotiations over how to proceed and what to do next, and these are natural conversational opportunities.

Once you become aware of conversational opportunities, you can make the most of them by using the following strategies:

- **Join children at their level.** At its best, conversation is a personal exchange between trusting people. For such conversations to occur, you'll need to *position yourself at the child's physical level.* This may mean squatting, kneeling, sitting, and occasionally even lying on the floor. This way, children are not "looking up" to you, and you are not "looking down" on them.

- **Wait for children to open a conversation, and respond to their conversational leads.** After you have joined children silently and positioned yourself at their level, you can *make yourself available for conversation by remaining attentive and listening patiently and with interest* to any ongoing talk among them. When adults take this approach, children are apt to address them directly or invite them into an ongoing discussion. For example, an adult noticed that 5-year-old Tina had paused and was studying the collage she had made. The adult approached her, squatted down, and looked at the collage. Tina then made the first move, saying "This is for my mom." The adult responded with "Oh, something for your mom," and a conversation ensued.

Note how the adult in the following example lets the child set the agenda for conversation by using many statements of acknowledgment and few questions. Though the adult does open the conversation by asking a question, it is directly related to interests the child is expressing through his actions:

(Max is watching the fish in a tank. The adult squats down next to Max and watches for a while. Then Max points to one fish.)
Adult: *What's that fish doing?*
Max: *He's waiting for his daddy.*
Adult: *Oh, he's waiting.*

Sharing Conversational Control

A fascinating study of early childhood education programs in Britain yields insights on how adults can encourage (or discourage) lively conversation with children. The study is reported in *Working With Under Fives* (Wood, McMahon, & Cranstoun, 1980).

In the study, researchers conducted extensive observations of 24 nursery school teachers and playgroup leaders, and the children in their care. They also had the practitioners themselves tape-record over 1,500 minutes of their conversations and interactions with children.

As they observed the adults at work and analyzed recordings of adult-child conversations, the researchers concluded that adults varied widely in their conversational styles. Not surprisingly, they found that some styles were much more effective than others in eliciting a rich dialogue with children: "Some adults manage to get children asking a relatively large number of questions, encourage them to elaborate freely in their responses to their questions, and, in general, prompt them to play active, productive roles in dialogue. Others are much more likely to receive only monosyllabic, terse, and somewhat reluctant offerings from children, despite a similar investment of time, effort, and dedication. Why?" (pp. 52–53).

The researchers answered their own question by exploring the issue of who was in control in adult/child conversational exchanges. To analyze the conversations transcribed, they devised the following framework:

- Speaker retains control.

    1. *Enforced repetition* ("Say 'Night, night' to baby." "Say please.")

    2. *Closed question* ("Is your baby crying?" "How old are you?")

    3. *Open question* ("What are you doing with your baby?" "What can you tell me about your picture?")

- Speaker passes control to listener.

    4. *Contribution* ("I used to take my baby to the park." "I'm making a tower, too.")

Max: *See that big one down there? He's the daddy, and he's waitin' for him so they can go around together.*
Adult: *I see.*
Max: *They both have those tails like that. Pointy. That's how you know.*
Adult: *Oh, the pointy tails mean they go together.*
Max: *Yeah, that means they're the boy and the daddy. Once I got lost.*
Adult: *Oh, dear!*
Max: *I couldn't find my daddy. He finded me.*
Adult: *He didn't want to lose you.*
Max: (Pointing to fish.) *Now they're together.*
Adult: *Like you and your daddy.*
Max: *Uh-huh. There they go.*

• **Use comments or observations as conversational openers.**
Though waiting for the child to open a conversation is often the most

5. *Acknowledgment* ("I see." "Uh-huh." "Oh, you're going shopping with your baby.")

In the researchers' framework, each conversational turn is classified on a scale of 1–5, according to the degree of control the speaker retains over the next conversational move. In conversational moves 1–3, the speaker retains control of the conversation. In moves 4–5, the speaker offers control to the listener.

When the researchers used this coding system to conduct an analysis of the transcribed conversations, they found that when adults used conversational moves 4 and 5, they were far more effective at stimulating discussion with children than when they used moves 1, 2, and 3. When adults used moves 4 and 5, children often responded by making contributions or asking questions of their own; this often led to further discussion and elaboration by the child. When adults used moves 1, 2, and 3, however, children tended to respond dutifully but briefly—then the conversations usually died.

Thus, as the researchers concluded, adult conversational strategies have a strong impact on the quantity and quality of child language: "The various styles of conversation that adults bring into the classroom and playgroup exert a tremendous influence upon the children's part in and contribution to talk, and, indeed, represent one of the main factors which determine how well a child plays his part as a conversationalist" (p. 52).

The key lesson of this study for early childhood educators is clear: To encourage animated conversation with children, adults should avoid asking children frequent questions. Instead, they should use their turn in a conversation to make statements of acknowledgment or personal contributions.

REFERENCE

Wood, D., McMahon, L., & Cranstoun, Y. (1980). *Working with under fives* (Vol. 5, Oxford Preschool Research Project series). Ypsilanti, MI: High/Scope Press.

effective strategy, it's sometimes appropriate for the adult to make the first conversational move. To invite a child to talk with you, *begin with a comment or an observation, rather than a question.* This gives the child control over his or her response and consequently over the direction of the conversation. Note how the adult uses nondemanding comments as conversational openers in the following two examples:

(Emma, a preschooler, brushes the coat of a fluffy stuffed dog.)
Adult: *My dog, Stanley, likes to have his coat brushed.*
Emma: *So does my doggy. He hates baths . . .*

(Tyson, a 4-year-old, is standing at the workbench with a car he has made.)
Adult: *You made a very long car, Tyson.*

Making a comment rather than asking a question can mean the difference between encouraging a child to expand on his play or bringing the play to a premature conclusion.

Tyson: *I got this long piece and this other piece on top.*
Adult: *Yes.*
Tyson: *These are the wheels. . .*

• **Converse as a partner with children.** Once you have been invited into a dialogue with children, it's important to resist taking control of the conversation. Look for opportunities to *give conversational control to the child.* You can do this by staying with the topic the child raises and making personal contributions ("I've made a snake, too") or statements of acknowledgment ("Oh," "Uh-huh," "I see"). These kinds of comments and statements allow the conversation to continue but do not pressure the child for a response. Once you've made a comment, it's also important to *wait patiently for the child to respond before taking another conversational turn*—young children need lots of time to choose their words.

As the previously discussed conversation with Tina continues, note how the adult uses these strategies to encourage Tina to describe her plans and activities:

Tina: (speaking of the collage she's making for her mom)
It's . . . it's not done.
Adult: *Oh.*

Tina: *I'm gonna put some of that twisty stuff on right here and those things he's got.*

Adult: *You mean the acorn tops like Ryan's using?*

Tina: *Yeah! Acorn tops. We picked 'em up, didn't we?*

Adult: *Yes. We found the acorn tops on our walk.*

Tina: *An' Linda found that stick, and you jumped over it!*

Adult: *YOU did, too!*

Tina: *Yep!* (Pauses.) *I'm gonna put a stick on and those tops. A lot!* (Turns back to her work.)

Adult: *I'll come back to see what it looks like with the twisty stuff and the stick and the acorn tops.* (Moves toward another child.)

• **Ask questions sparingly and responsively**. Too many adult questions can dampen a conversation with a young child by keeping the adult in control of the conversation and forcing the child to respond to the adult's agenda. However, *the right kind of adult questions—those that are responsive to children's*

Are Questions <u>Ever</u> Okay?

I know that asking closed questions—those with only one answer—does not promote conversation with young children, because their possible responses are so limited. But I did think that open-ended questions—questions that can be answered in any number of ways—helped children to formulate and discuss their own ideas. Now you seem to be saying that I shouldn't ask questions at all. I'm puzzled. If I'm not asking questions, how am I teaching children to think?
— *A preschool teacher*

We have always supported using open questions ("What do you think made the tower fall down?") rather than closed questions ("How many blocks does the tower have?"). Open-ended questions encourage children to speculate about things and explain them in their own words without worrying about being right or wrong.

At the same time, we also understand, through observation and research on adult-child conversations, that children are more apt to talk, more likely to think out loud, more ready to wonder about things and answer their own questions, when they have control over the content and direction of their conversations with adults. By making noncontrolling conversational moves (comments, observations, and acknowledgments) instead of asking questions of any kind, adults give children more control and pressure them less. Therefore, we encourage adults to *use questions sparingly with children.*

This doesn't mean you should give up on questioning children altogether, although you may want to do so for several days, just to find out for yourself how using fewer questions can influence the amount and quality of children's language.

play interests—can sometimes stimulate a rich dialogue, if they are used sparingly. Questions that discourage conversation tend to be questions about facts the questioner already knows (What color is that? Which board is longer? Is that a house?), or questions unrelated to the situation at hand (Child is coloring. Adult asks, "How's your new baby brother?"). On the other hand, when questions are asked out of genuine curiosity and relate directly to what the child is doing, they may stimulate discussion.

Among the best kinds of questions are those that encourage children to describe their thinking (for example, How can you tell? How do you know that? What do you think made that happen? How did you get [the ball] to . . . ? What do you think would happen if . . . ?). When a question grows out of the immediate situation, it is an aid rather than a hindrance to the flow of conversation. For example, in the previously discussed conversation with Max, the adult opens the conversation by asking about the fish the child is pointing to. As the conversation continues, the adult asks another question that grows out of the conversation:

Max: *That fish only gots one eye.*

Adult: *How can you tell?*

Max: *'Cause look. That's all you can see.*

Adult: *I see. You can see only one eye.*

Max: *Yeah, one eye right on the side up by his nose.*

Asking the question "How can you tell?" in response to the child's observation that the fish has one eye invites the child to describe his thinking. Only he has the answer to this question, so it's a question well worth asking. Furthermore, in the process of answering the question, the child has the opportunity to consolidate what he knows and how he knows it.

In active learning classrooms, each child's voice can and should be heard. Taking advantage of natural conversational openings, offering personal comments and acknowledgments, and asking questions sparingly are ways adults can help children reflect on what they are doing *in their own words.*

In Praise of
Praising Less

By Mark Tompkins

• •

"I like the way Molly is sitting . . . I can tell she is ready for circle time!"

୬

"Oh, Joseph, what a beautiful painting you've made today!"

୬

"Good job, Darren; you're really getting it!"

Do you frequently make comments to children like "Good job," "Way to go," "Nice work," "Beautiful," or "I like the way Molly is sitting . . ."? If so, you are like most adults who work with young children. Most of us have probably made statements like these for years. We may have even received training in how to praise children.

Many adults praise liberally because they believe this is an effective way to help children feel good about themselves and their work. Praise is also thought of as a management tool—a way to get children "settled" or ready to start an activity, as in the above example of Molly.

The Drawbacks of Praise

Despite the widespread use and acceptance of praise in early childhood settings, researchers and early childhood practitioners have identified many drawbacks to praising children. In her review of the literature on praise, Kamii (1984) concluded that praise leads to dependence on adults because it encourages children to rely on authority figures to solve problems for them and to evaluate what is right, wrong, good, or bad. In another literature review, Chandler (1981) stated that praise can discourage children's efforts, have a negative effect on self-image, and place students on the defensive. As Hitz and Driscoll (1988) stated in paraphrasing the conclusions of Ginott (1972), "Praise is not conducive to self-reliance, self-direction, or self-control. If the authority figure, in this case the teachers, can judge positively, they can also judge negatively. To judge at all implies

Watching intently, listening quietly, joining children's play when appropriate, and responding to children's statements by offering a supportive comment or suggestion are often more meaningful to children than words of praise.

superiority and takes away from the children's power to judge their own work" (p. 8).

Praise, well-intentioned as it might be, has thus been shown through research and practice to invite comparison and competition and to increase the child's dependence on adults. Too much praise can make children anxious about their abilities, reluctant to take risks and try new things, and unsure of how to evaluate their own efforts.

Reconsidering the Use of Praise

All of these drawbacks have led adults working with young children to begin to reconsider their use of praise. Learning to use praise less often is easier if the alternatives to praise are clear. Following are several examples of typical situations in which adults use praise inappropriately in early childhood programs. For each example, we present one or more alternative ways to handle the situation by observing children carefully and intervening without praise:

• *It's cleanup time, and Mr. A. notices that Alison is putting away most of the pine cones she has been hauling around in a truck. Mr. A. says, "Good job, Alison, I really like the way you're putting those pine cones away."*

In this case, the child is already engrossed in an activity in which she is successful, and the adult's ill-timed comment not only interrupts her but also may make her feel defensive. Alison may wonder whether she really is doing a "good job," and she may become more inclined to seek such adult approval for her efforts in the future. As an alternative, Mr. A. could decide not to intervene at all with Alison, reasoning that her experience of putting away her own play materials independently is beneficial in itself. Or, Mr. A. might support Alison by working alongside her and helping her put away the pine cones.

• *It's time to start circle time. Mrs. F. says, "I'm looking for good listeners . . . Ah, I see Molly is ready. She's listening."*

Praising one child to get others to conform, as Mrs. F. does here, can be damaging, because children usually resent being manipulated in this way. In addition, the implied comparison between Molly and the other children can encourage all the children to feel competitive. Instead of making a big effort to get all children completely quiet before a song, fingerplay, or other group activity, Mrs. F. could *just start the activity*. By starting right in, she would quickly and effectively redirect children's attention to the task at hand.

Sometimes it's best to leave children alone as they play. Engrossed in their work, they may resent unnecessary intrusions, or even words of encouragement. By observing children's play carefully, we can identify these occasions and keep our distance.

• *Mrs. T. is working with several children in the art area. Ben has made an elaborate picture by gluing many strips of colored paper onto a big sheet of construction paper. Mrs. T. says, "Why, Ben, that's terrific. How many strips did you use on your picture?" Ben looks puzzled and does not reply.*

Mrs. T.'s vague praise is not specific enough to be meaningful to Ben and also invites other nearby children to compete for her praise. In addition, in asking a closed-ended "how many" question, she is quizzing Ben rather than conversing with him. Ben feels "put on the spot," and the possibility of conversation is canceled.

As an alternative, Mrs. T. could sit next to Ben and make her own similar picture out of paper strips. Since they would both be using similar materials in similar ways, they would naturally have much to talk about. Mrs. T. could ask Ben how he did something, or she could make a comment about how the pictures she and Ben made were alike or different. The process is always more important than the product, and these conversational strategies would encourage Ben to talk about the processes he is using.

Three Alternatives to Praise

The examples just presented illustrate the positive outcomes that are produced by praising children less and supporting them in other, more appropriate ways. To assist adults further, we have identified three specific strategies from the High/Scope Curriculum that can be used as alternatives to praise: **participating in children's play, encouraging children to describe their efforts and products,** and **acknowledging children's work or ideas by making specific comments.**

This adults listens attentively as a young painter talks about his work.

When using these strategies, adults working with infants, toddlers, preschoolers, elementary-aged students, and children with special needs discover that they can rely much less on praise. By creating an environment in which children can make mistakes and learn from them without being evaluated or judged, these adults are helping children learn how to value themselves and their work and to be self-reliant.

Participating in children's play. If adults want to reduce their use of praise, making a greater effort to get involved in what children are doing is a good place to start. Consider this recent example from the High/Scope Demonstration Preschool: Becki, one of the teachers, noticed that Alison, Graham, and Chelsea were "making pizzas" in the block area. As a way of entering their play, Becki went to the house area and called the pizza store on the telephone, asking if she could have a pizza delivered to her. This led to many other children calling the pizza store and asking for pizza. Becki soon found herself in the pizza store, pretending to take orders and help with pizza-making while some of the other children delivered them. The next day, the teachers built on the children's interest in pizza by having the children make mini-pizzas out of English muffins, cheese, and different toppings at snack time.

Clearly, Becki's actions greatly enhanced the play experiences of Alison, Graham, and Chelsea. However, another adult might have handled the same situation less effectively, by using praise to convey her interest in the children's activities. Noticing the pizza-making play, this hypothetical adult might have commented on how "nice" or "terrific" the pizza was.

Compared to Becki's direct involvement in the children's activities, using praise in this way would have been, at best, a weak gesture of support. Instead, Becki told children *by her actions* that what they were doing was valued and accepted. She was responding to their interests and abilities in the most direct way possible. Becki's active involvement in the children's play conveyed to the children a message more powerful, con-crete, and meaningful than any number of praise statements she could have made. In addition, by taking part in their game, Becki not only showed children that she valued their activities but also encouraged them to expand on and develop the pizza-making theme. This opened up many possibilities for further learning—opportunities to use developing abilities in representation, number, language, and beginning literacy. Becki's involvement in the activity was a catalyst for children as they continued to build on their interests.

Encouraging children to describe their efforts and products. In one of the opening examples, a teacher tells Joseph his painting is "beautiful." There are several potential problems with the teacher's statement. First, what does *beautiful* mean to Joseph? For many children, words like *beautiful, terrific, good, super,* are not specific enough to be meaningful. A second issue is that this statement, however positive, is still an adult judgment that sets the teacher up as an authority. And what about the child on the other side of the easel from Joseph, who is also painting a picture? Prais-ing Joseph could lead the other child to seek the same kind of praise. In this case, the teacher's well-intentioned comment results in children comparing their efforts and competing with one another, and it puts the teacher in the position of judging and comparing their efforts.

The alternative is to encourage Joseph himself to describe what he is doing, how he is doing it, and anything else he finds important. A good way to elicit such comments is for the adult to **ask an open-ended question:** "Would you like to tell me about your painting?" Joseph might then answer, "It's a green bowl with lots of soup in it, and I worked on the painting real hard." Once the child has begun the process of discussing the painting, the adult can extend the conversation in various ways. For example, she might repeat in general terms what Joseph has said, to show him that she is listening carefully: "So you made a green bowl with lots of soup in it . . ."

With these kinds of open-ended questions and comments, the adult initiates a dialogue in which Joseph is the expert on his own work. Encouraging children to describe their activities stimulates the process of reflective thinking that is central to the High/Scope approach. When sensitively used, open-ended questions can help children contemplate and describe what they've made and done. Children recall the high and low points of their experiences and the problems encountered and solved. They become more aware of their own thinking and problem solving and more able to appreciate and evaluate their own experiences and achievements.

Acknowledging children's work or ideas by making specific comments. We have just discussed ways to encourage the children themselves to talk about their activities as an alternative to adult praise or evaluation. Often, though, the adult finds it appropriate to make a direct comment on

Stickers—The Right Stuff?

I'm in the habit of passing out stickers to all my children as they leave the classroom at the end of the day. They're meant to be a reward for their "good day at school." This seems to be a positive motivational tool—the children like getting stickers, and their parents have come to expect them. Should I be doing this, and if not, what are the alternatives?
—*A kindergarten teacher*

Passing out small rewards at the end of the day is a common practice in preschool and early elementary programs, especially in special education. In programs like yours, all children get stickers; in others, only those who had a "good day" get the reward.

However, we feel both practices are inappropriate—there are better ways to help children feel positive about their school experiences. When all children get stickers every day, the reward becomes meaningless—it bears no relationship to the varied experiences each child has had.

On the other hand, when stickers are handed out only to *some* children, the teacher is forced to judge children, and being judged in this way does not develop children's *self-esteem*. Self-esteem cannot be conferred by others and also doesn't come from having a sticker on one's hand. Self-esteem develops as children make choices, work successfully with others, and complete tasks they have set for themselves. These are experiences that grow from the child's *personal* initiatives, not from adult judgments.

As an alternative to passing out rewards as children leave, we would suggest that you plan a brief recall experience for the end of the day. This would give children a chance to review and reflect on some of the many things they did—a more meaningful experience than getting a sticker.

Encouraging children to describe their own work stimulates the process of reflective thinking that is central to the High/Scope educational approach. Here, preschooler Frances is explaining her block structure to an adult who has commented, "Frances, you've been working hard to put all these blocks together!"

a child's work, either because it fits into an ongoing conversation or because the child seems to be asking for an acknowledgment of her efforts. In these cases, we recommend that instead of subjective comments like "Beautiful," "Nice work," and "Good job," adults **make a *specific* reference to the details of the child's product or the process the child has used**. For example, instead of "How pretty," you might say, "On the top of your paper you have blue stripes, and on the bottom you have red stripes." Instead of "Good job," you could say, "That is the first time I've seen you put that puzzle together, Donnie. You worked on it for a long time." Such specific comments have the added advantage of being conversation-starters. Praise statements, on the other hand, often dampen conversation. A statement like "Good work, Lisa!" can communicate the message that the conversation is ended and the child is dismissed.

In this article, we've recommended that most adults who work with children should use evaluative phrases like "Beautiful," "Good job," and "Nice work" sparingly. If you decide to join those early childhood staff who are trying to curtail their use of praise, bear in mind that it will take

To Learn More About Praise . . .

Curry, N., & Johnson, C. (1990). *Beyond self esteem: Developing a genuine sense of human value.* Washington, DC: National Association for the Education of Young Children.

Chandler, T. A. (1981). *What's wrong with success and praise? Arithmetic Teacher,* 29(4), 10–12.

Dreikurs, R., & Greenwald, B. (1982). *Maintaining sanity in the classroom: Classroom management techniques.* New York: Harper & Row.

Hitz, R., & Driscoll, A. (1988, July). Praise or encouragement? New insights into praise: Implications for early childhood teachers. *Young Children,* pp. 6–14.

Kamii, C. (1984, April). Viewpoint: Obedience is not enough. *Young Children,* pp. 11–14.

Kohn, A. (1993). *Punished by rewards: The trouble with gold stars, incentive plans, A's, praise, and other bribes.* Boston: Houghton Mifflin.

Lepper, M. R. (1973). Undermining children's intrinsic interest with extrinsic reward. *Journal of Personality and Social Psychology,* 28(1), 129–137.

Martin, D. L. (1977). Your praise can smother learning. *Learning,* 5(6), 43–51.

Potter, E. F. (1985). "Good job!" How we evaluate children's work. *Childhood Education, 61,* 203–206.

Wood, D., McMahon, L., & Cranstoun, Y. (1980). *Working with under fives* (Vol. 5, Oxford Preschool Research Project series). Ypsilanti, MI: High/Scope Press.

some practice to effectively apply the alternatives to praise. However, you'll soon see the results of your efforts—children who are more independent, self-confident, and cooperative.

"Driving Master Brian": Supporting Children's Thinking

By David P. Weikart

• •

In this personal account of recent experiences with his 3-year-old grandson, High/Scope President David Weikart considers an important and challenging issue for those using the High/Scope approach: How can an adult pose problems that stimulate a child's thinking?

Around 7:45 each weekday morning, I stop by my daughter's house to pick up my grandson Brian for our daily drive to the High/Scope Demonstration Preschool. If you've never experienced a daily 45-minute drive with a 3-year-old, you can't imagine the pleasure this can bring. So many things to discuss—"I went with my dad to Big Wheel and we got some new baskets for my room"; to observe—"Hey Pa, the horses are still out in the yard in the cold. See the steam [their breath]?"; and *to wonder about*. It's this last topic that I want to discuss here.

About 10 minutes into our ride, we pass a microwave transmission tower, a rather small one, with only two satellite dishes and a single blinking beacon on top of the 100-foot structure. The beacon on top of the tower appears to be a warning signal for low-flying aircraft. The signal is operated by a light-sensitive control and comes on automatically. During the day, it's usually off, unless the sky is dark because of bad weather.

For the first few months of the school year, Brian didn't notice the tower, although it is fairly close to the road. One day, however, he started the drive talking about a discovery he had made. He and his mom had seen "flying pancakes" (the satellite dishes) the day before on the ride home, and he couldn't wait to show them to me.

It was a grey, rainy morning, and as we drew near the tower, Brian excitedly pointed out the flying pancakes to me. The red beacon at the top of the tower was blinking steadily. "I wonder why the light is on," I said casually to Brian.

Brian immediately informed me why the light was on: "It's a little bit sprinkling," which it was. During our drives over the next several weeks, we often found the signal operating. Whenever we noticed this, I would

"wonder" why the light was on. Each time, Brian would offer an explanation: "It's a little bit winter," or "There's snow on the ground," or, occasionally, "Because it's a little bit dark."

Brian's curiosity was sparked by these discussions, and we soon fell into a routine that became the high point of our daily trips. When I picked Brian up in the morning, I would usually say, "I wonder whether the light will be on today." Brian would then confidently predict that the light would be on or off because of some generally observable condition, such as "winter." On dark mornings he would predict that

Setting the stage for the child to think independently is one of the most important ways an adult—whether parent, grandparent, caregiver, or teacher—can help a child develop his intellectual capacity.

the light would be on because it was "dark." After a while, Brian began to initiate our discussion about the light as soon as I picked him up.

Each morning, as we rounded the bend to the tower, Brian would lean forward eagerly to see if his guess had been correct. When his prediction was right, he cried out in delight. When his prediction was wrong, he was disappointed. But whether or not he had predicted correctly, I would usually then ask him *why* he thought the light was on or off. Brian always had an explanation: "It's winter," or "It's raining," or sometimes, when his guess hadn't been right, "He's sleeping."

Brian's answers told me he did not yet understand that the degree of brightness outside determined whether or not the signal was operating. Then one morning in mid-January, Brian announced the light was off because it was "too light." After a pause, he added that it was "still a little bit winter." By February he had dropped the false part of this explanation, and he usually predicted the condition of the light accurately, based on the brightness of the morning.

Of course, aside from the fun and suspense this small mystery provided Brian, a larger educational purpose was being served. *Each day, Brian entertained a problem, predicted an outcome, held his prediction in mind, and verified his position based on his direct observations.* I never saw it as my role to suggest to Brian that his predictions, or his explanations for them, might be right or wrong. I left it up to Brian to draw conclusions. Based on whatever else he was observing—winter, snow, rain, and so forth—he extended various working theories to explain the beacon's operation. Gradually, this allowed him to make the connection between the light being on or off and the degree of brightness outside.

I knew that Brian realized something was causing the beacon to turn on or off. But within this basic logical framework, he felt free to invent whatever theory seemed appropriate at the time. It would have been easy to give him a "rule" that would predict the operation of the light and then to drill him on it each day. But then he would have been denied the chance to make his own observations, discoveries, and judgments. And I would have missed that excited, wondering cry, "Pa, it's on!" as we came around the bend.

Psychologists could propose many theories as to the exact nature of Brian's mental processes in these incidents. But I didn't need to know exactly what was going on with Brian to support him as he developed a greater understanding of the factors governing the light's operation. By the same token, it wasn't really important whether Brian could correctly grasp the rules behind the operation of the beacon. My main goal in this interaction was not to "teach" Brian how the beacon worked, but to support an *independent thinking process* that is essential to the success of any child. A secondary goal was to demonstrate to Brian that important adults in his life wonder about things and try to figure them out.

This brings me to a second interesting line of discussion that has been unfolding on our daily drives. Between the towns of Clinton and Saline there is a traditional Michigan farmhouse that is separated from its outbuildings by the highway. The barn is close to the road, and a slope leads away from the barnyard toward the highway. On the slope are five or six light-colored boulders that are large enough to be, well, pigs!

Passing the boulders one day, I said to Brian excitedly, "Hey, look at all those pigs! That big one has its snout way deep in the ground!"

Brian looked at the stones, frowned, looked at the stones again, and said, "Pa! Those aren't pigs! They're stones. The pigs are in the barn!"

Several weeks went by in which I couldn't resist pointing out the "stones-that-are-pigs" several more times. I was careful not to let my joke become a problem to my literal-minded grandson. Finally, one day around the same time that he solved the microwave tower mystery, Brian announced as we passed the boulders, "Hey Pa! There are *your* pigs! Mine are in the barn because it's cold!" At this pronouncement, I looked over at Brian. He was looking directly at me with a huge "gotcha" smile on his face!

At Brian's age, an adult's jokes may be hard to accept and harder yet to match. Things have to be clearly understood before they can be joked about. With the light on the microwave tower, Brian was wrestling with his observations, trying to reach an explanation for what he saw. In the case of the stone "pigs," a different situation was being presented: With my joke, I was, in a sense, asking him to *deny* what he saw. Eventually, he solved the dilemma this created for him by giving ownership of the false observation to me and by beginning to see the humor in this.

As adults using the High/Scope Curriculum in classrooms and centers, we are oriented to asking questions that don't call for a single correct answer. As with the beacon on the microwave tower, our questions often pose problems, leaving it up to the child to come up with an explanation and to verify it. In the example of the "pigs," the situation is different: The *adult* suggests the hypothesis, while the child is clearly in a position to verify it or uncover the error. In both these examples, though, the key issue is the same: *setting the stage for the child to think independently.* Whether or not the child reaches a conclusion that is objectively true really doesn't matter.

It's not easy to provide this kind of sensitive support for children's development as independent thinkers. Here are some things to consider as you pose problems to children:

1. **Can the child verify the information or solve the problem independently by manipulating, observing, touching, or listening?**

2. **Is the issue exciting to the child? Does the child discuss it joyfully? Learning is boring only when the child has no control over the topic or when the topic is presented at a level that is beyond the child's understanding.**

3. **Can the child control the entry and exit to the problem? Does the child raise the topic or problem spontaneously? Does the adult look to the child for cues on how far to proceed? Does the adult "give it a rest" if the child signals that he wants to drop the issue?**

I find it tough to drive Brian to school each day. Sometimes I think it would be easier to turn on the radio, let the time pass without comment, and think about my own day rather than wonder about the perceptions and interests of a 3-year-old. How easy it would be to be directive, to control, to explain. But the rewards of talking and playing with Brian *at his level*, of "tuning in" to his way of seeing the world, more than compensate for the effort involved.

Helping Children Resolve Disputes and Conflicts

By Betsy Evans

• •

Alice and Sam are playing in the playhouse. They are dressing up, and at the same moment, they reach for the only colorful scarf available. They tug back and forth, yelling simultaneously, "I got it first! Give it to me!"

Emma and Joe are in the block corner building a dinosaur house together. Joe accidentally knocks down a section of the building. Emma pushes him and angrily yells, "Get out!"

Adults working in early childhood programs see many conflict situations like these. Such incidents often create feelings of frustration and failure for both children and adults. Many times it isn't clear what has happened, who is responsible, or how the problem can be resolved. The feelings of everyone involved are often strong and confused. Yet these are very important occasions for learning.

Teachers and caregivers in High/Scope centers and classrooms can turn disputes and conflicts into positive experiences by understanding the **developmental needs** of young children, using **problem-prevention strategies,** and engaging the child in a **conflict resolution process.** By settling disputes with their peers, children gain an understanding of how to respect the needs of others while meeting their own needs. They learn that there is often more than one "right" side in a dispute, that feelings are important, and that there are many possible "win-win" solutions to conflicts.

Understanding Developmental Needs

When we engage in problem solving and conflict resolution with young children, it is important to keep their developmental needs in mind. First, *young children are very egocentric,* which makes it difficult for them to understand the needs of others. Young children are not being "bad" or selfish when they ignore another child's rights or needs—it is simply very difficult for them to look beyond themselves. Since the child who is having a dispute with another child often isn't aware of the other child's point of view, it's important for adults in such situations to **acknowledge and talk about what each child is feeling.**

A second developmental characteristic of young children is that *they are at an important stage in developing autonomy.* They are just beginning to develop relationships outside their families and to explore the world as independent people. As a result, they often need to feel in control and have their independence affirmed. When children are upset, helping them recognize their own feelings (and those of others involved in the situation) can contribute to their sense of being in control—this is another reason adults should talk about the feelings of each child in a conflict. Another way for the adult to affirm the child's independence and sense of control is to **engage the child as an active participant in the problem-solving process.** Statements like "Let's try to solve this problem together" encourage each child involved in a dispute to take an active role in resolving it.

A third characteristic of young children that affects their ability to resolve conflicts is their tendency to think concretely. We know that children of preschool age are unable to deal with abstractions: *They learn best when information is concrete and specific.* So, in helping to resolve a conflict

Young children are egocentric, and it is difficult for them to understand the needs of others. Because of this, it is important for the adult to acknowledge and talk about what each child is feeling.

Conflict—An Occasion for Learning?

Which of the following *key experiences in social relations* occur as children resolve conflicts with peers?

- Making and expressing choices, plans, and decisions
- Solving problems encountered in play
- Taking care of one's own needs
- Expressing feelings in words
- Participating in group routines
- Being sensitive to the feelings, interests, and needs of others
- Building relationships with children and adults
- Creating and experiencing collaborative play
- Dealing with social conflict

between children, avoid general statements like "You must learn to share." Instead, **give children specific information that will help them work out the details of sharing.**

We've outlined several general principles to follow in working with young children in conflict situations. Now let's see how an adult applies these principles to one of the examples that open this article—the situation in which Alice and Sam are fighting over a scarf they both want. In responding, the adult speaks to the children in a calm, matter-of-fact tone: "Alice and Sam, I can see that you both are upset and that you both really want to use the scarf. It is hard when there are not enough scarves for both of you. Let's think of some ways that we can solve this problem." This kind of approach helps to calm all the parties in a conflict and makes shared problem solving possible. Note that the adult started by **recognizing the feelings and desires** of both Alice and Sam **in specific terms.** She then gave a clear message that **they could work together to solve the problem.** Then, in moving toward a solution, the adult was again careful to be specific: "Sam, Alice says she would like to wear the scarf for five minutes. Would you like to use the sand timer, so you will know when her five minutes are over?"

Problem-Prevention Strategies

In the example of Alice and Sam, the adult intervened skillfully in the children's dispute. But this incident might have been prevented if additional colored scarves had been available. Providing extra sets of similar materials in each area of the classroom or center is a good example of a strategy adults can use to prevent conflicts. Some others are listed on the next page:

• **Keep expectations for behavior developmentally appropriate.** Respect and plan for children's different abilities, interests, and pacing levels.

• **Have many choices for play available.** Materials should be plentiful, and it should be easy for children to get them out and put them away.

• **Set clear limits for children's behavior.** Use them consistently, and give reasons why the limits are important.

• **Establish a consistent daily routine** and communicate it clearly, using pictures or drawings to make the segments concrete.

• **Model respectful ways of interacting with others and using materials.** The behaviors you model are the easiest ones for children to learn.

• **Plan for transitions.** Keep them short or make them playful.

When these types of prevention strategies are in place, children will be more focused and purposeful in their play, and there will be fewer disputes and conflicts. Nevertheless, conflict will not disappear.

Following are steps you can take to help children settle disputes whenever they arise. The steps, gleaned from conflict-resolution literature (see References), have been adapted for young children by incorporating the child development principles described earlier. To illustrate each step, we will again refer to one of the opening examples—the one involving Emma and Joe.

Steps in Resolving Conflicts

1. Approach calmly. Your body language says a lot about your intentions and feelings. Stay neutral in order to respect all the viewpoints:

Seeing Emma and Joe arguing in the block area, the adult calmly walks over to them.

2. Acknowledge feelings. Make simple statements, such as "I can see you're feeling sad/angry/upset." This helps the child let go of feelings and prepares him or her to think clearly about solutions:

"Emma, you sound very angry with Joe, and Joe, you look quite sad. Let's try to solve this problem together, so you can continue to build your dinosaur house."

3. Gather information. Listen to all points of view, both for your own information and so the children can learn what others feel they need.

Effective Mediation

Some Examples

1. Evan goes to the playhouse and takes the spoon that Collin and Trevor have been using. They find Evan at the stage and ask for it back. He says no. They ask a teacher for help, and they all go to talk to Evan. Evan, and then Collin and Trevor, explain that they want the spoon. Another child steps in the middle and says, "I think they should share."

The teacher asks, "How do you think they can do that?"

Trevor says, "I know. We'll use it for a minute, then bring it right back."

Evan says, "No."

Collin says, "But we were using it to make applesauce."

The teacher says, "Evan, it seems that there are two ways we can solve this. Trevor and Collin can take the spoon for a minute and bring it back, as Trevor suggested, or you can use it for a minute and bring it to them."

Evan says, "No, I think they should bring their stuff for applesauce here and make it."

Collin and Trevor say, "Yeah! Let's do that!" They quickly go to get their applesauce-making things.

The teacher says to Evan, "You thought of a way to solve the problem for everyone!" Evan smiles.

2. Sara and Mei Mei complain to the teacher, "Josh and Shakeel are bothering us through the window in the playhouse. Josh squeezed my arm, and Shakeel hit Mei Mei."

"What did you do?" asks the teacher.

Sara answers, "We told them to stop, but they didn't."

"Did they hurt you again?" the teacher questions.

"No . . . but they kept peeking!" Sara says.

"Did you ask them to stop peeking?" the teacher asks.

Sara doesn't answer. She and Mei Mei go back and tell the two boys to stop peeking. Josh and Shakeel look up from their building and listen. They go back to building and don't bother the girls again.

Levels of Mediation

It's not always necessary for adults to mediate conflicts directly; some children are able to solve problems more independently than others. Below we describe three different levels of support adults can offer children:

- *Level 1.* Work directly with all the children who are involved in a dispute, mediating in a way that is developmentally appropriate and supportive of all children involved.

- *Level 2.* Listen to one child describe a conflict with another child. Ask questions and offer suggestions that support the child in solving the problem independently.

- *Level 3.* Position yourself near a conflict, but let children settle it without your intervention. Your presence alone may provide enough support.

For Those Persistent Problems . . .

Even though I use a problem-solving approach in my classroom, there are some behaviors that come up repeatedly. Some children persist in running around the classroom, and others frequently hit or push others when they are frustrated. What should I do if I have tried on-the-spot mediation and the behaviors are still repeated?

—*A preschool teacher*

You should try the problem-solving approach each time a problem occurs, even if the problem is a recurring one. However, here are some additional strategies you might try for persistent problems:

• **Group problem-solving.** Group times can provide opportunities for children to discuss a problem together. For example, children running around the classroom was a persistent problem at our school, despite constant reminders by adults. Even though the adults explained why it was not safe to run, the children could not seem to stop. One day at recall time, I told the children, "At work time today, there was a lot of running, and even though children were reminded why it is not safe to run, they did not stop. Can we think together of some ways to help children remember not to run in the classroom?"

In the discussion that followed, one child earnestly suggested, "We could build fences and then they won't run!" We discussed this and the problems that would be created by having fences. Another child said, "You could

ask children to go read a book when they are running too much." Everyone agreed that this would help. And a third child (one of the frequent runners) suggested, "We could make a big stop sign and show it when someone is running!" There was a lot of enthusiasm for this idea, and we decided that at small-group time we would make a large sign that could be held up by children or adults when children were running in the classroom.

• **Limiting choices.** Young children are physically expressive and have trouble controlling their impulses. It is very difficult for some children, when they are upset, to stop hitting and pushing, even when it has been clearly stated that this behavior is *not okay*. When one child hurts another, it's important for both children to talk through their feelings. If the child who hits and pushes is still unable to communicate his or her needs in words rather than actions, it may be necessary to give the child choices that are more limited. For example, the adult might say "Natalie, I feel unhappy because you are still pushing children. I need to stop you. Your choices now are to go to the book area or the puzzle area until you are ready to be with other children without hurting them." The phrasing used in this example can help in a variety of situations. Adults first state their feelings and expectations ("I feel _____ because _____"), then state the limited choices ("Your choices now are to _____ or _____. Later, we can try again to solve this problem together.")

The details revealed about the conflict are very important in finding a solution. Listen carefully:

Joe says, "Emma's being mean. She won't let me play here. She tried to push me out of here."

Emma says, "I don't want Joe to play here 'cause he knocked down my dinosaur house."

4. Restate the problem. Use as much of the children's language as possible, and rephrase child language that may be hurtful:

"Joe, you feel that Emma is being mean, and Emma, you don't want Joe to build because he is knocking down the building. Is that right? . . . Do you both want to keep building here?" Emma and Joe nod their heads to both questions.

5. Ask for ideas for solutions, and choose one together. Respect all of the children's ideas, even if some are unrealistic. Explore how each idea might work, considering the consequences. Help children think through the specifics of any general solutions they may suggest, such as "They should share":

"If you both want to continue building, what do you think we should do now? How can we work this out?"

Emma says, "I want to build this part by myself. Joe can build over there."

Joe says excitedly, "Hey, I can build the dinosaurs a swimming pool!"

Engaging children in the problem-solving process helps them learn how to deal with difficult situations. Also, when children are upset, helping them recognize their own feelings and those of others involved in the situation can contribute to their sense of being in control.

Emma says, "Yeah!"

*The adult suggests, "Joe, if you build your part farther from the wall, it will be easier for other children to walk by it without knocking it down. Emma, it is easier for Joe to understand what you need when you **talk to him** rather than push him."*

The adult pauses for a moment and continues, "Emma and Joe, it seems that you both want to play here and that you each want to build separate parts of the dinosaur house. Is that what you both want?" Emma and Joe both say yes and begin to build.

6. Be prepared to give follow-up support. Sometimes children need further help in clarifying the details of a solution:

"Emma and Joe, you both had ideas for solving your problem together! I'd like to see the dinosaur house when it is finished."

The adult stations herself nearby as Joe and Emma start to play. Soon they are arguing over the building space. The adult places a line of tape across the block corner, so it is clear whose space is whose.

Just as with any new set of skills, it takes practice to learn to apply the process of conflict resolution. But with time and repeated positive experiences, both children and adults will come to rely on this shared process.

REFERENCES

Prutzma, P., Stern, L., Burger, M., & Bodenhamer, G. (1988). *The friendly classroom for a small planet.* Philadelphia: New Society Publishers.

Wichert, S. (1989). *Keeping the peace.* Philadelphia: New Society Publishers.

Crary, E. (1984). *Kids can cooperate.* Seattle: Parenting Press.

Hopkins, S., & Winters, J., (Eds.). (1990). *Discover the world: empowering children to value themselves, others and the earth.* Philadelphia: New Society Publishers.

Watch Your Language!

By Betsy Evans

· ·

In working with children who are upset, choose your words carefully—the language you use can be a major factor in successfully resolving problems and conflicts. In this article, we identify some key communication strategies (including both spoken and body language) that support children in finding solutions to conflicts. When adults use these strategies repeatedly, children become more and more able to resolve conflicts independently.

Body Language Strategies

• **Approach children calmly;** don't raise your voice or use abrupt or threatening gestures.

• **Put yourself on the children's physical level.** For example, sit or kneel on the floor.

• **Gently reach out to children who are upset or angry.** For example, make a welcoming gesture, or place a hand on a child's shoulder.

Speaking and Listening Strategies

• **Make descriptive statements about the details of what you see,** striving for an objective, nonjudgmental tone: "Joe, I can see that your building got knocked down." "Amy, I can see your clothes are very wet."

• **Ask open-ended, specific questions:** "Amy, can you tell me what made you feel so angry?" "Hugo, can you tell me what happened?"

• **Describe and expand on the feelings children are expressing.** "Amy, it's hard to wait for a turn on the swing." "You worked a long time on this building, Hugo. I can see that you're upset that it fell down."

• **Listen carefully to what children say.** Often small details that are unimportant to adults create major conflicts for children. For example, an adult may wonder why two children are fighting over a truck when there is a similar truck available nearby, but the color or some other minor feature of the truck may be what makes it appealing to both children.

 • **Encourage children to talk to each other.** Frequently, simple misunderstandings can be cleared up if you encourage children to describe the problem to each other rather than to you: "Tell Jason what you need" or "Show Sam what it is you want." As the child describes his or her problem to the other child, encourage the other child to listen, and if necessary, repeat and expand on what both children say.

 • **State expectations clearly and specifically, leaving some room for a choice if possible.** "Sam, it is not okay to throw toys. Can you stop yourself, or do I need to stop you? . . . If you cannot stop, I will need to make a choice for you about what you can do next."

 • **When children have solved or tried to solve a problem, comment on the effort they have made,** emphasizing the *process* they used rather than the *outcome:* "You listened to each other so carefully." "You thought of ideas for solving your problem and found one that would work for both of you!"

Verbalizing their own needs and listening to the points of view of other people are valuable communication skills that children develop as they resolve disputes. By modeling appropriate problem-solving language, we are helping them learn to respect and celebrate the differences among people.

Punishment:
What Does It Teach?

By Betsy Evans

· ·

At lunchtime, Liana asks for more "Pasgetti." Should the adult say "You should know better!" and send Liana to the time-out area? Kazu, preparing to go outside, puts his boots on the wrong feet. Should the adult tell Kazu that because of his mistake, he must stay inside to "think about it"?

Louise holds a marker in a fist-like grasp instead of correctly positioning it between her thumb and index finger. Should the adult take the markers and put them away until Louise "learns to do it right"?

Most early childhood teachers would agree that children should certainly not be punished for making mistakes like these or for lacking particular skills.

Yet when children make *social* mistakes—when they quarrel, hit and kick, or "lose it" because they can't solve a problem—it's common for early childhood teachers to respond with punishment. When a child's social behavior is unacceptable, teachers may send her to the time-out chair, exclude her from outside time, or take a toy away.

Children who are punished may only remember the fright or resentment created by an adult's anger or may only retain the message that they are "bad" or "naughty."

Consider this example: At outside time, Luke and Lawrence are both pulling on a new stroller, hitting each other, and shouting. Should the adult punish Luke and Lawrence?

In a High/Scope program, the answer to this question is no. Punishing children for their social mistakes is inconsistent with our commitment to active learning. Teachers in High/Scope programs know that children learn best when they are intrinsically motivated and are actively involved in learning new skills. If Luke and Lawrence are removed from the situation and punished, they will not develop the skills they need to approach the problem more constructively the next time it occurs. During this moment of conflict, however, the children's keen interest in the stroller means they are highly motivated to find a constructive solution to their problem. Punishing Luke and Lawrence might solve the adult's immediate problem of restoring order, but such an approach will not support the children's need, at a critical moment, to begin to acquire new social skills.

Later in this article, we consider alternative responses to Luke and Lawrence's dilemma, but first it is important to consider *why* adults punish and the implications of punishment for children.

Why Adults Punish

When it is clear that conflicts like these result from children's immaturity, why do many adults use punishment for the Lukes and Lawrences in their programs?

There are many reasons why adults punish, and the reasons vary with each adult-child situation. The most common is that many adults simply have no other model for dealing with children's unacceptable behaviors. Research informs us that children who have been punished often become adults who punish (see, for example, *Punished by Rewards* by Alfie Kohn [Boston: Houghton Mifflin, 1993]).

Having had no role models for constructively communicating strong emotions such as anger and frustration, adults do what they have seen modeled—they respond to an "out-of-control" child by taking over control. Instead of helping him learn to be more in control, these adults respond by venting their own strong feelings.

Children are likely to acquire new social behaviors when they can choose to engage in them independently, without adult coercion.

Another reason why adults punish children is that they feel a strong sense of responsibility for children's behavior. They fear that if they do not respond to the offending behavior firmly enough and with a sufficiently memorable consequence, the child may be tempted to repeat the behavior. They may express the fear that if an "impression" is not made, the child may grow up to be "bad," possibly even become a criminal.

Unfortunately, however, punishment often doesn't help the preschooler remember how to behave more acceptably. Since young children have difficulty holding more than one thought in mind at a time, children who are punished may only remember the fright or resentment created by an adult's anger or may only retain the message that they are "bad" or "naughty."

Punishment and Behavior Change

Even if the child does realize that a particular behavior is not acceptable, the punishment may still not have a *lasting* effect. Punishment usually results only in short-term changes in behavior, because the child's *desire* to repeat the offending behavior has not changed, even though she has outwardly complied with the adult's wishes. As a result, maintaining the new behavior requires a punitive *system*, in which punishment, or at least the threat of it, is repeated over and over. Child-management techniques like "time out" and "1-2-3 magic" are examples of punitive systems that rely on such cycles of punishment.

Systems like these are popular because punishment (and its partner, reward) do appear to work, at least in the short run. Children are easily manipulated by promises, stickers, sweets, the loss of "goodies" or privileges, or threats of possible isolation in a time-out area. Yet such punishment-and-reward systems do little to help children learn how to express needs and feelings or to resolve problem situations more appropriately.

To help children begin to develop these important social skills, we need to adopt an active learning approach, in which **child choice** and **initiative** are essential elements of the learning process. New social behaviors are likely to be acquired permanently only when children can choose to engage in them independently, without adult coercion. Punishment and reward alike result in *mindless obedience*. Because the child who has

Negative Implications of Punishment

- Makes children dependent on adults, while increasing adult control and authority.

- Has a negative effect on self-esteem: Makes children "other-directed" rather than "inner-directed" and focuses on "badness" of the child rather than on the problem or action.

- Addresses the adult's short-term needs rather than the child's long-term needs.

- Promotes compliance and conformity.

- Promotes fear, aggression, resentment.

- Develops mindless obedience rather than a desire to act constructively.

- Teaches a desire to avoid being caught.

- Inhibits the child's ability to express strong emotions appropriately.

- Creates an adversarial relationship between child and adult.

- Physical punishment: teaches that violence is an acceptable way of expressing anger; teaches that if you are bigger, you are allowed to hurt.

been punished or rewarded has not chosen the new behavior freely but has simply adopted it to avoid punishment or to gain a reward, he will repeat the desired behavior only if the adult continues to use such external motivators as bribes, threats, or punishments. As a result, the child becomes dependent on the adult for the motivation to behave constructively. As Jean Piaget wrote, "Punishment renders the autonomy of conscience impossible." The child never internalizes the desired behavior, because he has never made a *conscious choice* to engage in the behavior.

It is important, too, to evaluate punishment from the perspective of our basic educational goals. What do we want for children? When teachers who are learning the High/Scope approach are asked this question, they most often respond that they want to encourage children's independence, creativity, problem solving, social adaptability, and risk-taking. The development of these capabilities is valued and supported throughout all parts of the High/Scope daily routine. In the High/Scope approach, problem situations as well are seen as valuable opportunities to develop these same capabilities. From this perspective, children's mistakes and problems are critical experiences that concretely demonstrate their need for a new skill. If children are placed in the time-out area as soon as a problem arises, they miss out on the opportunity to explore and learn from their mistakes.

Alternatives to Punishment

- Engage children in active learning experiences.

- Follow consistent daily routines.

- Intrinsically motivate children through play that is fun, is personally interesting, gives children choices, has a high probability of success, and promotes a sense of competence.

- Support developmentally appropriate play with adult-child interaction strategies based on sharing control with children.

- Engage children in a problem-solving approach to conflict that focuses on problems, not people, and that encourages them to express needs and feelings and listen as others do the same.

- Use "I" statements to express strong emotions, to give reasons for feelings, and to give limited choices and logical consequences.

What Works Better?

What, then, are the alternatives to punishment? An effort to respond to children's social mistakes should include **prevention strategies** as well as **interaction strategies.** All of the components of the High/Scope learning environment and daily routine (see "Alternatives to Punishment") are effective in preventing social problems and mistakes. In addition, the steps in High/Scope's problem-solving approach to conflict (introduced in "Helping Children Resolve Disputes and Conflicts" on p. 27) can be very useful in resolving the conflicts and problems that will inevitably arise despite prevention efforts. The goal of this

The problem-solving process is an alternative to punishment that helps children learn to express feelings appropriately and to be sensitive to the feelings of others.

process is to help children find and *consciously choose* alternative, positive ways to express needs and solve problems. During this process, children's feelings and ideas are sensitively acknowledged and respected, and solutions are chosen by the children with the support of the adult.

Here's how this process was used to assist Luke and Lawrence, the two children fighting over the stroller, who were described at the opening of this article:

During work time Luke and Lawrence decide simultaneously that they want to use the stroller. Shouting loudly, they alternately pull at it and hit each other.

Hearing the commotion, Rachael, the teacher, approaches them, kneels down so she is at their level, and gently puts her hands on each of them, stopping the hitting. She says, "Luke, you look angry and, Lawrence, you look angry, too. It's not okay to hit when you are angry, but we **can** *talk about what is making you feel upset." The children quiet down and look at Rachael. Continuing in a calm manner, Rachael asks, "What seems to be the problem here?"*

Luke says, "I had it and I want it!"

Lawrence insists, "I want it!"

Rachael continues to acknowledge their feelings. "So, Luke, you want the stroller and, Lawrence, you want the stroller, too. The problem is that you both really want this stroller. Hmmm, I wonder what you could do to solve this problem?"

Both children are silent, and Rachael waits. (Though it is difficult to wait for the children's suggestions, Rachael has learned through experience that her patience at times like these is very important.) Suddenly Luke's face lights up and he says, "We could buy a new one!"

Rachael, remembering that she is supporting the exploration of ideas, replies, "I wonder how that could happen?"

Luke thinks for a moment and then curls up his nose and says "Nah." Other ideas are explored—making a stroller, using the stroller together—but Luke and Lawrence do not agree on either of these.

Finally a child playing nearby offers, "They could take turns." Luke responds excitedly, "Yeah, I could push the stroller all the way down to the wall and back and then give it to Lawrence. He can do it, then give it back to me!"

Rachael restates this, making sure both children agree to this idea. They do agree, and they take turns for the rest of work time.

During the next week, Luke and Lawrence have another conflict over a favorite toy. Rachael reminds them that they have solved a problem like this before. Luke replies, "Oh, yeah, we can take turns like with the stroller."

This example demonstrates how effective the steps in problem solving can be. Sometimes, however, because of limited time or because the emotions of the adult or child are so strong that problem solving will not be productive, it may be best to postpone your problem-solving discussion. In this case, to deal with the immediate situation, the adult can use the language strategies suggested in the next article. Whether problem solving occurs right away or at some later time, however, it offers an effective alternative to child management systems that are based on punishment or external rewards. As children solve problems together and engage, *by choice,* in new ways of interacting, they find that successful problem solving has its own rewards.

Language That Sets Limits

By Betsy Evans

• •

The problem-solving approach to conflict outlined in the previous article is usually the most effective way to deal with conflict, disruptive behavior, and other social problems in the preschool classroom. Sometimes, however, it is necessary to postpone a problem-solving discussion because time is limited. For example, if a conflict arises just as large-group time is about to start or when it's time to walk down the hall to the lunchroom, problem solving may have to be delayed.

It's also appropriate to postpone problem solving when children are engaging in physically hurtful behavior that the adult must attend to immediately or when children or adults are experiencing very strong emotions about a problem situation. Usually the problem-solving process takes only a few minutes, but conflicts involving strong emotions can take much longer to resolve. Particularly if the mediating adult has strong feelings or opinions about a conflict, it may not be appropriate to begin problem solving until the adult feels capable of a neutral attitude.

When problem solving must be delayed for any of these reasons, teachers need other options for dealing with the problem behavior. Some alternative strategies are presented here.

Limit-Setting Statements

If a child's actions are disruptive or unsafe to others and there isn't time for problem solving, limit-setting statements can be effective. Describe the **action** that is disruptive, state **limits,** give the **reasons** why the behavior is not appropriate, and offer **choices.** For example:

• "Cory, it's not okay to run inside [action and limit] because you may get hurt [reason]. Your choices are to stop running or to have me stop you. Then you can choose something else you would like to do [choices]. If you cannot choose, I will need to choose for you."

• "Susannah, shouting during circle time is not okay, because the other children cannot hear the story. You need to stop or I need to stop

Stopping Hurtful Behavior

When a conflict has become physical, special strategies are necessary to ensure children's safety and to establish a calm atmosphere in which problem solving can begin. It is important to stop the hurtful behavior immediately, gently interceding with your hands and body so as to prevent further hitting, kicking, and so on. Even if you are upset, it is important to use calm body language, remembering that young children express their feelings physically, not because they are "bad," but because they have no other skills.

As you stop the behavior, explain what you are doing, and acknowledge the child's feelings; say, for example, "I can see that you are very upset, but it's not okay to hurt. I need to stop you." If the need to restrain the child continues, calmly continue to acknowledge her feelings and explain your actions: "I can see that you're still really upset. I need to hold you, so you don't hurt yourself or anyone else." By continuing to acknowledge the child's feelings, you are helping her "empty out" those feelings: "I see that you are still very, very upset/sad/angry/frustrated!" If possible, you could give an angry child something to punch: "You are so upset that you want to punch and hit. It's okay to hit this bag as hard as you want."

When the child has regained control of her physical behavior and has her thoughts and feelings back in balance, you can begin to discuss the problem together.

---

you. Your choices are to stop shouting and listen with us, or to go to the book area and look at a book. Which will you do?" After circle time is over, it might be useful to problem-solve with Susannah about circle time, if her disruptive behavior is an ongoing problem.

"I" Statements

"I" messages are another kind of limit-setting statement that may be used when problem solving must be delayed. In "I" statements, the adult first describes his or her feelings and the reason for them ("I feel _____ because _____"), then states the child's limited choices ("Your choices now are to _____ or _____"). "I" statements are often effective for situations when the *adult* has a problem, as for example when the adult has feelings or opinions that might make it difficult for him or her to be neutral during problem solving.

"I" messages describe actions, situations, feelings, needs, and reasons, rather than people. They offer an alternative to language that accuses, blames, or labels children who are engaging in unacceptable behavior. "I" statements may include the logical consequences of children's actions, which can be conveyed using *either/or* or *when/then* lan-

*If a child's actions are disruptive or unsafe to others and there isn't time for problem solving, limit-setting statements can be effective. Describe the **action** that is disruptive, state **limits,** give the **reasons** why the behavior is not appropriate, and offer **choices.***

guage. When adults make "I" statements, it is best for them to avoid using the word *angry* too often. When possible, they should instead name the feelings behind their anger (for example, *afraid, sad, worried, upset*). Following are some examples of "I" statements:

• "James, swinging sticks [action] near people's faces is not safe. I feel afraid [adult's feeling] that someone will get hurt [reason]. You may *either* move away from people *or* put down the stick [*either/or* statement giving logical consequences and choices]."

• "Charisse, I feel very upset, because hitting hurts. I'm too upset to problem-solve with you right now. Your choices now are either to go to the water table or to use the punching bag. In a few minutes, when I am not upset, we will talk about this problem together."

• "Sara, I feel frustrated, because all the children are ready to go outside. When you have finished putting away the blocks, then we will all be able to go outside."

As you use these verbal strategies for dealing with disruptive behavior and conflict, remember that your nonverbal messages to children are just as important. Keep your body language calm and reassuring: Assume the child's physical level, use a calm tone of voice, maintain good eye-contact with children, use gentle body movements, and in resolving conflicts, position yourself so as to stop hurtful behavior (for example, *between* two children who are arguing). Thoughtful use of both the verbal and the non-verbal strategies will help to establish an atmosphere in which constructive problem solving can proceed.

From Superheroes to Problem Solving

By Betsy Evans

S ay "superhero" to teachers of young children, and they groan with frustration. Each year, it seems, there are new superheroes that children are imitating, and the play that revolves around these characters seems increasingly violent. Many teachers report that today's children, instead of just putting on capes and pretending to fly, are kicking, chopping, and hitting as a part of their play.

In addition to the disruption and conflict this kind of play so often creates in the classroom, many teachers see another problem with children's fascination with superheroes: the unrealistic model of problem solving these characters present. For some children, the superheroes' ability to solve every problem through violent, physical action has become a model for solving the everyday problems they have with their friends.

Young children are small and vulnerable. Superhero play meets their needs for power and control.

This article describes an alternative problem-solving process that gives children a positive, constructive means of working out conflicts with peers. The process helps children learn valuable social skills and also meets their needs for power and control—the same needs they are expressing through superhero play.

To understand superhero play and how it relates to problem solving, we must first explore the important developmental needs involved. Why are superheroes so appealing to young children? Children understand the world in terms of clear, concrete actions and physical characteristics, and they are interested in how their actions affect others. Superheroes have simple, bold behaviors that involve a lot of action, and their personalities are understood through their physical characteristics. The color-coding of the Power Rangers, for instance, makes it easy for children to tell the "good guys" from the

Helping children express their own feelings, ideas, and needs will also help them gain sensitivity to the feelings, interests, and needs of others. In addition, they will experience the feelings of control and competence that come from helping solve a problem.

"bad guys" (a necessary coding system, since both sets of characters use the same violent tactics to solve problems). Another reason superheroes are appealing is that they have the strength and power to fight off any danger—a dream come true for the small, vulnerable child just learning to be independent.

Powerful characters thus appeal both to children's need to feel strong and in control of their lives and to their desire to quickly and easily solve problems that arise with peers. Adults can help children meet these same needs for power and control by establishing a conflict-resolution process in the classroom. Through this process, children learn to express their own feelings, ideas, and needs; in addition, they gain sensitivity to the feelings, interests, and needs of others. They learn the *real* power of expressing their own needs and having others respond. They also experience the feelings of control and competence that come from contributing to the successful resolution of a problem.

The basic steps in this process are described in "Helping Children Resolve Disputes and Conflicts," pp. 27–34. To summarize these steps:

1. **Approach calmly.**

2. **Acknowledge feelings.**

3. **Gather information.**

4. Restate the problem.

5. Ask for ideas for solutions, and choose one together.

6. Be prepared to give follow-up support.

Now let's look at how adults and children use this conflict-resolution approach in a typical classroom incident:

It's cleanup time, and Simon and Carlyn are struggling over the last large hollow block to be put away. Shouts are heard: "I had it first!"

The teacher approaches them and says, "I can see that you're both feeling upset. I think you can work this out, and while you do, I will hold the block." They both let go of the block.

Each child explains his or her desire to put the last block away. The teacher restates the problem: "I can see you both really want to put away this block. Can you think of some way that you can both put away the same block?" They discuss the possibility of doing it together, but neither will agree to this. Each asks to do it alone.

As the teacher and children discuss the problem, five or six other children gather around them, listening. The teacher turns to the children who are looking on and says, "Does anyone have any ideas of how we can solve this problem?" Two more ideas are suggested, but neither Carlyn nor Simon will agree to them.

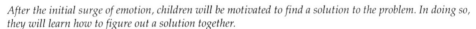

After the initial surge of emotion, children will be motivated to find a solution to the problem. In doing so, they will learn how to figure out a solution together.

Finally, another child, Sarah, says, "How 'bout if we get down another block just like that one, and then you each have the same kind of block to put away."
"Yeah!" Carlyn and Simon say in unison.

Carlyn then takes the block Sarah has taken out and puts it on the pile. Simon picks up the original block but can't lift it to the top by himself. "Carlyn, will you help me with this?" he asks. Together they put the last block on the pile. The teacher says to all the children, "You were very powerful problem-solvers! You figured this out together!"

A Motivating Process

One reason this problem-solving process is so effective is that it engages children's **intrinsic motivation** to learn. (Intrinsic motivation is learning that is motivated by the child's *internal* desires, intentions, and interests rather than by *external* factors, such as adult rules, directives, or rewards.) Motivational research indicates that five factors contribute to an intrinsic desire to learn: enjoyment, personal interest, a sense of control, feelings of competence, and probability of success.

All five of these factors are present in our example of successful problem solving. Carlyn and Simon's genuine *interest* in resolving the conflict is obvious from the intense emotions they are expressing. The *enjoyment* factor can be seen in the experience of the children who are looking on and contributing their ideas. For these children, suggesting possible solutions is like a game; finding the solution that works is much like the fun of placing a key piece in a jigsaw puzzle, resulting in everything else fitting together. Another key motivational element is *control.* By involving Carlyn and Simon and the other children in finding a solution to the problem and by respecting their needs and ideas, the teacher shares control. By giving them the support they need to reach a solution, she creates a *probability of success.* When the solution is successful, all the children experience feelings of *competence.* Resolving a conflict, then, is an *intrinsically motivating experience* for children and one that is therefore an important occasion for learning.

Respecting Children's Ideas

When children have real problems and conflicts to solve, their need to be respected as competent problem solvers is strongest. It is important for adults, as the supporters of these problem-solving experiences, to respect and explore all the ideas that children offer, even the ideas that seem unrealistic. Through the process of exploring what might happen if their suggestions are tried, children develop an understanding of cause-and-effect connections, sharpen their critical thinking skills, and strengthen their abilities to express feelings and needs clearly. In the process, they also come to appreciate the points of view of others, and they learn how powerful their positive actions can be. With each problem-solving experience, their skill, as well as their trust in the process, increases.

Returning to our concern about superhero play, our next example shows experienced problem-solvers dealing with a problem created by such play. Note how children's ideas contribute to the resolution of this incident:

Through the process of exploring what might happen if their suggestions are tried, children develop an understanding of cause-and-effect connections, sharpen their critical thinking skills, and strengthen their abilities to express feelings and needs clearly.

Alex and Nathan are playing Ninja Turtles at work time, as they do almost every day. They move about the room doing kicks and chops. They rush into the playhouse with their arms swinging, disrupting the children who are playing there. As they enter, Latisha moves quickly, trips, and falls backward. She begins to cry. The teacher, Denzel, comes over and comforts her, then says, "I can see that something has happened that has upset Latisha. I think we can figure this out together by talking about the problem, one person at a time. Latisha, can you tell me what happened? You seem very sad."

Latisha describes what happened from her point of view; then Denzel questions Nathan and Alex, hearing several different versions of the incident. As Denzel listens, he tries not to make any judgments about what has happened. He listens in a way that is neutral and respectful of each child. As he talks to each child, he is careful to acknowledge each child's feelings; he knows that children will not be ready to explore possible solutions until they have "let go" of their feelings.

The children in the playhouse then describe their need to play without being scared by Alex and Nathan. Alex and Nathan say they want to be Turtles, but they also want to play in the playhouse with the group. "In order to solve the problem," Denzel says, "we need to think about a way to play so that everyone can feel happy and safe." The playhouse children respond: "Make them stop kicking. We don't like it." A child from the playhouse group then suggests, "You could come here and make the pizza you like to eat, but no kicking!" The teacher suggests that Alex and Nathan could pretend to be Turtles by dressing up like them, instead of kicking and chopping. "Hey, we could make some armor and then come and make pizza!" Alex says. Then the teacher checks with the play-house group to see if they think the problem is solved. "Yeah, we like Turtles that don't chop and kick. Let's help them make pizza."

Power and control are important themes in children's play, and superhero play is just one way they act out these themes. By helping children explore the negative and positive implications of being power-ful, adults are supporting children's intrinsic motivation to develop skills in social problem solving. As children solve problems during conflicts, they come to understand that problem solving and positive, caring actions can be a satisfying source of power.

"Super Strategies" for Superheroes

By Betsy Evans

• •

Superhero play, which often focuses on weapons and fighting, frequently causes hurtful behavior, disruption, and conflicts in the classroom.

There are many options for teachers who wish to deal more effectively with the problems created by superhero play. The problem-solving process described on pp. 47–52 helps teachers and children deal with the individual conflict situations that sometimes arise during such play. In addition, it satisfies the needs for power and control that children are expressing through their pretend battles. However, this process by itself does not completely solve the problem, since superhero play and weapons play are partially the result of influences outside the school. Therefore, teachers and parents must work together to respond effectively to this kind of play.

What Parents Need to Know: Television and Movies

As a first step, you'll need to educate parents about the impact of violent television and movie content on children. Post pertinent articles on your parent bulletin boards, or use newsletters, workshops, parent conferences, and informal playground conversation to get this message across. Here are some important guidelines for working with parents in this area:

Parents and teachers must work together to ensure that children aren't exposed to violent television programs and movies. This partnership approach is very effective.

• **Parents need to take responsibility for their children's viewing.** Television and movies have become very violent, and this violence can disturb children and distract them from learning. Programs and movies should be carefully selected by parents to avoid those with violent content and images. Children can handle scary books, because they are in control of the images. With television, however, images are larger and louder and can seem overwhelming.

• **The average young person, by the age of 18, has watched the equivalent of seven years of television and in doing so has witnessed the enactment of 26,000 killings.**[1] This is a devastating emotional burden for children to carry.

• **Parents need to know that violent television and movies can inhibit children's ability to learn.** Children whose play ideas come mainly from television are not using their own creativity and are not taking full advantage of other learning opportunities.

• **Experts point out that many cartoons are actually just program-length toy commercials.** These programs exploit the children's interest in action and power for financial gain.

Dealing With Weapons Play Through Small-Group Discussion

Another strategy is to use small-group discussion to involve children in the process of setting limits on the use of toy weapons or character toys in the classroom. For example, gun play is a problem in many preschool programs, with some children complaining that they don't like to be shot at. This problem can be discussed with a small group of children, either after recall time or during snack time.

To open the discussion, the teacher might say "You all know that we do not allow toy guns to be brought to school, but we do allow children to make pretend weapons. I've noticed that there is sometimes a problem with the play that happens with guns. Some children like to make guns to play with, but some other children (it is important not to use specific names) don't like to be shot at. We need to find a way that pretend guns can be used so everyone will feel happy and safe."

Children will usually respond to such an opening with many ideas. It's best to write down and discuss each idea and then to identify which ideas children as a group agree should be tried. For example, they may agree that "We can make toy guns but not point them at other children"

---

[1] For more information, see *Teaching Young Children in Violent Times* by Diane E. Levin (Cambridge, MA: Educators for Social Responsibility, 1994) and "NAEYC Position Statement on Violence in the Lives of Children," *Young Children*, 48(6), pp. 80–84.

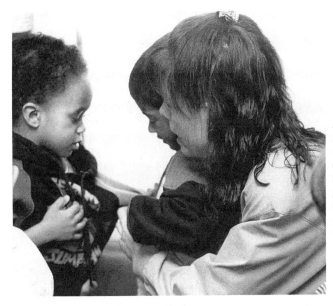

Ask children who are engaged in pretend fighting whether their intention is to hurt someone, and make sure the children who are frightened by the violent play hear the answer. Most children want to be a powerful character but do not intend to hurt anyone.

or "We can make toy guns at school, but once they are made, they go in our cubbies to be taken home."

Additional Recommendations

• **Don't attempt to ban superhero or weapons play altogether.** This isn't appropriate in High/Scope-oriented programs, in which adults are committed to supporting children's play choices. Such bans may force children to lie about or disguise their true play interests and may also turn teachers into "police officers" who are constantly on the lookout for infractions.

• **When dealing with violent play, focus on the action that is disturbing or hurtful rather than on the child.** If Sammy says, "Duane is being really mean. He's going around kicking and chopping and we hate him," rephrase Sammy's words to separate the action from the person: "Duane, kicking is not safe to do in the classroom, because there are so many children close by. Some children are afraid they will be kicked. Let's see if we can think of other ways for you to pretend to be a Ninja."

• **Ask children who are engaging in pretend fighting whether their intention is to hurt someone, and make sure the children who are frightened by the violent play hear the answer.** Most children want to be the powerful character but do not have the intention of hurting someone. Once this is clear, they can explore other ways of playing.

What About Toys That Tantalize?

I've been having a problem with children bringing in toys from home. These toys cause many conflicts. Children use them to get attention, sharing them with special friends and excluding others, and this results in hurt feelings and resentment. What can I do?

— *A preschool teacher*

Here are some suggestions to discuss with classroom staff:

- At the beginning of the year, inform parents that you would like children to leave their toys at home, explaining why. Consider allowing only stuffed animals or dolls, which are often "security objects" for children adjusting to school.

- In small groups or individually, discuss with the children the problem of using toys at school. Explain any limits you have set on toys from home, noting that it is hard to share important toys and it makes others sad when there is a single item that everyone wants to use. Ask children if there are any other things (besides special toys) that might be brought from home to use in school. If children do not think of it, suggest that even though it may not work well for them to bring in single toys, collections of items may be brought in to share (e.g., empty containers, bottle caps, yarn, paper tubes, twist ties, wood scraps, etc.).

- If, in spite of your rules, a child does bring a favorite toy to school, remind the child and parent of the rule. If the child does not easily give up the item, consider letting the child show others the toy before the first part of the daily routine, agreeing that when the day begins, the toy will be put away. An item such as a special truck or dinosaur could be used, with the child's permission, as a planning prop, so everyone would be able to hold the item before it needs to be put away.

• **With other staff members, discuss the appeal of power-oriented play, and brainstorm constructive ways that children can explore these interests.** Superheroes are appealing not only because of their strength, speed, and appearance but also because of their ability to deal with scary situations and emergencies. To meet children's need for *strength* activities, then, you might decide to provide large hammers, big wood pieces, nails, and a stump to serve as a workbench; for *speed,* you could provide ramps for racing marbles, cars, and balls; for *appearance,* you could supply costume-making materials, such as scarves for capes and headbands, and sparkly and shiny fabric and clothing. To provide *scary situations,* you could read scary stories that are appropriate for preschoolers or play dramatic musical selections (for example, "Sorcerer's Apprentice" or "Skeleton Parade") for movement activities or cleanup time. For pretend *emergencies,* you could provide hospital or fire station materials or rescue materials, such as nets and life preservers.

Chapter Two

Designing Routines for Active Learners

· ·

A *major part of the adult's role in a High/Scope early childhood program is to plan a balanced* **daily routine,** *a consistent sequence for each day's events that provides a framework for children's active learning experiences. In all High/Scope settings, this routine consists of certain basic elements—a plan-do-review sequence, small- and large-group times, outside time, transition times, and, when appropriate, greeting time, mealtimes, and naptime.*

Though the basic components of the daily routine are part of every High/Scope early childhood program, each program implements these components in an individual way. Staff of each program decide how to order the components; they also plan which materials or experiences will be available to children during each part of the routine.

To guide program staff in this planning and implementation process, the High/Scope approach provides specific guidelines for each part of the daily routine. Under these guidelines, work time and outside time are intended to be **child-initiated** parts of the routine; this means that during these times, children are busy throughout the classroom (or, in the case of outside time, busy throughout the playground) choosing materials and activities from the wide range available. On the other hand, small-group time, large-group time, and transition times are designated as adult-initiated; these events take place in a specific part of the classroom or center, and adults set things in motion by providing children with specific materials or experiences. Even in these adult-initiated parts of the day, however, children's intentions are important; throughout the group experience, adults provide children with opportunities to make choices and decisions, and they let the interests expressed by children shape the direction of the activity.

In the first article in this chapter, "Work Time: Teacher Habits That Are Hard to Break," Michelle Graves focuses on work time, one of the central components of the High/Scope daily routine. Work time is the **do** segment of the High/Scope plan-do-review sequence. During work time, children pursue their personal interests, working and playing independently or in small groups throughout the classroom or center. (Work time begins immediately after a brief time in which children **plan** what they want to do, for example, by indicating that they want to "play with blocks" or "paint in the art area." In the last part of the sequence, **review** time, children discuss in a small-group setting what they did at work time.) In her article, Graves discusses common pitfalls that teaching teams encounter in implementing work time. She provides a variety of suggestions adults can use to move toward sharing control with children during this part of the day. In the next article, "Successful Elementary-Grade Work Times," Charles Hohmann discusses related issues in elementary-level programs.

The next three articles in this chapter deal with the group activities that constitute the important **adult-initiated** parts of the High/Scope daily routine. In High/Scope programs, as in most early childhood programs, adult-planned group activities are a standard part of the day. However, in High/Scope settings, staff take a nontraditional approach to these group experiences. In early childhood programs based on other approaches, adults often see a group time as an opportunity for structured activity or for serious "teaching"—for drilling children on letters, numbers, and shapes or for helping them memorize songs or dances. In High/Scope programs, by contrast, group experiences are designed to encourage children's active involvement with people, materials, and ideas; the adult's role is to foster children's discoveries rather than to dispense knowledge.

In "Group Times: What Makes Them Work?" Becki Perrett provides some general principles for carrying out this active learning philosophy at small- and large-group time. She explains how to plan an activity with children's interests and developmental levels in mind and how to keep children's interest-level high during the activity by giving them choices, tuning in to their involvement, and minimizing their waiting and turn-taking.

In the next selection, Mary Hohmann focuses specifically on small-group experiences, giving further suggestions for making small-group time active and productive for children. In "Small-Group Time: Active Children, Active Adults," she explains what adults and children do at the beginning, in the middle, and at the end of a typical small-group time and emphasizes the supportive adult-child interaction that occurs throughout this group experience. She also addresses the content of small-group time, highlighting four important sources of ideas for content: the interests of children, new and unexplored materials, the High/Scope key experiences, and local traditions and events.

In the last of the articles dealing with small-group time, Charles Hohmann discusses "workshops," which are the small-group component of High/Scope elementary programs. Like the preschool small-group time, a workshop is planned according to active learning principles. Unlike a small-group experience at the preschool level, however, the elementary-grade workshop time focuses on specific instructional content. This article gives a detailed example of a typical workshop time in a High/Scope elementary classroom.

Transition times, which link one major program element to the next, are considered incidental in many early childhood programs, but in High/Scope programs, transitions are just as carefully planned as the other program elements. Becki Perrett's "Shifting Gears Smoothly: Making the Most of Transition Times" discusses some key strategies staff can use to make transitions go more smoothly. In the succeeding article, Perrett focuses on one of the most difficult transitions of the day, the cleanup at the end of work time. She suggests that adults assess whether their expectations of children at cleanup time are realistic and then offers a range of strategies for making cleanup engaging for preschool children. Another transition, the opening of the day, is the topic of the next article, "Greeting Time: A Smooth Transition for Children," by Carol Beardmore. In the High/Scope Demonstration Preschool, the day opens with children listening to stories and exploring books with a teacher while the other teacher greets the arriving children and their parents. Beardmore explains how this way of handling greeting time eases the transition from home to school for children and provides an opportunity for parent involvement.

The last two articles in this chapter were originally included in Extensions because of the growing number of children under age 3 who are enrolling in child care programs. In these articles, Jackie Post and Mary Hohmann offer some general principles and basic program events to consider when planning schedules and routines for these younger children, pointing out the need to make room for each child's individual schedule within the overall program schedule.

Work Time: Teacher Habits That Are Hard to Break

By Michelle Graves

· ·

Work time is a time of opportunity for both children and adults. For children, it is time to follow through on their own intentions in a supportive social setting. During work time, it is normal to see some children playing alone and others working together in clusters. Whether children have chosen to play individually, in pairs, or with several play-mates, you can be sure that the play has a definite purpose in their minds. Through this purposeful play, they encounter and solve problems. They also construct knowledge about themselves and the people, materials, ideas, and events that surround them.

For adults, work time is also full of oppor-tunities. In the High/Scope Curriculum, adults see children as unique individuals with differing interests and ability levels. Work time is a time for adults to observe the special characteristics of children and to use these observations in supporting and interact-ing with them.

Attempting to carry out work times that reflect this High/Scope perspective may cause you to rethink classroom routines that you may have been using for years. Imple-menting this active learning approach to work time takes trust—trust that children have the ability to make decisions, solve problems, and learn academic, social, and emotional concepts within a framework based on their initiative.

On the road to developing the trust needed to create a true learning climate for children during work time, you may encounter some pitfalls involving common,

In the High/Scope daily routine, work time gives children the opportunity to initiate their own activities and to make lots of choices and decisions.

hard-to-break adult habits. This article explains how you can replace those habits with new work time strategies and routines.

Pitfalls to Avoid

Pitfall 1: Setting up learning stations for specific activities. Most teachers who are learning the High/Scope approach understand that giving children choices is an important principle. Sometimes their way of implementing this principle is to set up daily "learning stations." Early in the morning, before children arrive, they select certain materials to set out on tables or on the floor in each of the classroom areas. On a typical Monday morning, for example, they might set out a selection of Play-Doh and Play-Doh tools in the art area; toy trucks, cars, road signs, and interlocking road pieces in the block area; pegs and pegboards in the toy area; and a doctor's kit and doctor clothes in the house area. As children arrive, teachers tell children what the choices of the day are and then ask children to make a selection from these limited activities. The next day the choices are different. While this approach does provide some choices to children, it closes off many more.

The Adult Role at Work Time

At work time adults interact with children thoughtfully, in ways that encourage each child's development. To do this successfully, consider the following strategies:

1. Begin by designing interest areas stocked with materials that appeal to young children.

2. Wait and watch before entering children's play. Make conscious decisions about where to place yourself, based on what children are doing, how that play can be supported, and who might be most receptive to that support.

3. Observe the actions and language of children to gain a better understanding of what interests them and how they react to the involvement of others in their play.

4. Offer comfort, contact, and simple acknowledgments to children as needed.

5. Play side by side with children on their level.

6. Have conversations with children, taking your cues and lead from them, asking questions responsively and sparingly.

7. Encourage children to solve problems by watching and listening to them, referring them to one another, and remaining calm throughout the process.

8. Develop a system for recording your observations of the children.

Pitfall 2: Limiting the number of children who can play in an area. Teachers often express concern that if children are free to choose where they will play and what they will play with, there may not be enough materials or adequate space in the interest areas for children to play without conflict. To prevent such problems, their strategy is to limit the number of children who can go to an interest area during work time. This may be done in a variety of ways. Some teachers have area boards with pockets or hooks attached to them. When the hooks or pockets representing the number of children allowed in that area are full, it is "closed." In earlier versions of the High/Scope Curriculum, we experimented with this strategy but found that it creates too much frustration for children who want to play at an area that is "full."

Pitfall 3: Discouraging children from moving materials from one area to another. Left to their natural inclinations, children often shift materials from area to area. They may take trucks from the block area and ride them throughout the room, or they may take toy food, pots, and pans to play with in a house they've just built in the block area. In such situations we often hear adults telling children to keep the trucks in the block area or the food toys in the house area. Teachers often have a rational explanation for their rules: They may feel that moving trucks throughout the classroom could disrupt other children's play or that taking food items from the house area will create a problem when other children go there to complete their

These children understand that they are free to move about the play space and to shift materials from area to area, as they wish.

work time ideas. Confining materials to one area, however, interferes with the plans we have asked children to make.

Pitfall 4: Having a special "project of the day." During work time in some classrooms, children can choose freely among all the interest areas and materials, but teachers also introduce a special "project of the day." These projects can range from using baby dolls and wash basins in the house area to painting with eyedroppers in the art area to taking a walk outside with one of the teachers. At planning time children are free to choose from any of the standard areas and materials or to make a plan to do the special project, which is usually available on a limited-time basis.

Implementing an active learning approach to work time takes trust—trust that children have the ability to make decisions, solve problems, and learn academic, social, and emotional concepts within a framework based on their initiative.

Such special projects generally occupy all of one adult's energies, preventing him or her from supporting and learning from children's self-initiated projects. For this reason it's better to save such special projects for small-group time.

Pitfall 5: Pulling children away from play to test and improve their skills. In some programs, there is pressure to complete screening tests and develop individualized educational plans (IEPs) that target the children's "weak areas." Work time becomes the natural choice for completing these tasks: The feeling is that because all the children are busy carrying out their plans, adults are free at this time to conduct tests or drills with individual children or small groups of children. But again, this practice ties up an adult and disrupts children's work on the plans we have asked them to make.

Pitfall 6: Assigning team members to one area for all of work time. Some teaching teams decide to station themselves in a single area for the entire work time. Sometimes these choices are made because of a teacher's special qualities. A teacher who is good with tools may be assigned to the construction area; a teacher with an art background, to the art area; and so on. Though this practice does take advantage of each

When Work Time _Is_ Working

Everyone who works with young children is well aware that there are days when everything seems to go awry. Just as common are those days when everything seems to run smoothly and you can't believe your good fortune to be able to "play" while you work. Recently, I experienced one of those "it just feels right" work times. Here's what happened:

At the start of work time, as we looked around the room, we saw five children in the block area building a car "to go to California"; six in the computer area; four using markers, tape, and scissors in the art area; one pouring sand through a sieve at the sand table; and four in the house area pretending to be a family (a mother, baby, cat, and dog).

After watching for a few moments, I went to the art area and began drawing with markers, and my team member Carol went to the house area, where she was immediately welcomed with a "cup of coffee." As work time evolved, some children shifted playmates and activities, while other small groups stayed together, working on the same activity throughout the entire 45-minute period.

Following are some of the morning's highlights for us:

- Watching Meghan and Carleen pretending to be dog and owner. Carleen carefully tied a string around Meghan's wrist, then led her on a walk around the classroom, stopping in front of the dog-food bowl, so her "dog" could get a drink of water and some dog food.

- Participating in the car ride to California. On the way, we learned that it would take a "long, long, long, long, long, long" time to get there, so it was important to stop first for lunch at McDonald's.

- Offering support to Alex as he worked on designing a mask for his friend Steven. When the mask kept slipping from Steven's face (it was tied loosely with string), one of the teachers said, "I notice it keeps slipping down. Is there anything you might use to hold it in place?" Alex then got masking tape and taped the mask to Steven's forehead.

- Observing that Victor stopped shooting at children in the room when Kayla said to him, "You know, real guns really hurt people—they get dead, and then you can't see them anymore."

- Listening to Tyler say to Jordan at the computer, "You've been there for a lot of turns. Here, you hold the mouse one time, then give it to me, then I'll give it back." Then we watched them play for an additional 10 minutes, using Tyler's idea.

- Having the time to support Saraya (who recently had a new baby join her family) by sitting next to her, covering her with blankets when she crawled into the baby crib, and softly singing her a lullaby while she rocked and made sucking sounds with her mouth and occasional crying sounds.

Each work time in High/Scope classrooms is unique. Watching children's ideas develop, becoming an active partner in activities generated by children, and observing the learning that took place in these and other incidents made this a work time that really worked!

adult's special strengths, it limits his or her ability to focus on and learn from the wide range of children's play.

Pitfall 7: Settling conflicts for children. Work time is a busy, sometimes noisy time of the day that is often full of conflicts over materials and relationships with others. Adults have a natural inclination to want harmony in a classroom. Because they can sometimes see solutions to problems that children cannot, stepping in to direct the solution may seem like a good idea. For example, the adult might say, "Here, give James this doll so he'll stop crying. You can use this pretty one over here." However, if the adult would instead take the time to help children arrive at their own solution, the children would learn much more about solving their own problems.

Pitfall 8: Setting no limits or expectations. The High/Scope philosophy emphasizes decision making as a goal for children, but this doesn't mean that children should always do whatever they want, whenever it suits them. Carefully setting and maintaining *reasonable* expectations and limits helps children feel safe and secure in their environment. However, set expectations cautiously, considering the safety of individuals and materials to be of primary importance. Also, set them in a way that makes sense to the children and can be realistically enforced. For instance, "no hitting" or "no breaking the toys" rules are not likely to work successfully in a preschool classroom. On the other hand, setting the expectation that children will work through the consequences of such actions has more learning value (having Ivan bring an ice pack or Kleenex to the child he hit, or asking Alexis to tape back into the book the page that she tore).

Why Break These Habits?

Many of the adult habits just described suggest a tendency on the part of the adult to retain control of the classroom environment and the actions of the children. When we retain too much control over children by limiting their choices of materials or areas, they have little opportunity to develop self-control, learn from the consequences of their actions, or master the skills necessary to accomplish their goals. The following four tips for sharing control at work time can help you to avoid some of the pitfalls.

1. Begin by making a list of all the ways you do have control over your classroom. Things on the list might include arranging and equipping the interest areas, setting the basic elements of the daily routine, planning group times, and deciding which interaction strategies to use. Making this list may help you realize that the classroom is not "out of control."

As they pursue their own interests during work time, children work and play independently or in small groups throughout the classroom or center.

2. Instead of deciding beforehand to limit children's choices of activities or play spaces, observe children carefully as they play. Then, if space is inadequate or a specific material is especially popular, add space or additional materials in the interest areas as needed. If you find that 10 of your 20 children choose to go to the block area every day, make that area the largest in your classroom and add building options to the house, toy, and art areas.

3. Try letting children move materials from one area to another. Then, after a short trial period, compare the level of chaos or frustration created when children can move things and complete their ideas with the level of frustration created when you tell them they can't.

4. Keep your special "project of the day," but instead of setting it up at work time, save it for a small-group time. After you have introduced a new experience, such as eyedropper painting on coffee filters, add those materials to the art area, so they become yet another choice for the children to make during future work times.

It is important to remember that even when control is shared, children need a secure environment with consistent adult support to deal with the difficulties that inevitably arise when we encourage them to make choices. For example, if children move all the materials from one area to another and this disrupts the work of others, an opportunity arises for children to negotiate an acceptable outcome, but you will need to be available to support their negotiations. If your energies are tied up in leading special activities or pulling individuals or small groups out for assessments or skill drills, you will not be available as a support person.

Also, releasing yourself from the expectation that you have to plan, lead, or manage children's activities at work time gives you the opportunity to enter into play and converse with children in meaningful ways. When you have to make daily decisions about which materials to set out or are constantly dealing with negative behaviors of children who are frustrated by the limits on their choices, you rob yourself of the joy of sitting side by side with children and learning about them as they learn through play.

Successful Elementary-Grade Work Times

By Charles Hohmann

• •

In High/Scope elementary classrooms, work time is the heart of the plan-do-review process, just as it is in High/Scope preschools. In this part of the daily schedule, children carry out their plans to work in one or more of the classroom's activity areas.

Like the preschool work time, the elementary school work time is when children pursue and develop personal interests. But work time in elementary school tends to be somewhat different from work time in preschool, simply because elementary-level children have a wider range of skills and interests. As a result, the projects they undertake may be more complex and often may extend over several days. Elementary-level children frequently write their work plan in a planning notebook or planning journal. Planning a cooperative effort that includes several students, such as putting on a puppet play or playing a board game, is also common for elementary-level children.

The best way that teachers can prepare for children's work time is by planning activity areas stocked with materials that inspire children's ideas. Include areas for art, music, reading, writing, computers, construction, and science, as well as areas that reflect your local community or children's special interests (examples: weaving, Native-American art, beading, cooking).

Work Time Practices to Avoid

Because the High/Scope concept of work time is completely new to many primary-grade teachers, they may at first find work time difficult to implement. Unsure of how to make work time successful, teachers sometimes fall back on old teaching habits that can impede effective implementation. Here are some common pitfalls for primary-grade teachers to avoid when conducting work time:

• **Setting up work stations containing assigned projects, tasks, or worksheets for children.** Instead of work stations, set up *activity areas* in which children can choose from a range of stimulating materials; then encourage children to make their own choices about how to use the materials.

• **Turning work time into an indoor recess or free-play period for children.** Without the structure of planning before work time and reviewing afterward, and without purposeful but nondirective support from the teacher, work time becomes a break time instead of a time for productive activity.

• **Using work time as catch-up time.** Some teachers permit only those children who have finished their previous work to participate in self-initiated tasks during work time. So children who have difficulty completing math or language assignments must use work time to "catch-up." However, these are often the children who can benefit most from being able to make choices about their learning experiences. Self-initiated tasks give children who work at a slower pace or who are less motivated a chance to succeed that they may not have when doing adult-initiated tasks.

• **Failing to follow work time with an effective period of review.** Children's review of work time activities is important at any level but especially important in the elementary grades. Reviewing helps children draw out and solidify the essence of valuable work time experiences. It is a time when children and their teachers actually see what has been accomplished or learned. This time of "publicly" accounting for their work also helps children to develop an awareness of the viewpoints of peers and teachers. At least 10 minutes of review is recommended in elementary classrooms.

Keep in mind that children's work time is just one element of an overall process of planning, doing, and reviewing—and each of these elements requires your continuous support. With your thoughtful involvement in all three elements, work time can become one of the most productive parts of the day for children and adults.

Group Times:
What Makes Them Work?

By Becki Perrett

· ·

"Circle time is so hard for my children," moans a preschool teacher. "They just won't sit still and listen. And I just can't believe that when we review the calendar, most of the children can't tell me what day it is. We've been working on this for months. I just don't know what to do anymore."

Group times can be a challenge for adults working in any early child-hood program. Many adults complain that children just don't meet their expectations at group times. These adults often see these parts of the routine as their main opportunity for serious "teaching," and they use these times to drill and quiz children on numbers, colors, or the days of the week or to help children memorize dances or songs.

In High/Scope early childhood settings, however, group times are not adult-led "lessons." Instead, both large- and small-group times are planned around the same goal: to encourage children's active involve-ment with materials, people, and ideas. This means that throughout any group activity, children make choices, have "hands-on" experiences, and talk about what they are doing. Active learning is the guiding philoso-phy at group times, just as it is during all other parts of the High/Scope daily routine.

Yet group times *are* distinct from other parts of the routine in several important ways, and because of these differences, they offer special learn-ing opportunities.

Special Features of Group Times

Unlike children's activities at work time, **group times are adult-initiated—they are planned and set in motion by the adult.** At *small-group time,* the adult brings 6 to 10 children together for 15 or 20 minutes each day. The adult provides a set of materials that the children can use for explor-ing, creating, experimenting, or building. At *large-group (or circle) time,* adults meet with the entire group of children for 10 or 15 minutes to sing songs, do fingerplays, read stories, move to music, or participate in action games or other group activities.

Because of this adult-initiated format, *group times allow adults to introduce something new or different to children.* At circle time, the adult might work with children to create a new variation of a familiar song or game. At small-group time, the adult might introduce new materials or new combinations of materials to children—a computer program, counting bears and small blocks, toy farm animals. Sometimes the materials the adult sets out at small-group time have already been available in the classroom; the group time allows children who have not yet used the materials to explore them in a comfortable setting.

A second special feature of group times is the **social opportunities** they offer. During the child-initiated parts of the routine, children can choose how solitary or sociable they wish to be—whether they want to work by themselves, with a friend or adult, or with a group. However, not all children choose to play cooperatively during these times. Group times offer another social opportunity. At small-group time, when everyone is working with the same set of materials, children often share and discuss what they are doing, learn from one another, and help one another. At large-group time, an action game or song is a safe, low-risk social experience in which children have opportunities to contribute and demonstrate their ideas to the group and to imitate and learn from their peers.

A third special feature is that **group times enable adults to observe children closely.** For example, adults often maintain the same small groups for several months. This allows the adult to get to know each child well and to observe all the children in terms of their interests and developing abilities. For example, during a small-group time in which children are working with large wooden letters, Mr. T. may observe which of them use the letters simply as building materials, which are able to recognize and describe the shapes they see in the letters, which recognize some of the letters they see, and which attempt to form words with the letters. Mr. T. then uses the observations he has made in deciding how to support each child, what materials to add to the classroom, and what additional small-group times might be planned to build on the abilities observed.

Strategies for Effective Group Times

Group times, then, are a valuable part of the routine for children. To make group times effective, adults consider the children's **interests**, their **developmental levels**, and their **degree of involvement** in the activity. Here are some specific suggestions for effective group times:

First, when planning group activities, **think about what is interesting to your group of children**. In many schools and centers, group times are planned around a theme chosen by the adults—a theme like "spring" or "zoo animals." But this theme may not be of interest to the children. We recommend instead that ideas for group times come from the children. By observing children and families, adults learn about the interests and experiences of the children, and these can become the starting point for group activities. For example, at the High/Scope Demonstration Preschool, an idea for a group time came from Linda, a 5-year-old who enjoyed dancing with scarves in the classroom. To build on this interest, the teachers planned a circle time around scarf dancing. The adults passed out brightly colored scarves to each child, and each child moved in his or her own way to different selections of music. In later work times, children built on this experience by building a stage in the block area for their dancing performances.

As another example, during home visits, the teachers at the Demonstration Preschool learned that Scott, a 4-year-old, was interested in building with wood and that the parents of several other children did woodworking as a hobby. The teachers decided to develop a small-group time in

To make group times effective, adults consider the children's interests, their developmental levels, and their degree of involvement in the activity.

which children worked with wood scraps and glue. After the wood scraps were introduced at small-group time, woodworking became a favorite activity of many children at work time over the next few weeks. During these times, children extended the range of materials they used along with the wood, sometimes using masking tape to connect wood pieces together and often painting their wooden creations. "The ideas these children came up with were incredible," commented one teacher.

Children's developmental levels are another thing to consider when planning group activities. Activities that are too difficult for children (like the calendar activity in the opening example) often create management problems. Therefore, avoid games and activities with complicated rules, unless children can understand the rules. Some games are easily simplified. Most preschoolers who are playing "Hokey Pokey," for example, don't understand such directions as "put your right foot in," because they can't yet distinguish between left and right. In this case, it would be better for the adult to say "put your foot in, . . . put your foot out" and also to give some of the children chances to lead the activity: "Tyrone, what body part should we put in next?"

This last example points up another strategy for making group times responsive to your children's interests: **Share control of the group time by giving children choices throughout the activity**. Although adults plan group activities, this doesn't mean that they dictate what happens at group times. While adults provide a general context for the activity—a song, story, fingerplay, or movement game, or a selection of materials to work with—it is the children themselves who determine exactly how the activity will unfold. For example, an adult may set out collage materials for a small-group time, but the children decide what to create with the materials. As they go about doing this, the adult moves around the group and talks with them individually, supporting and helping them expand

Are Group Times for Toddlers?

We are trying to implement the High/Scope approach in our center-based toddler program. How can we make group activities for this age group successful? It is very difficult to get toddlers to participate in circle or small-group times.
— *A child care provider*

Many group activities that are typically conducted with 3-, 4-, and 5-year-olds are developmentally inappropriate for toddlers. Because they require behaviors (such as waiting, sharing, and taking turns) that are beyond the abilities of most children in this age group, highly structured small-group activities and large-group music activities, games, and story times are often unsuccessful with toddlers. Most toddlers are not yet ready to interact socially in a group. Instead they engage mainly in solitary or parallel play.

Too often, the group activities provided for toddlers are simply scaled-down versions of group activities for preschoolers. Adults who are working with toddlers may need to rethink their

notions of group activities for this age group. Here are two suggestions to consider:

- **Eliminate structured group activities for toddlers.** Instead, provide children with materials and experiences that will allow them to play in close proximity to one another or to interact with one or two other children or adults.

- **Make structured group times optional.** Allow children to join a group activity (and to leave the activity) when they wish. For example, while one adult remains with the children who prefer solitary or parallel play, another adult may invite children to come to the reading corner to listen to a story, or to the art area to play with a new batch of modeling dough.

Remember, children of *any age* are most likely to be actively engaged in group activities in which they experience feelings of enjoyment, interest, control, and success.

on their efforts. Likewise, the adult may select some chant or music for a large-group activity, but she asks the children to choose different ways to move to the chant or music, or different ways to modify verses or lyrics.

In addition to giving choices, we also recommend that when a group activity is under way, you **tune in to the involvement level of the children.** Group times are usually scheduled to last 15 to 20 minutes, but you should be open to making the activity longer or shorter, depending on how children respond to it. Often, for example, some children become very involved in what they are doing at small-group time and aren't ready to stop when it's time for the next activity. One way to allow for this is to schedule something after the small-group time that doesn't require participation by the *entire* group (for example, schedule circle time or outside time, rather than a trip to the library). This way, children who need to can take a little more time to finish their small-group projects. By the same token, if children are inattentive, bored, or fidgety, you may want to end the group activity earlier than planned. When a group time hasn't gone smoothly, you might ask yourself why. Were there enough materials? Was the activity of interest to children? Were all the ingredients of active learning (materials, manipulation, choices, child language, and adult support) present?

To keep children involved in group activities, another key suggestion is to **minimize waiting.** In one child care center we know of, the beginning of circle time is scheduled to overlap with the end of snack time. While one of the adults continues sitting with children who are eating, another adult begins circle time when just a few of the children have finished their snacks. This way, children don't have to wait for everyone to finish eating before they can start the next activity. The adults at this center also keep waiting to a minimum at small-group time by having individual sets of materials ready for each child to work with. They place the materials in paper bags, small baskets, margarine tubs, or other small containers, so they can be passed out quickly.

You can also **lessen waiting by keeping turn-taking to a minimum in group activities.** When some form of turn-taking is a part of a circle activity, be flexible about children's turns. At the High/Scope Demonstration Preschool, we often ask children to take turns leading a movement activity or suggesting a word or phrase to complete a song or chant. In these cases, we don't create the expectation that all children will have a turn. Instead, we observe how involved children are in the activity and allow as many turns as the children can handle. If we sense that children are almost ready for a new activity, we might say something like this: "We

Ideas for Adapting Traditional Group Activities

We welcome suggestions for adapting traditional adult-led songs, chants, fingerplays, or games to make them more developmentally appropriate and to offer children more opportunities to initiate ideas. Here are some of the suggestions we've received from High/Scope staff, workshop participants, and other early childhood professionals in the training network:

- When chanting "Jack Be Nimble," ask children to suggest how Jack might get over the candlestick (march, hop, walk, etc.). Then ask various children to demonstrate their suggestions for the group to imitate as they repeat the chant. The activity could be personalized further by substituting a particular child's name for "Jack" each time the action in the chant is changed. *(Submitted by Willadene White, Education Coordinator, Ninth District Opportunity Head Start, Gainesville, Georgia)*

- When singing "How Much Is That Doggie in the Window?" ask the children for ideas on what and where the animal should be. For example, a child might suggest, "How much is that bird in the cage? The one with the purple feathers" or "How much is that cow in the barn? The one with the loud moo." *(Submitted by Virginia Lewis, Education Coordinator, EOA Savannah-Chatham Head Start, Savannah, Georgia)*

- When doing fingerplays that require children to count backwards, e.g., "Five Little Monkeys Jumping on the Bed" or "Five Little Ducks," consider whether counting backwards from 5 to 1 may be confusing to children in your group, as it is to many preschoolers. Instead of reciting the verses of these chants in the traditional way, ask individual children to suggest what the "starting" number of monkeys, ducks, etc., will be for each verse (don't worry about the order of the numbers not being 5, 4, 3, 2, 1 for successive verses). *(Submitted by Beth Marshall, High/Scope Educational Consultant)*

- Instead of playing "Duck, Duck, Goose" in the traditional way, ask children to make up their own way of counting off the players ("Pizza, pizza, pizza, Coke" or "Slipper, slipper, slipper, *sock*.")

have time for one more child [two more children, etc.] to pick a way to move. Then we'll do a different song."

In sum, don't make your group activities a time for rigid routines, complicated games, or teacher-led lessons. Instead, the hallmarks of group activities should be flexibility and openness toward children's signals and ideas.

Small-Group Time:
Active Children, Active Adults

By Mary Hohmann

• •

Small-group time in High/Scope programs is a lively, busy time in which both children and adults are active. It is an opportunity for adults to introduce new concepts, activities, or materials to children, but it is not a time for school-like lessons, drills, or ditto sheets. The adult's role is to support children's learning, building on children's individual discoveries rather than dispensing knowledge.

In High/Scope small-group activities, 5 to 10 children meet with an adult to experiment with materials, to talk about their observations, to solve problems they encounter, and through these processes, to learn new skills and concepts. This article explores how adults plan and support these kinds of active small-group experiences.

Small-group time ideas are generated by adults for various reasons: For example, a small-group time might be planned to build on a particular interest of children that the adult has observed, to introduce a new or unexplored material, to create opportunities for a particular set of key experiences, or to enable children to participate in a local custom or tradition.

Whatever the idea behind a small-group time, *it is the adult's style of interacting with children throughout the activity that makes the experience uniquely "High/Scope."* This interaction style becomes clear as we discuss how to start small-group time, support children as they work, and bring the small-group time to a close.

Setting Small-Group Times in Motion

Give children materials right away. As the starting point for small-group time, adults usually provide an individual set of materials for each child in the group. Children come to small-group time eager to begin. Giving them their materials as they arrive allows them to focus their energies on the task from the outset. If you immediately present the child with, say, a pile of blocks, some markers and paper, musical instruments, or a hat full

Planning Lively Small Groups

These are some useful sources of small-group ideas. As you'll see, the test of a good idea is how well it sparks ideas from children.

Plan Small-Group Times Around the Interests of Children

"This is the second day Brianna has asked me for a Band-Aid to patch up a 'tiny cut' on her hand," Barbara reported at daily team planning. "And Audie told me that the masking tape he was using looked like a Band-Aid. Tomorrow I think I'll give the children in my small group Band-Aids, since they really seem to love using them." The next day at small-group time, Brianna put one Band-Aid on each finger. Julia made a line of big Band-Aids on her leg followed by a line of small ones. James and Audie taped some Band-Aids on their "muscles," then taped Band-Aids to paper to make the bodies of "muscle men." Sarah and Erica took apart their Band-Aids to see what was underneath the gauze.

Plan Around New and Unexplored Materials

"Alex, Trey, Sarah, and Audie have been painting with tempera paints. I'd like to introduce them to watercolors," Barbara said at another daily team planning meeting. The next day at small-group time, children used the watercolors in many ways. Megan watched the other children and made a few strokes of yellow. Alex painted mostly with green, his "favorite color." Sarah filled her whole paper with color. James and Audie made lots of lines, using many colors. Erica painted with water, adding dots of color to her water splotches as she watched them spread.

Plan Around the High/Scope Key Experiences

"We haven't recorded many anecdotes lately about the seriation key experiences," Peter said in daily planning. "Let's plan an activity to see if children will *arrange things in a series or pattern* (a seriation key experience)." Peter provided each child in his small group with lengths of wide, flat ribbon in several colors, along with paper and a glue stick. He asked, "What could you do with these ribbons?" and then watched to see if any patterns emerged. Amy made a border on her paper that repeated the pattern red/white/red/white. Namen made a "wild man" with ribbon hair in an alternating green/blue pattern. Josh used the glue stick to glue ribbons together in a long line in no particular pattern. "This is Snakey," he said.

Plan Around Local Traditions and Events

"The children are so excited when they hear the marching band and see it on the days it marches down our street," Beth said one day at daily team planning. "I think I'll plan my small-group around having our own band." The next day at small-group time, the children gathered as usual with Beth at the table in the art area, then went together to the playground, where they chose their instruments and took turns being "the leader of the band." When it was Brian's turn to lead, he marched everyone through the sand box and up and down the hill. Douglas led the parade under the slide, the climber, the climbing net, and the tree house.

It's easy to see from these examples that the adult's ideas (garnered from many sources) are only the beginning of small-group times that inspire children's inventiveness.

In High/Scope small-group activities, 5 to 10 children meet with an adult to experiment with materials, to talk about their observations, to solve problems they encounter, and through these processes, to learn new skills and concepts.

of little toy animals, the child will most likely begin exploring, drawing, building, making music, or whatever, as soon as the materials are in hand.

Make a brief introductory statement. Sometimes you will want to offer children a simple challenge: "What can you do with ribbons, glue, and paper?" In the case of the hats and animals, the teacher might hold out a hat full of animals and say, "Today we'll be working with hats and animals. We'll also try a computer program with magic hats and animals that jump in and out of the hats."

Supporting Children As They Work

Once children have gotten their materials and have begun working, use these strategies to support them as they experiment and discover:

Move to the children's physical level. If children are sitting on the floor, sit on the floor with them. If they are kneeling around a large piece of butcher paper, kneel with them. Joining children at their physical level helps you understand what they are experiencing and makes you readily available for interaction.

Watch what children do with materials. You can expect to see multiple responses to the same materials: Frances fills her whole pegboard with pegs, Kacey makes a pattern with hers, Julia counts her pegs, and Douglas sees how high he can stack his. You'll also see **High/Scope key experiences** take shape: In a small-group time in which children tie cans to their feet to make stilts, Audie counts the number of steps he takes on his stilts *(key experience, counting objects),* Sarah talks about the noise the stilts make *(key experience, exploring and identifying sounds),* and Alex fills his stilt cans with pea gravel *(key experience, filling and emptying).* By observing the different ways children use materials, you'll gain ideas about how you might interact with each one to support his or her learning.

Listen to what children say. You will find out what is important to individual children and what they are thinking about: "My water is turning into orange!" "I'm keeping my egg in the water for a long time." "How do you keep the can part on your stilts?"

Move from child to child. Even in a small group of children, you can't attend to everyone at once. In an egg-dyeing activity, Becki, the teacher, first makes sure that each child in her small group has vinegar, dye pellets, water, and hard-boiled eggs. Then she moves around the table, squatting for a time next to each child. Moving from child to child in this way enables Becki to see and hear each one. Also, she is telling children through her actions that she will come to them eventually. This allows them to focus their energies on their work rather than on getting her attention.

Imitate children's actions. Often at small-group time, conversation takes a back seat to action, because children are focusing so intently on what they are doing. For example, they may be concentrating on getting their eggs into the dye without cracking them or on checking their eggs to see if they have enough color. At these times, adults can support children's work by getting their own set of similar materials and then using the materials to imitate what children are doing. Imitation engages you in a partnership with children without interfering with their intentions. As Becki works alongside Caleb, dyeing her own egg green, Caleb advises, "Becki, don't take it [the egg] out. It needs more green." "Okay," Becki agrees, putting her egg back into the cup.

Converse with children, following *their* lead. When children talk, respond to them by sticking to their conversational topic, tone, and pace:

Catherine: *Mine is turning green, Becki!*
Becki: *It is turning green.*
Catherine: *It's spreading.* (She looks at her cup from the bottom.)
Becki: *I see the green spreading.*
Catherine: *It's really, really green. Even on the bottom.*

When introducing your small-group activity, keep your explanation brief and to the point. The children will take the lead in expanding on the activity, once you've introduced it.

Encourage children do things for themselves, and refer them to one another for assistance if necessary. Children learn through their own actions, so the more adults encourage them to do for themselves at small-group time, the more learning opportunities they have. Referring children who need assistance to their peers encourages independence in another way—it helps them to see their classmates, as well as adults, as valuable resources. When a child spilled dye in Becki's small-group time, she would matter-of-factly pass the child a paper towel. The child would then wipe up the spill without assistance and go on with egg coloring. This experience also enabled children who had spilled to sympathize with other spillers. "That's just what happened with mine!" Caleb said when Catherine spilled dye on her hands. Bolstered by Caleb's encouragement, Catherine then went to the sink without further ado, washed her hands, and returned to color her other two eggs. Thus, even though we like to do things for children at small-group time, we are more effective teachers if we let children do things for themselves and encourage them to rely on one another as resources.

Ask questions sparingly. For children, the most relevant questions are the ones they ask themselves. "Does the green really go all through, even to the bottom?" Catherine wonders after she drops her dye pellet into the vinegar. When you do ask a question at small-group time, make sure it is part of an ongoing conversation and directly related to what the child is doing or thinking. Questions that encourage children to tell you more about how they are thinking about their activities are especially useful:

Namen: *I'm keepin' mine in [in the dye cup] for a long time.*
Becki: *What will happen to it after a long time?*
Namen: *It'll catch more color.*

Bringing Small-Group Time to a Close

In High/Scope programs, adults strive to bring small-group time to a smooth conclusion while continuing to meet children's individual needs. These strategies help adults achieve this goal:

Realize that children finish at different times. As small-group time winds down, it's important to avoid rushing children who work slowly; nevertheless, because small-group time isn't quite over is no reason to hold children to a task in which they're no longer interested. In the egg-coloring small-group time, for example, Becki allowed children to finish at their own pace. As children finished one by one, she had them put away their materials, then talked to them individually about their plans for work time. This way, some children could begin a new activity while others were finishing their egg dyeing.

When necessary, give children fair warning about the end of small-group time. Sometimes small-group time must end at a set time, perhaps because lunch is ready or because right after small-group time the whole group will be walking to the park. In such cases, **give children a warning several minutes before they will need to put materials away.** This gives those who are working slowly the opportunity to find a natural stopping point in what they are doing. You can also **remind those who are not finished that the materials will be available at another time** (for example, during that day's or the next day's work time), so they can plan to finish their activities then.

As small-group time draws to a close, children may want to share what they've accomplished, make plans to take their projects home, or talk about ways to follow up on their work. Don't rush children through these concluding discussions, as this is an opportunity for children to evaluate and bring closure to their work. Such discussion facilitates a smooth transition to the next activity, which is the final step in small-group times that engage children fully in the active learning process.

Small Groups in Elementary Classrooms

By Charles Hohmann

• •

In High/Scope elementary classrooms, small-group time takes the form of a 50- to 70-minute "workshop" period, in which three or four small groups of 4 to 8 children work at separate "stations" and rotate through them. At the kindergarten level the station activities are briefer than in grades 1 to 3; the children spend 10 or 15 minutes on each activity and usually change stations two or three times during the workshop period. By third grade the time allotted for single activities stretches to about 30 minutes; if the teacher has planned four activities, each small group does two of the activities in one day's workshop, and the groups usually trade activities in the next day's workshop.

Workshop activities are teacher-initiated and focus on specific concepts or skills in mathematics, language, science, and other curriculum areas. During workshop periods, teachers usually work intensively with one of the groups, *facilitating*—not *directing*—what the group is doing. The remaining groups work independently (on activities planned by the teacher).

Partly because a workshop group must be able to function independently as well as with the teacher, group composition is an important consideration. Following are some things to keep in mind when dividing an elementary-school class into small groups:

• Groups should be easy to handle. If possible, separate children whose personalities clash.

• Attempt to balance each group by such factors as gender, ability, personality, tendency to lead or follow, and so on. Avoid ability grouping—research indicates it is detrimental to the average and low-performing children. It's okay to occasionally group a few children together who need practice on particular skills, but avoid making this a pattern.

• Change the group membership throughout the year, so children get a chance to work with a variety of other children.

• While group membership should vary, this should not be at the expense of an established daily routine. It's important for children to know where they are supposed to be and to have the feeling of belonging to a group.

The following account shows how one teacher conducted a language workshop session with her third-grade class, which is used to splitting into four workshop groups:

It is 10:30 a.m., and children have just come in from recess. To launch the workshop session, Mrs. McCain brings the whole group (24 children) together and briefly reviews the concepts to be covered and materials to be used by the four workshop groups. Then she reminds the class where each small group will go for each half of today's workshop.

Group 1 *starts out at the computer area, working in pairs on the class-room's four computers. The children use two different computer programs: a word-processing program and a skill-practice program on vowel sounds. In the second half of the workshop, Group 1 goes to the "Go Fish" activity, a spell-ing game introduced to this group on the previous day.*

In High/Scope elementary classrooms, small-group time takes the form of a 50- to 70-minute "workshop" period, in which three or four small groups of children take turns working at separate "stations."

Teachers who have adopted the workshop approach in their elementary school classrooms report that children interact, cooperate, and communicate with one another more than they do in traditional, large-group settings.

Group 2 does the "Go Fish" game for the first half of the workshop and then works with Mrs. McCain at the language table. During this second segment of the workshop, the children first silently read the story "Stone Soup" from their reading textbooks. Then they discuss the story and begin planning a play based on the story. In tomorrow's workshop, the group will begin creating props for the play.

Group 3 starts the workshop session by working with Mrs. McCain on the "Stone Soup" activity. For their second activity, they go to the art area. They start this portion of the workshop by reading, silently, a Halloween story in their reading books. Then they produce a taped "radio play" of the story, using all kinds of interesting sound effects (clinking blocks together to make footsteps; flapping a piece of sheet metal to make the sound of thunder). They were introduced to some of the materials needed to make sound effects in the previous day's music class.

Group 4 starts with the radio play activity and then goes to the computer area.

At 11:30 Mrs. McCain calls a halt to the activities and brings the group as a whole together again. Each group briefly reports on what they did and the insights they gained in the workshop.

Teachers who have adopted the workshop approach in their elementary school classrooms report that children interact, cooperate, and communicate with one another more than they do in traditional, large-group settings. Children not only take more responsibility for their own learning but also are able to participate in evaluating their own work. The teachers also find that small-group work makes it possible to introduce a greater variety of "hands-on" materials and to give children more individualized attention.

Shifting Gears Smoothly:
Making the Most of
Transition Times

By Becki Perrett

• •

Throughout the day in every early childhood setting, there are many transitions for children. When a parent drops a child off in the morning, when the class walks down the hall to the lunchroom, when a small group finishes recall time and starts eating their snacks—all of these are important transitions. At these times, children experience one or more changes—of activity, location, caregiver, or playmates.

Since children often react strongly to changes like these, it's important for adults to plan carefully for all transitions. Adults may think of these changeover times as incidental parts of the routine, but they are crucial events for children. Well-planned transitions often make the difference between a "bad day" and one that goes smoothly.

Keys to Successful Transitions

To ease transition times for your group of children, start by looking at your overall daily routine. **Be sure the routine is consistent**—transitions go more smoothly if children know what to expect and can prepare themselves for what comes next. If your program is based on the High/Scope approach, you and your team members have probably already developed a consistent routine for your group of children.

In addition, in discussing your daily routine with your team members, **consider the *number* of transitions** between activities, places, and caregivers. Ask yourselves, Are there are too many transitions? Can we coordinate our daily routine so there are fewer changes and smoother transitions? For example, teachers in one Head Start program decided to reduce the number of transitions in their day by not having their children regroup after breakfast, in another location, to make their plans. In this program, a teacher asks for each child's plan at the breakfast table, as soon as the child has finished eating. Then that child moves directly into work time.

Making transitions fun keeps the focus on active learning and smooths the way for children. This child is "driving" to the "next stop" of the day.

This way, children make only one shift in location (from the breakfast table to the chosen play area) instead of two (from the breakfast table to the planning table to the play area). And, children don't have to wait for others to finish eating before they can make their plans. As this example shows, **reducing the number of changes children have to make** and **eliminating waiting time** are keys to planning successful transitions.

Also, once a transition has occurred, it's important to **get started right away with the new activity.** At the beginning of a small-group or circle time, for example, problems may arise if children have to wait as the teacher prepares materials. Keep in mind that even if not all children are finished with an activity, you can start a new activity. At the High/Scope Demonstration Preschool last year, circle time followed snack time. The children were assigned to two groups for snack, one group with each teacher. As each child finished eating, he or she moved to the circle. As soon as a few children were at the circle, the teacher who was designated to lead that day's circle time would move to the circle and start right in with a song, movement game, or fingerplay. This way, teachers didn't have to tell children to "wait until everyone is finished with snack time."

Waiting time can be reduced, but it can't always to eliminated. **When waiting time can't be avoided, plan ways to keep children actively involved.** If children have to wait for the school bus at the end of the day, find a spot for them to wait with you. Use this time for singing songs, learning fingerplays, talking with one another, or reading books together. Remember that children of this age do not like to sit still and keep quiet.

You'll also need to plan ways to keep children mentally and physically active when they have to walk from place to place. Instead of asking children to walk quietly, single-file, with their hands at their sides, encourage them to move in creative ways: "Which animal can we move like as we walk down the hall to the bathroom?" (Each child chooses an animal to imitate.)

Supporting Children Who Have Trouble With Transitions

So far, we've outlined some general strategies that usually make transitions go smoothly for the group as a whole. But you may notice that transitions are a particular problem for a few children in your group. These are the children who have a hard time getting involved in cleaning up after work time, who resist leaving the playground when everyone else is going inside, and whose parents have to "pry them away" at the end of the day. When you identify these children, you can **plan strategies to help them through these transitions.** Here are some examples of strategies to try:

• **During your daily planning session, decide which adult will spend transitions with the child:** If Jessica has trouble getting started with cleanup, choose a teacher to be with Jessica at the end of work time to remind her of the upcoming transition and to help her. ("A Frequent Question," on the previous page, contains suggestions for helping the *whole group* with cleanup.)

• **Talk individually with the child before the transition, offering appropriate choices:** "Mikey, when you finish your snack, it will be circle time. Is there someone you want to sit next to at the circle?" or "Chelsea, it is almost time to go inside. Show me how you are going to move to get to the door."

• **If the end of work time or some other part of the routine is near and the child is obviously not going to be able to finish his or her activity, alert the child to the upcoming change, while also giving the child some control in deciding what to do:** "Deola, work time is almost over, but you have enough time to finish the face on your drawing. Then it will be time to clean up. If you want to finish your drawing tomorrow, where could you put it so you will remember it?"

Notice that all three of these strategies incorporate two important ingredients of active learning—*choice* and *adult support*. In fact, these strategies, along with the other transition-smoothing ideas discussed in this article, are all consistent with the same teaching approach we use during all parts of the daily routine. During transitions, just as at work time or small-group time or plan-do-review time, **remember to use the principles of active learning and build upon children's interests.**

Cleanup:
The Toughest Transition

By Becki Perrett

· ·

It's no surprise that cleanup time is the most difficult transition of the day for many of us who work with children. Cleaning up—whatever the setting—is an emotional issue for many adults: We often judge ourselves by how clean and orderly our homes are. As teachers, too, we often measure the day's success by how smoothly cleanup time goes.

To plan for successful cleanup times, it's primarily important to **be realistic in your expectations of children.** Cleanup is an adult-initiated activity; yet a child's need at cleanup is often to continue to play. Though we as adults may hate to clean, we often expect children to clean up willingly and are surprised when this doesn't happen.

Although it's natural for children to resist cleaning up, cleanup is a valuable learning experience. As they clean up, children are developing self-help skills and a sense of responsibility for their environment. In addition, they are engaging in many of the High/Scope key experiences. For example, they are *classifying* as they sort spoons from forks and place the utensils on the shelves; they are *representing* as they pretend to be airline pilots "flying" the toys to their boxes.

To engage children in cleanup and keep them actively involved, we need to plan ways to support them. Here are some ideas:

First, prepare for cleanup beforehand. Cleaning up usually doesn't come naturally to children; so for a successful cleanup effort, you'll need to "set the scene" by labeling the classroom. Because cleaning up is a lot easier if everyone knows where materials belong, it helps to label classroom shelves and containers with developmentally appropriate labels. Use *concrete labels* (for example, a Lego block taped to the side of the Lego container); *pictures of the materials* (drawings, catalog pictures, or Polaroid photos taped to appropriate containers or shelves); and *tracings* (outlines of objects taped to the exact places where the objects go on shelves, pegboards, or racks). *Word labels* are okay, too, if you also have a concrete or pictorial label for each set of materials.

Is Cleanup for All Ages?

I work in a center-based child care center serving children 18 months to 5 years old. Should I expect all of my children to clean up the room every day?

—A teacher

There isn't one right answer to this question. It's up to the teaching team to decide exactly what their expectations are for their group at cleanup.

The first thing you should consider is the developmental level of the children in your care. Cleanup, like any other part of the daily routine, should be developmentally appropriate. A rule of thumb: The younger the child, the less you can expect of him or her at cleanup time.

Toddlers and younger preschoolers are often easily distracted when cleaning up. They will begin to put a toy away and then become engrossed in playing with it. Gentle reminders and assistance from adults are needed to keep younger children engaged. With this age group, adults often do most of the picking up.

Older preschoolers are more capable of understanding the concept of cleaning up, but some would rather do almost anything but put toys away. These are the children who hide under tables, go to a new area and begin something new, or continue with their ongoing work when everyone else is cleaning up. This can be very frustrating for a classroom adult who sees such behavior as a sign that she has lost control. At these times, ask yourself, Why do I have the expectation that children will willingly engage in cleaning up, when I often avoid cleaning my house, car, and so forth? Then plan strategies to support individual children.

In sum, to make cleanup less stressful, think through the expectations for your group, plan for individual children, and then *relax*.

Second, clean up as you go. Before children start a new activity, encourage them to put away the toys they are using: "Tiffany, you're done playing in the house area. Let's put away the dishes, and then you can tell me your next plan." This strategy reduces classroom clutter, making it easier for children to see the choices available to them. And there's less to do later at cleanup time if children pick up as they go along. There are occasions, however, when it isn't appropriate for children to clean up immediately after they finish doing something. For example, if five children have built a stage out of blocks for a "concert," and then one of them decides to paint, the block stage should be left out for the other children to use. Deciding if and when children should be expected to clean as they go is an issue for the teaching team to resolve through discussion.

Finally, throughout cleanup time, look for ways to make the process engaging, active, and enjoyable for children Some ideas to try:

• **Follow children's interests.** Use what you know about individual children and build on it. If Petey loves to pretend he's a basketball star,

Cleanup can be a time of exciting active learning experiences. These children are "swabbing the decks like sailors on a ship." Imaginative adventures such as these, that arise from the children's interests, can make cleanup time as enjoyable for children as other parts of the daily routine.

hold out the trash can and encourage him to "shoot baskets" with paper scraps and other litter. Another way to follow children's interests is to **imitate what children are doing.** For example, sometimes children enjoy carrying toys in unique ways. If you see Athi carrying something behind his back, try imitating him as you carry a toy to its place on the shelf. This will probably catch the attention of other children, who will then imitate what they see you and Athi doing.

• **Extend on children's work-time activities.** If children are pretending to be dogs during work time, encourage the "dogs" to clean up: "Doggie Ben, [handing the child a toy] here is a bone for you to put away." You might follow this by saying "Can *you* find another bone to put away?"

• **Make a game of cleaning up. Be playful.** For example, try these cleanup ideas:

> **Surprise!** One teacher encourages children to clean up an area quickly before the other teacher sees what they are doing. The other teacher is told not to peek into the area. When the children have cleaned the area, they permit the other teacher to look and be "so surprised!"

Responding to the Unexpected

Dealing with children's mess-making can push teachers to the limits of their patience. In these two vignettes of cleanup times from the High/Scope Demonstration Preschool, teachers responded calmly to unexpected messes, helping children learn about the natural consequences of their actions.

During one day's cleanup time last year, Sam, one of the teachers, asked three children to wash paintbrushes. While they went into the bathroom to wash the brushes, Sam got involved working with the rest of the children in the classroom. Shortly afterwards, a child ran to Sam, reporting excitedly, "The kids are painting the bathroom!"

The children had gotten carried away and had painted the toilets and the linoleum walls with red, green, and blue paint.

Sam walked into the bathroom, and (resisting the temptation to get angry) calmly asked the children what happened.

"We're painting just like my dad does at home," Max said.

Sam asked the children what they needed to do, and several answered, "Clean up the bathroom." Sam found sponges, and the children washed off all the paint.

Later, at their daily planning session, the teachers decided to support the children's interest in painting by making large paintbrushes and buckets of water available at outside time the next day. To limit the temptation for children to paint the bathroom walls again, the teachers also decided to confine further paintbrush-washing to the art-area sink.

The next day, the children enjoyed "painting" the climber, the surface of the playground, and the building with water. They never again tried to paint the bathroom.

❧

One day near the beginning of the school year, Kenneth decided it might be fun to make a pile of toys in the house area. The idea was contagious, and soon a small group of children were gleefully pulling toys off the shelves and adding them to the rapidly growing pile.

When it came time to clean up, Beth reminded the children who had made the pile that it was their job to put the toys away. It took 45 minutes for the children to put all the toys in their places. To help keep the children involved in their task, the teachers supported them throughout the process, using all the active learning strategies they could muster.

The next day, the teachers overheard Petey asking Kenneth if he wanted to make a pile again. The adults chuckled as they heard Kenneth reply, "No way! If we dump out all these toys, we'll be cleaning up forever!"

When children understand that it is their job to put toys and materials away, they accept the responsibility for keeping their environment in order and also develop self-help skills.

Paper bag. Give each child a lunch sack or grocery bag. Ask children to move around the room, filling up their bags with toys that are out. When the bags are full, ask them to return the toys to their places in the room.

Football game. One teacher pretends to be a football player, "hiking" a toy between her legs to a child behind her. The child then puts that toy away and returns for another one. Children will often line up behind the teacher to play this game.

Statues. Play music as children clean up, stopping the music occasionally. When the music stops, children pose as statues, resuming cleanup when the music begins again.

Music cleanup. Music can be used in a variety of other ways during cleanup. For example, sing a cleanup song, with or without children's names in it. It's also fun to play selections at different tempos as children put things away. The children then match their pace to the music, speeding up or slowing down as the music changes. Another idea is to put a familiar song on the tape player and ask children to clean up the room before the song is over.

One more hint for teachers to keep in mind at cleanup time: **Stay flexible.** Just because cleanup (or some other transition) isn't going as expected doesn't mean it can't result in a worthwhile experience for children. "Responding to the Unexpected" on p. 94 provides vignettes of two such difficult incidents from the High/Scope Demonstration Preschool. In both of these situations, which occurred early in the school year, children were testing the boundaries of appropriate classroom behavior by making bigger-than-usual messes.

Notice that in both cases of boundary-testing, teachers resisted the temptation to scold children. Instead, they stepped back and looked for ways to turn the situations into active learning experiences with a lasting impact. Instead of squelching children's initiatives, they built on them, but they still made it clear they expected the children to clean up after themselves. These cleanup experiences gave children opportunities to learn about the natural consequences of their actions.

Greeting Time:
A Smooth Transition for Children

By Carol Beardmore

· ·

The morning session is beginning at the High/Scope Demonstration Preschool. As the children arrive, teachers Carol and Beth take their places: Carol greets families at the door while Beth stations herself in the book area. Carol greets the first child, Rachel, and her dad. Then, as Rachel approaches the book area, Beth greets her. Rachel walks over to the bookshelf, chooses the book Who's Counting, *sits down in Beth's lap, and asks her to read it. Beth reads the story to Rachel, and when they get to the page with the number 5, Rachel counts the five eggs that are in the picture. Meanwhile, Carol is greeting Brendan at the door. Brendan says to Carol, "I'm gonna use those bricks in the blue tub over there" and points to the tub of plastic connecting blocks. They discuss the things he made with the blocks the day before. Then he walks over to the book area, chooses a book, sits down, and begins to page through the book. (Because he is used to the routine, Brendan understands that he will start working on his plan at work time and that using the blocks is not a choice now.)*

Several more children arrive. After Carol greets Frances, Daniel, and Kelly, they go to the book area, and Frances and Kelly join Rachel in listening to the story Beth is reading. Looking at the last page of the book, Kelly counts 10 puppies, and Frances counts their 10 dog dishes. As Beth reads to the small cluster of children gathered around her, some of the other children explore various books on their own while other children sit and talk with one another. (Brendan says, "Look, I got new shoes," to which Daniel responds, "Hey, you have the same shoes as me!" They put their feet next to each other and look at their shoes more closely.)

Then Kayla and her mom join the children in the book area. Kayla's mom sits down with her and reads the book Kayla has chosen from the shelf. Meanwhile, Carol stands at the window with Leah, so Leah can wave to her caregiver.

Once all the children have arrived, Carol joins the group at the book area. She and Beth let the children know that they have two more minutes to look at books. Frances looks around the area and says,"If Megan's not here, I'm working with Kelly and Leah today." After two minutes, Beth and Carol sing "It's Time to Put the Books Away" and "read" the day's messages with the children. (The messages are usually in the form of simple pictures the teachers have drawn on a wipe-off message board in the book area.)

Together they look at the first message, which shows Megan's symbol with a red circle around it and a slash through it. Frances "reads" the message: "Megan is not going to be at school today." Kayla "reads" the next message, a drawing of a stick figure looking through a camera: "Mary and camera boy are coming here again." (Two staff members are scheduled to videotape in the classroom that day.)

Now that the messages have been read, Carol asks the children to choose different ways to move to their planning tables. Children crawl, walk, run, and jump to the two planning tables, and planning begins with one teacher at each table.

This scenario illustrates a typical greeting time in the Demonstration Preschool. The main purpose of greeting time is to assist children in making the transition from home to school and from parent or caregiver to teacher. For children, greeting time is a time to ease into the routine of the preschool. For parents, it is a time to exchange a few words with a teacher or to read a story with their child before saying goodbye for the morning. Greeting time is also the setting for a variety of important learning experiences.

Principles for Planning Greeting Time

There are several principles to keep in mind when planning for greeting time:

• **Hold greeting time in a space close to and visible from the entrance of your classroom.** In the High/Scope Demonstration Preschool we have our greeting time in the book area, which is easily seen by anyone walking in the door. This arrangement is important for several reasons. First, it enables children to go straight to the book area without passing by materials in other areas that will not be available to them until work time. Second, children are more eager to join in greeting-time activities if they can see them from the entrance. In addition, holding greeting time close to the entrance makes it easy for children in the book area to say goodbye to adults who are leaving.

• **Make the space in which you hold greeting time open and inviting to the children.** In addition to a bookshelf, our book area has a rug, two beanbag chairs, several throw pillows, and a plant. We have books, story tapes, and puzzles available for the children to choose from at greeting time. This small range of materials enables children to make choices and stay active during this transition time.

Sharing Daily Announcements With Children

In most preschool programs in which children's arrival times do not vary too widely, greeting time is a good time to share with children the news and announcements relevant to the day's events in the classroom. For example, you may need to inform children that one of their classmates or a teacher is absent that day, introduce a substitute teacher or classroom visitor, or remind children of new materials added to the classroom. To support children's emergent reading, these announcements can be shared in the form of simple drawings (sometimes accompanied by a few words).

"Reading" these picture-messages helps make children aware that writing is one way that important information can be conveyed. Such messages can be shared in a variety of ways. A wipe-off message board is used in the High/Scope Demonstration Preschool; however, an easel pad, a chalkboard, or just a large piece of paper could also be used. Whatever method you choose, make sure that any pictures or letters are large enough for the children to see and that they are at children's eye-level.

• **Plan on encouraging parents to stay during greeting time.** Contrary to conventional wisdom, it is *not* necessary to ask parents to ease their child's separation by leaving as quickly as possible. We have found that inviting parents to linger awhile at the beginning of the day actually eases this transition for children. Greeting time not only gives the parent and child a little more time to be together but also encourages both of them to become involved in talking, interacting, and exploring books with the other children. This helps the child to feel more relaxed and comfortable in the classroom and also prepares him or her to say goodbye to the parent.

• **Plan the role each team member will assume during greeting time.** In our classroom, one teacher is the "greeter." She stations herself near the door, so she can talk to the children and parents as they arrive. At this time, parents and children may share any news they have, and the teacher may pass on information about school events or share an anecdote about the child's activities. For example, the teacher who is greeting Brendan may learn that his grandparents are visiting, that he has a new pet, that he was up late the night before, or that his grandmother will be picking him up that day. In turn, the teacher might tell the parent about an upcoming field trip or describe the structure Brendan built in the block area the previous day. It's important for teachers not to rush through these conversations at the door: These interactions not only ease the transition from home for the children but also offer excellent opportunities for parents to be involved in their child's educational experiences. In programs in which the children arrive by bus, without their parents, it's still important for the teacher to greet and talk with each child at the door.

In our classroom, the second teacher's role is to interact with the children in the book area. This teacher talks with children and reads the books they request. If several children request different stories at the same time, the teacher explains to children that she is reading another book right then and that she will read their chosen book or books next. She may also offer children the choice of either looking at their books independently until she is finished or listening to the story she is reading. She also encourages parents to join in reading with children at this time. If the teacher realizes there isn't enough time to fill everyone's request, she lets some of the children know that she can read their selections with them later during work time. So not only does the teacher model reading and questioning styles for any parents who are present, but she also models a way to problem-solve—how to handle "too many requests."

At the Demonstration Preschool, the two teachers alternate these roles; the teacher who greets families at the door is stationed in the book area the following day. Conducting greeting time close to the entrance of the classroom enables teachers to be somewhat flexible in these roles. For example, the adult whose role that day is to greet the families can spend some time interacting with some of the children in the book area in the times between children's arrivals. Likewise, if the greeter is busy with some parent or child, the second adult is close enough to the door to greet anyone else who comes in.

Key Experiences at Greeting Time

If you observe children carefully during greeting time, you will notice that a great deal of learning is taking place. By jotting down a few anecdotes from your observations, you will be able to identify the key experiences that are occurring. Since much of the activity at greeting time centers around books, there are frequent opportunities for key experiences in the **language and literacy** category; however, key experiences in many other categories also occur.

Consider, for example, how many key experience categories are evident in the typical greeting time described in this article. As Frances, Kelly, and Rachel listen to Beth read stories, and as Kayla and Frances interpret the picture writing on the message board, they are engaging in **language and literacy** and **representation** key experiences. As Brendan

Greeting Children in Home Child Care Programs

While the need for a smooth transition at the opening of the daily session is universal in early childhood programs, staff of each program must plan this time in an individual way. The opening routine established in each program will vary according to such factors as staffing patterns, parents' work schedules, children's arrival times, climate, the physical facility, and the schedules for such other activities as mealtimes and outdoor play.

Recently, Kathie Spitzley, a High/Scope endorsed trainer in Holland, Michigan, and the director of a family child care group home serving 12 children, described how she ensures a smooth morning transition for the children in her program. The children in Kathie's group range in age from 9 months to 5 years.

Kathie's program opens at 6:30 a.m., and most of the children arrive between 7:30 and 8:00. Kathie is the only greeter until the second caregiver arrives, although the second caregiver is also familiar with the routine for greeting children.

Kathie's back door opens to the kitchen, so she stations herself in the same corner of the kitchen each morning to greet parents and children. (When the second caregiver arrives, she interacts with children at the breakfast table or in the game area, which is adjacent to and visible from the kitchen.) As each child arrives, Kathie greets the parent and child, and the parent takes the child downstairs, where the child hangs up his or her coat. After they come upstairs, the child may choose to sit down in the kitchen and have breakfast or go to the game area. In the game area children can play with small toys such as Legos, little dinosaurs, puzzles, and pull toys; they may also choose to explore the books available in the nearby reading area.

Kathie encourages parents not to rush off but instead to participate in as much of the transition as they can, either sharing breakfast with their child or perhaps reading a story to him or her before they leave. She sometimes holds "hot muffin Mondays" to encourage parents to stay and have a fresh muffin with their child. As the parent leaves, Kathie and the child go to the front door to wave to the parent, and then she helps the child find something to do.

Kathie emphasizes that small children (usually those younger than 3 years) must be transferred by the parent directly to her arms, or the transition does not go smoothly. She also has discovered that even small changes in the greeting routine—such as missing the goodbye wave to Mom or Dad—can be upsetting to a child. According to Kathie, a consistent routine for greeting children "is critical for each and every child." She points out that a predictable routine enables children to be more independent: "Following a routine that includes opportunities to make choices empowers children to manage their own transitions."

and Frances talk about their play plans, they are engaging in **initiative** key experiences. As Brendan and Daniel compare their shoes, they are participating in **classification** key experiences. As Rachel, Kelly, and Frances spontaneously count objects in the book Beth is reading, they are encountering key experiences in **number.**

In the daily routine, greeting time sets the stage for all that comes after. This important time involves teachers, children, and parents. It offers many enjoyable learning experiences for children and also provides many opportunities for meaningful interactions between parents and teachers.

Unlike the whole-group teacher-led "story time" that is held in some preschools, our greeting time is a time when individual children are free to use books in all kinds of ways. Typically, the teacher reads to one or a few children at a time, while other children talk with one another or explore books together or independently. In this more intimate, informal setting, children typically engage in a wider range of learning experiences than they do when listening to teacher-read stories in a large group. This approach to story-reading also makes it easier for the teacher to interact with individual children and to observe the key experiences that are occurring. When the adult is able to observe what the children are noticing and understanding in the story, she is better able to respond appropriately.

As you can see, greeting time is more than just a transition to other parts of the routine; it offers important learning experiences and interaction opportunities for children.

Planning the Day in Infant and Toddler Programs

By Jackie Post and Mary Hohmann

· ·

Early childhood educators familiar with the High/Scope preschool approach know that a consistent daily routine is one of the important elements of programs for children of preschool age (2½ to 5 years old). As more and more High/Scope programs serve children in the infant and toddler age range (from birth to 2½ or 3 years old), staff members must decide how to plan the day to meet the needs of these very young children.

Guidelines for Daily Schedules

In this article, we present some guidelines for developing daily schedules and routines for infants and toddlers in High/Scope child care settings.

The following scenario, which was observed in a High/Scope infant and toddler program, illustrates some of the principles of maintaining daily schedules for infants and toddlers:

Six toddlers sit at a small table eating lunch. Their caregivers, Ann and Ruby, sit with them at the table. As the children finish, they put their cups and plates into a dish tub, leave the table, and return to the riding toys they were playing with before lunch time. Ann stays at the table with the children who are still eating, while Ruby sits on the floor near the children who are using riding toys. When all the children have finished, Ann removes the dish tub and wipes the table. Ruby then takes the children individually or by twos into the bathroom for the caregiving routines that precede naptime, returning them to play with the riding toys until naptime. Ann takes Ruby's place on the floor with the riding-toy riders until each child has been to the bathroom and it's time for stories and naps

This after-lunch scenario illustrates typical daily occurrences in High/Scope infant and toddler programs. These toddlers are engaged in a **pattern, or sequence, of activities**—lunch, riding toys, bodily care routines, riding toys, stories, and naps. They move from one part of their day to the next with a **child-focused transition** between each part: Using the riding toys serves as a transition from lunch and toileting to stories and naps. The children also experience certain **predictable elements within each activity.** For example, every day as they finish lunch, the toddlers put their dishes into the dish tub.

Before discussing the planning behind the sequences of activities in High/Scope care settings, we need to define what a *daily schedule* means for an infant or a toddler. In a group of six to nine infants and toddlers, **each child has a consistent daily schedule, or pattern of activities, based on his or her particular needs, temperament, and natural rhythms.** This means that six to nine individualized daily schedules occur simultaneously, calling for both flexibility and organization on the part of caregiving staff.

Fortunately, there are common elements among infants' and toddlers' individual daily schedules, and these elements often overlap. This overlap makes it possible for caregivers to **create an *overall* daily schedule that is stable and responsive to children's individual needs.**

For infants and toddlers, **the components of the day in a High/Scope program include certain regular events:** *play* or *choice time, outside time,* and additionally for older toddlers, *small-group time* and *large-group time.* Interspersed among these daily events are individual *caregiving routines,* that is, the supportive, child-focused interactions that occur during eating, napping, and bodily care (including diapering, toileting, washing, and dressing).

The following is the overall program schedule that evolved from children's individual schedules in a High/Scope mixed-age child care program serving infants, toddlers, and younger preschoolers (ages 3 months to 2½ years).

Overall Daily Schedule

Arrivals (7:00–8:00 a.m.)	Bodily care
Choice time	Nap
Breakfast	Bodily care
Bodily care	Small-group time
Choice time	Choice time
Cleanup	Outside time
Large-group time	Bodily care
Bodily care	Choice
Outside time	Departures (5:00–6:00 p.m.)
Lunch (12:00–1:00 p.m.)	

"Daily Schedules for Latisha, Bobby, and Carlos" on p. 105 presents the actual daily routines followed by three children of different ages in that High/Scope program. These individual schedules include routine

Daily Schedules for Latisha, Bobby, and Carlos

Daily Schedule for Latisha
(A Non-napper), Age 2½

Arrival (7:15 a.m.; says "Bye" to Dad as she sits in caregiver's lap)

Choice time (plays in house area next to Carlos)

Breakfast

Choice time (plays in block area, then house area)

Bodily care (is in the process of toilet training: uses toilet and washes hands independently, using step stool at the sink)

Cleanup time (with an adult, puts blocks into baskets in the block area)

Large-group time (uses bells and drum with music tape)

Outside time (plays on slides and swings)

Bodily care (uses toilet, washes hands)

Lunch (noon–1:00 p.m.)

Choice time (wipes off lunch tables with sponge)

Small-group time (uses water, stones, paintbrushes)

Bodily care (uses toilet, washes hands)

Choice time (uses riding toys)

Outside time (digs in gravel with shovel)

Choice time (looks at books)

Bodily care (changes into a clean pair of socks)

Departure (5:15 p.m.)

Daily Schedule for Bobby,
Age 5 Months

Arrival (7:45 a.m.; mom passes him to the caregiver; caregiver holds him and he smiles at mom as he watches her go)

Choice time (lies on blanket with several soft balls)

Feeding (caregiver holds him and gives him a bottle)

Bodily care (usually gazes at pictures on the wall as caregiver changes his diaper)

Choice time (sits in infant seat, reaches for and grasps toys on tray)

Outside time (lies on a blanket near the slide, where he can see children and caregivers)

Nap

Bodily care (diaper change)

Feeding (12:10–1:00 p.m.; has bottle in caregiver's lap)

Choice time (splashes hands in tub of water with float toys)

Bodily care (diaper change)

Nap

Bodily care (plays peek-a-boo with caregiver as she changes diaper)

Feeding (has bottle in caregiver's lap)

Choice (plays peek-a-boo with caregiver, looks at books with another infant as caregiver reads)

Departure (5:30 p.m.)

Daily Schedule for Carlos,
Age 18 Months

Arrival (7:50 a.m.; waves to mom from the window as she goes to her car)

Choice time (plays in house area next to Latisha)

Breakfast

Bodily care (chooses a tape for the tape player at the changing table; has diaper change)

Choice time (first plays in block area with Latisha, then asks caregiver to read him stories)

Large-group time (shakes bells, then returns to book he was looking at)

Bodily care (diaper change)

Outside time (uses shovels and rakes at the sand table)

Lunch (noon–1:00 p.m.; eats spaghetti with a spoon and fingers)

Bodily care (diaper change)

Nap

Small-group time (fills and empties containers with water in washtub)

Choice time (uses riding and pushing toys)

Bodily care (brings a diaper from his cubby when caregiver asks him to get one)

Outside time

Choice time (explores books, asks caregiver to read stories to him)

Bodily care (diaper change to tape)

Departure (5:40 p.m.)

elements that are fairly consistent from day to day (such as using a potty chair after lunch) as well as activities that may vary each day (such as choosing to play with water toys at one of the choice times). Note that caregivers have planned the overall program schedule to overlap as much as possible with children's individual schedules. In most cases, we have not given specific starting times for the events on these schedules, because the times when various activities occur and the length of each time segment will vary according to the ongoing interests and activities of individual children.

Caregivers in High/Scope care settings, then, must **learn and respond to each infant's or toddler's personalized daily schedule and at the same time develop an overall daily schedule that accommodates all the children in the group.** Coordinating multiple schedules can be a challenge. This is one reason why infant and toddler groups are relatively small (three to nine children) and why the ratio of adults to children in these groups is one adult for every two to four children. The complexity of dealing with infant and toddler schedules also makes it critically important for teaching teams to spend time each day discussing their observations of children and planning around them.

Though it *is* challenging to organize a program around multiple routines, the benefits to children are great. When routines for infants and toddlers are predictable and well-coordinated, infants and toddlers gain a sense of safety, security, and control. Since variability can overwhelm them, these very young children rely on adults to **maintain a sequence of events that remains substantially the same from one day to the next.** This daily consistency allows very young children to anticipate what happens next— for example, riding toys, then lunch. Even such an event as the daily separation from their parents is easier when children know what they will be doing after their parents leave.

Parts of a Daily Schedule

We've now discussed some **general principles** that guide our approach to daily schedules for infants and toddlers in child care settings. Next, we'll briefly describe the **typical components** of these schedules (see p. 107 for examples of each of these components).

Choice time. Young as they are, infants and toddlers, as they choose and explore materials at choice time, are able to take initiative and use problem-solving skills. Of course, in an active learning setting, adults offer children choices and materials during all parts of the day. During choice time, however, children and adults alike are focused on play in

Components of Daily Schedules for Infants and Toddlers

Here are some examples of typical behaviors of infants and toddlers during important elements of the daily schedule.

Choice Time

Michael rolls himself toward the mirror reflection. Elizabeth crawls to a doll, gets into a sitting position, picks up the doll with both hands, and babbles. She puts the doll on the floor, picks it up again, and babbles.

Tejas walks around the room hitting all the blocks on the floor with a plastic wrench. An adult watching Tejas offers him a plastic hammer to use along with the wrench.

Outside Time

Ian and John make roaring noises on their riding toys while traveling on the riding-toy path.

Lawanda pours buckets of water from the wading pool onto the grass.

In the arms of his caregiver, Andy gurgles and waves to Miko, who is swinging on the swing.

Patrice sits in the grass and runs her hands over the dandelions that grow all around her. An adult sitting next to Patrice imitates her actions with the dandelions. Patrice watches the adult and laughs.

Small-Group Time

Three older toddlers and their caregiver, Joanne, are gathered around a plastic baby bathtub into which they are crumbling pieces of stale bread and toast to feed to the birds. "See!" Larue says, letting a handful of crumbs fall into the tub and then wiggling her fingers. Henry pats all the crumbs in the tub while Bettina claps two pieces of toast together.

Joanne observes each child's way of exploring the materials, and she supports individual children by imitating their actions and responding to their conversational leads. Elsewhere in the yard, other toddlers are absorbed in other activities.

Large-Group Time

Six toddlers and their caregivers, Pat and Marie, are moving to music. Eddie and Juan bounce up and down, while Cantrell and Yvonne sit on either side of Marie, swaying side to side with her as the music plays. Morris and Becki hold hands, laugh, and fall down. Pat falls down with them. They repeat this sequence until the music stops. Annie, who has been watching the group from the house area, toddles over and joins the action, holding up her arms to Pat to let her know she wants to be rocked to the music. Pat picks her up and continues her dance with the other children.

Transitions

Ricardo's day at the infant and toddler center begins when his dad hugs him and then gives him to Rochelle, who rocks him gently in her arms as she sings him the "Good Morning" song. Then Rochelle carries him over to the toy area and waits until he is engrossed in playing with his favorite toys, the small dinosaurs, before turning to another child.

Choice time offers toddlers a wealth of possibilities for all kinds of play. Appropriately stocked interest areas enable toddlers to choose things to explore and play with according to their interests and intentions at any given moment. These children have chosen to "read" some interesting storybooks in the house area.

which the infants and toddlers use all their senses to experiment with a variety of sensorimotor materials.

Adults provide for nonmobile infants at choice time by bringing them materials to explore—for example, materials with a variety of textures, such as large sea shells, wooden spoons, or shiny apples. For infants who can sit by themselves, adults might provide baskets containing such commonplace treasures as pine cones, a toothbrush, metal keys on a ring, and a tennis ball. For toddlers, choice time offers possibilities for more complex play in a specific play or interest area—an appropriately stocked toddler block area, house area, art area, toy area, or sand-and-water area. In these interest areas, toddlers can choose things to explore and play with according to their interests and intentions at any given moment. Some older toddlers are able to express their intentions in a very brief plan, for example, by pointing to the toy area and saying "balls."

Outside time. Except for the fact that it occurs outdoors, outside time for infants and toddlers is very similar to choice time. At outside time, children explore and experience the world of nature and try out large-muscle equipment. Outside time takes place in a safe, enclosed outdoor area stocked with age-appropriate toys and equipment. Weather permitting, children enjoy riding, climbing, sliding, swinging, rocking, pushing, pulling, pouring, splashing, filling, emptying, and building. Nonmobile infants spend time on the grass, on a blanket, in a stroller or backpack, or in their caregivers' arms. They may explore loose materials caregivers have provided—such as scarves, balls, or large stones—or they may just observe their surroundings.

Small-group time. Caregivers plan small-group experiences for older toddlers that are based on their observations of children's actions and interests. Often the small-group activity involves toddlers in some simple process, such as crumbling toast to feed the birds or taking a walk. Or the activity may offer children an opportunity to explore new materials, such as newspaper or crayons, or to work with a familiar material they particularly enjoy, such as a favorite storybook, Play-Doh, or water.

Large-group time. Large-group time offers toddlers a chance to participate in music and movement explorations with other children. Large-group time is brief (often less than five minutes) and physically active. As with every other part of the day, at large-group time children make choices about what to do; for infants and toddlers, these choices might include just observing the activity, moving in and out of it, or not participating at all.

Large-Group Time— Is "Keeping It Together" a Goal?

I work with a very active group of toddlers. There are several activity books I like to use that have ideas for group games and circle time activities. However, when I try these with my children, I often can't get them to stay together until we get through a game. Any ideas?
—*A child care teacher*

Activity books can be a good place to start when planning experiences for toddlers, but many books suggest ideas that are more suited to older children and thus would have to be simplified for your children. Remember that your own observations of your group of children will best enable you to plan activities that fit their interests and needs for active involvement.

You mention that the children in your care are "active"—a description that characterizes most toddlers! We find that children this young are often not interested in remaining with a group activity that lasts more than a few minutes. However, you may have some children in your group who happen to love what they are doing at the moment and will gladly continue the activity for some time.

To meet these individual needs, you can structure your activities so children may come and go as their interests dictate. You'll need to provide other choices for those not currently interested in what the group is doing. For example, teachers may plan a group activity around listening to a music tape and exploring some rhythm instruments. During the activity, if two children wander away from the group, one of the teachers could offer them some wooden beads and shoelaces to play with. Keep in mind that younger children often have no concept of "finishing" an activity or game but can nevertheless be deeply involved in the *process* that is occurring.

Transitions. Infant and toddler caregivers strive to keep transitions—events that link one part of the day to the next—to a minimum. When transitions do occur, adults plan them as carefully as possible to avoid disrupting children's play or activities. The transitions are consistent, so children know what to expect. When it is necessary to move children from one activity to another (for a diaper change, for example), caregivers attempt to help children retain a sense of control by planning a transition that is both simple and active (riding toys between lunch and diapering), making room for children's choices ("What toy would you like to bring to the changing table?"), reminding children what will happen next ("Stories and nap are next"), and avoiding having children wait (children play with riding toys instead of standing in line at the changing table).

Caregiving routines. In addition to having such regular events as choice time and outside time, infants and toddlers spend much of their time in caregiving routines: eating, napping, and bodily care. The next article describes these routines in more detail.

We've summarized here the basic elements that make up daily schedules for infants and toddlers. Caregiving staff must put these elements together in ways that reflect the needs of their particular group of children.

Child-Focused Caregiving Routines for Infants and Toddlers

By Jackie Post and Mary Hohmann

• •

Infants and toddlers spend much of their time in routine activities such as eating, napping, and diaper-changing—activities necessary to their physical well-being. We call such activities "caregiving routines" because they involve repeated interactions between child and caregiver. In High/Scope programs, adults view these frequently repeated activities not as chores to get through but as interesting, vital parts of children's daily experiences that offer varied opportunities to support children's development.

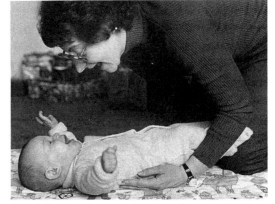

Caregiving experiences can be among the most enjoyable times babies and adults spend together.

To avoid turning these caregiving times into mechanical routines, adults using the High/Scope approach keep their focus on *children* during such activities—always looking for ways to support children's active learning. Here we discuss three caregiving routines—mealtime, diapering, and naptime—and suggest strategies for encouraging active learning during each set of activities.

Mealtime

Even when children are able to feed themselves, it's important for you to sit and eat with them, so you can observe and interact with each child. At mealtime, children have the opportunity to explore their food as well as to watch and imitate what others are doing with their food. As the caregiver, your role is to offer foods in ways that nurture children and support their explorations (for example, holding infants for bottle-feeding and offering older children, when appropriate, several choices of foods

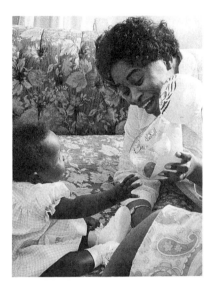

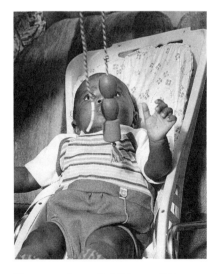

The many faces of child care: *Taking care of infants and toddlers is not only a major responsibility but also a great source of fulfillment for both children and the adults who care for them.*

they can handle with their fingers). Another way to support learning at mealtime is to help toddlers take part in setting the table for the meal and cleaning up afterward.

Diapering

Although following your center's health practices is your first responsibility at diapering time, it's also important not to miss the opportunity for one-to-one interaction with the child. While changing a diaper, adults can sing to or talk with the child and respond to the sounds the child makes. Placing pictures on the wall next to the changing area is one way to encourage the development of communication skills, as many children will vocalize about what or whom they see. You can also encourage children to bring something they like to handle to the changing table, as long as it is small enough to remain in the baby's hands and doesn't touch the diapering surface.

Naptime

Children usually don't have a choice about going to naptime, but you can help them develop a sense of control over their going-to-sleep routine by offering choices about how they will sleep. For example, encourage them to choose what they want to sleep with: a favorite blanket, a stuffed pet, or a book. You may want to provide alternative quiet activities for children who are not tired enough for a nap. These may be individual activities they can do while on cots or in cribs—such as looking at a book, listening to tapes, or dressing baby dolls—or the activities may involve some children moving away from the sleeping area to a space for working with quiet materials or listening to a story.

Some Anecdotes

The following anecdotes illustrate how the strategies just outlined can provide active learning experiences for typical children during normal caregiving routines:

At mealtime, the caregivers have provided easily handled sticks of French toast and small plastic bowls of applesauce for each toddler. Lizzie, 17 months, breaks her French toast stick in two and dips each piece in her applesauce bowl before taking a bite.

৯০

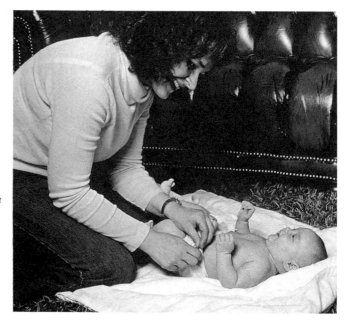

Diapering time represents a good opportunity for one-to-one interaction with a child. While changing a diaper, adults can sing to or talk with the infant and respond to the sounds the child makes.

Shawna, a caregiver, carries 3-month-old Margaret to the changing table, smiling at her and explaining where they are going. After laying Margaret down on the table, Shawna begins singing "We're going to change your diaper. . ." Margaret first watches Shawna's face intently as Shawna begins to sing and then smiles.

George, a teacher in a child care program for toddlers and preschoolers, is getting Sarah, age 20 months, and Hannah, 22 months, settled on their cots for naptime. Sarah climbs off her cot to get her soft doll, which she left on the floor before lunch. Hannah, already tucked in, watches Sarah get her doll and then says, "Baby, baby," pointing to her similar doll nearby. George says, "Would you like to get your doll, too?" Hannah nods, and slides off her cot to get her doll.

These anecdotes and the other examples and strategies suggested in this article convey just a few of many ways adults can capitalize on the active learning opportunities inherent in caregiving routines.

Chapter Three

Arranging Environments for Children
· ·

*C*areful planning of the physical setting for learning is one of the important elements of the High/Scope approach. High/Scope settings are organized and equipped to encourage children to choose from a wide variety of stimulating activities and materials. To provide an organized structure for the setting, staff arrange the space in distinct play areas—called interest areas—that are easily recognizable to adults and children. Within these, toys and materials are available on low shelves or on the floor, enabling children to take out and put away materials independently. While planning each interest area, adults select materials and arrange the space carefully, making sure that there is enough space for children to play both independently and cooperatively and that the materials support a range of play opportunities.

Interest areas in High/Scope settings typically include a block area, art area, book area, house area, music and movement area, sand-and-water area, and small-toy area. The setting may also include other areas that reflect the special interests or needs of the group, such as a computer area, construction area, and so forth.

The first three articles in this chapter deal with several specific play spaces in High/Scope preschool classrooms, each offering ideas for arranging and stocking a particular area and strategies for working with children who are using the materials in that area.

In "Open-Air Learning Experiences," Vincent Harris takes a close look at the outdoor play space, encouraging teachers and staff to consider the wide range of cognitive, social, and physical learning experiences that are possible outdoors. He urges staff who are planning an outdoor play space to consider not only the physical activities possible on outdoor play equipment but also the cognitive and social dimensions of children's use of playground equipment. Harris also urges staff to provide equipment and materials enabling children outdoors to engage in constructive play (making things) as well as a diversity of movement experiences. In "'High-Yield' Outdoor Materials" on p. 123, he gives examples of specific materials that are well suited to outdoor play areas. For each material, he illustrates a recommended planning process that highlights the issues for adults to consider when evaluating possible materials.

The next article, "Developing a Creative Art Area" by Mark Tompkins, offers ideas for art area tools and materials that generate interest, excitement, and creativity. His suggestions include some nontraditional materials to consider (for example, a group easel that makes painting a social experience) as well as some new ways of using familiar materials (using sponges or string for painting tools). The accompanying checklist enables teachers to evaluate their own art areas to see where additional materials are needed.

The classroom's reading space is the focus of Susan M. Terdan's "The Book Area: From Beginning to End." Explaining that planning and stocking any interest area should be an ongoing process that reflects the changing needs of the children, Terdan discusses how to select a supply of books for the preschool center and explains how staff plan for changes in the classroom book supply over the course of the year.

In the next article, "In the Elementary School—A New Activity Area Develops," Charles Hohmann looks at the distinct areas (called activity areas) in High/Scope elementary classrooms. This article describes how one activity area developed in a particular High/Scope classroom, illustrating how teachers and children can work together to plan activity areas that reflect their interests. In this case, children were interested in beadwork and, together with the teacher, made plans to set up and equip a beading area that became a popular choice for children's projects.

The last two articles, by Beth Marshall, focus on the preschool setting as a whole rather than on a specific interest area. Marshall explores how teaching staff can incorporate into the preschool setting specific materials reflecting children's diverse family experiences. She explains how, in such "family-friendly" settings, children realize that their own family lives are valued and learn to value family experiences that are both similar to and different from their own.

Open-Air
Learning Experiences

By Vincent Harris

. . . .

High-quality outdoor activities for young children result from a commitment by program staff to extend the classroom curriculum outdoors. Outside, whether on the playground or in the backyard, the essentials of providing a high-quality early childhood program are the same as they are indoors: Adults plan a developmentally rich environment that offers a wide variety of play options and experiences; within this environment, they work supportively with children.

In a High/Scope early childhood setting, the outdoor play space is rich in opportunities for children's physical, cognitive, and social development. The playground design and equipment not only present large-motor physical challenges for children but also offer them opportunities for play with loose materials and for participation in both child- and adult-organized activities.

The adult's role outdoors is to encourage children's learning and development by actively supporting and participating in their activities.

In considering particular equipment for the playground, it's important for teachers and caregivers to think about all aspects of children's play, including the social and cognitive dimensions of an activity.

Some adults who consistently apply this principle when working with children indoors *change* their style when the group moves outdoors. Often, the way caregivers respond to outdoor play falls at one of two extremes on the spectrum of interaction. Some adults monitor children's play from a bench, using outdoor time to socialize with other staff members. Others plan activity upon activity for children, focusing primarily on organized sports, games, and movement experiences.

Neither extreme is ideal. Instead, there should be a balance of teacher and child initiatives in outdoor play, and adults should encourage many kinds of experiences.

Supporting Outdoor Learning

Here are some general guidelines for designing and equipping the outdoor play space and for working with children outdoors.

In planning for outdoor activities, adults seek to provide opportunities for play and learning that are not possible indoors. The playground is a sanctuary for types of play that may not be permitted in the classroom, center, or home. The outdoor space has room for the running feet and "outdoor voices" that are not tolerable inside. So when children engage in play that is not acceptable indoors, this may be a signal to the adults to look for ways to allow that kind of play outdoors. For example, when children at the High/Scope Demonstration Preschool began building structures in the block area specifically for climbing and jumping off of, the teachers responded by stacking two large stumps out on the playground's safety surfacing (pea gravel, which absorbs the impact when children land on it). The children labeled this the "jumping area." Once children had a safe and spacious place to jump, their jumping play expanded, in the days that followed, to include many variations: They practiced jumping off the stumps frontwards, sidewards, and hand in hand; they tried to see how far they could jump, measuring and comparing the length of their jumps; and sometimes they jumped "like Mary Poppins," with one arm up in the air, holding an imaginary umbrella.

The many variations of children's jumping play illustrate another important consideration for program staff who are working with children outdoors: Outdoor play fosters not just physical abilities but also the full range of developing abilities. Just as they do indoors, **adults on the playground recognize and support the different key experiences they see occurring.** For example, if children are comparing the lengths of their jumps (key experiences in *number*), an adult might provide materials to mark the length of each jump; if a child is using jumping as a way of acting out a role (key experiences in *representation*), the adult might offer costumes or other props the child could use to embellish that role.

Similarly, in considering particular equipment for the playground, it's important for teachers and caregivers to **think about all aspects of children's play, including the social and cognitive dimensions of an activity.** Some pieces of playground equipment, for example, encourage particular kinds of social interactions. A single-child swing primarily pro-

Outdoor Play Areas For Special Needs Children

High/Scope consultants have often observed that some of the best playgrounds they see are designed for children with disabilities. Some ideas that work:

- No matter what a child's physical, cognitive, or social abilities, it's important to provide a range of play options, including some materials and equipment designed for easy success and others that offer inviting challenges.

- Avoid the "catalog approach" to playground design. Outdoor equipment specially designed for children with disabilities is commercially available, but much of this equipment is expensive and offers only a few play options. For example, a commercial wheelchair-accessible play structure may simply consist of a ramp, and you can provide the same experience of riding on a slope with an inexpensive home-built structure or with found materials. Remember, you know the individual needs of children in your group better than a commercial equipment designer does.

- When choosing and designing equipment, consider children's physical limitations. For children in wheelchairs or with limited mobility, provide reachable equipment—horizontal bars, hanging toys (like makeshift bags), low tethered balls. Sheets hung over ropes may make a dramatic-play enclosure that is more accessible than a plastic playhouse.

- Provide a wide range of loose materials for children to manipulate, build, and create with. Loose materials are a hallmark of high-quality playgrounds for all children (see "'High Yield' Outdoor Materials" on p. 123), but they are even more important for children with special needs, who may be unable to take part in traditional playground activities.

- Instead of purchasing special play structures for disabled children, plan ways to assist them in using conventional structures. Many nondisabled young children need help on swings, for example; so helping a child with a handicap use a swing can be seen as a normal part of the adult's role.

- Remember that some children who appear to have behavior problems indoors are often more involved and cooperative in outdoor play. If you have children like these, plan your outdoor play area to accommodate the plan-do-review sequence and other activities that are normally conducted indoors.

motes solitary play or, if an adult pushes the child, one-to-one adult-child interaction. Pushing a child on the swing can absorb a great deal of the adult's time, but the time spent can be valuable, especially if the adult enriches the activity with a rhyme, chant, or other steady-beat experience. On the other hand, a tire swing, which accommodates a number of children at once, encourages children to engage in a wide array of social experiences with their peers. When two or more children swing together, they are presented with many real social problems. Waiting for others to get on and off, compromising on an acceptable speed, deciding whether to swing back and forth or in a circle—all these decisions involve the challenge of negotiating and resolving conflicts.

A wheeled vehicle is another type of play equipment that offers much broader play opportunities than many educators realize. In using wheeled toys, it's important to think in terms of more than one kind of experience. For example, if various types of wheeled vehicles are available, children can develop a broad range of physical skills. Traditional tricycles, low-seated tricycles, and "big wheels" all have different steering angles and thus require slightly different coordination skills in the rider. Vehicles like the "Irish mail cart" (a traditional nursery school vehicle that is steered by the feet and propelled by the arms) demand an entirely different kind of coordination to make them work. The little red wagon, with its capacity to accommodate more than one child and to be pulled, pushed, or ridden down a hill, has more flexibility than almost any other single vehicle.

Playing is learning, *and outdoor play opens up a vast array of learning experiences. It's commonplace to see a child riding a bicycle, or in this case, a tricycle. Not so widely recognized is the fact that through these types of enjoyable play experiences, children develop a broad range of physical, social, and cognitive skills.*

"High-Yield" Outdoor Materials

By Vincent Harris and Ruth Strubank

In equipping their outdoor play spaces, many adults tend to think only in terms of stationary structures: swings, slides, climbers. Yet the best outdoor play spaces have—in addition to stationary equipment—a wide variety of "loose," nonspecific materials: art and building materials, balls, sand, dress-up clothes. Loose materials, unlike many stationary structures, do not limit children to a single activity. Instead, they stimulate children to use the full range of their abilities: pretending, making things, playing cooperatively, and inventing games and physical challenges. Because of their low cost and the wide range of play activities they inspire, these are truly "high-yield" materials.

In planning for loose materials on the playground, keep three guidelines in mind: **Think about children's physical limitations in using particular materials, plan for a diversity of play experiences, and select materials that can be used at a range of developmental levels. Then, observe how children use the materials.** If the materials are appropriate and challenging, children will be engaged by them and find many different ways to use them, and your observations will yield many insights about the children's developing abilities.

To illustrate these principles, we'll list a few of the loose materials that we used outdoors last year at the High/Scope Demonstration Preschool and describe some of the play activities they inspired.

Pinwheels. We bought a selection of different-sized pinwheels made of neon-colored transparent plastic. Children were mesmerized by the turning of the pinwheels and began trying to figure out what made the pinwheels work. They experimented with various ways of making the pinwheels move: blowing on them; attaching them to bicycle handlebars, so they could watch them turn as they rode down a hill; holding the pinwheels against the breeze as they swung in circles on the tire swing. Children also pretended

with the pinwheels: Some attached them to their backs to serve as superhero propulsion devices; others planted a pinwheel "garden" by sticking a row of pinwheels in the pea gravel.

Hula hoops. Since purchased hoops are far too large for preschoolers to manage, we made our own small hoops out of flexible plastic tubing joined by wooden dowels. Preschoolers swung the hoops on their waists, arms, and ankles; tied them to jump ropes so they could lasso various targets; and invented a catching game in which they threw the hoops around each other.

Painting tools. We bought a wide selection of paintbrushes and paint rollers in all sizes and styles. Children filled plastic paint trays and other containers with water and used the materials to "paint" everything in sight—play structures, the pavement, wheeled toys, a nearby fence. They also enjoyed experimenting with the effects of painting water on existing chalk marks on the pavement. The painting materials inspired lots of social play—children cooperated in carrying water buckets and in painting various areas of the playground. On sunny days, children discovered that there was a difference between painting in the shade and painting in the sun (where the "paint" quickly disappeared). From then on, "keeping up with the sun" was a challenge to them—and an opportunity for adults to support time and space language.

Bubble wands. Another way to expand on children's interest in water play is to provide bubble wands of all types. We include the conventional small blowers as well as the over-sized wands that make giant bubbles; bubble soap made from dish detergent and glycerin; and containers for dipping.

Purchased inexpensively at variety stores, materials like these inspire many hours of absorbing play and broaden the range of abilities children use on the playground.

Having some variety in the surfaces children can ride on is another way to promote richer experiences with wheeled toys. At the High/Scope Demonstration Preschool, for example, the paved surface includes a gently sloping walkway as well as a flat area. Children especially enjoy riding on the sloping sidewalk; since the slope ends with a closed gate, stopping on time entails some physical challenges. The sloping sidewalk has also inspired some creative "cross-pollination" of play activities. For example, one day a child drew a chalk line along the whole length of the walkway; a while later another child added a parallel line; then a third child added a series of crosswise lines, creating a "track" on the walkway. The next day children rode wheeled toys along the track.

Another important kind of experience that adults should strongly encourage on the playground is constructive play—making things. Many art materials can be used outdoors. Children can use chalk, for example, to outline their body shapes or shadows on the pavement; to make rubbings (on paper) of leaves, shells, and other textured materials; or to write letters or words on the pavement. Making collages of leaves, flowers, and other natural materials is another outdoor art activity that children enjoy.

Construction materials and tools also lend themselves to outdoor play. At the High/Scope Demonstration Preschool, the teachers set out a pair of tree stumps on the playground for hammering and nailing and found that children were fascinated with this activity. The children's physical limitations and safety were prime considerations for the adults in planning the materials for this area. The stumps were large and of soft wood (poplar), the children were required to wear safety goggles, and the teachers chose small hammers that would be manageable for the children and would do less damage in case of accidental finger blows. This example illustrates a key point: Adults don't have to be engineers to consider the feasibility of children using various materials; they just need to **look carefully at the size of the materials and the children's probable success with them.** In this case, for example, they chose roofing nails with large, easy-to-hit heads. The nails were long enough so children could hit them once or twice while holding them, yet short enough so they would not bend over before they were driven all the way in.

These same principles of supporting a diversity of experiences and choosing materials that insure children's success are also important when planning for large-motor movement experiences on the playground. The development of children's physical abilities through activities like running, riding, throwing, and climbing is traditionally thought of as a primary goal of outdoor play, and while movement skills do develop

Throwing is an enjoyable, satisfying activity for young children. When adults provide a variety of objects to throw—in this case, a paper bag stuffed with paper—children are naturally inclined to engage in developmentally appropriate large-motor learning experiences. For example, these children have decided to throw the paper bag through a hula hoop and have asked their teacher to hold the hoop for them.

through such experiences, adults need to go beyond the obvious and traditional in planning for them. **Throwing**—a popular, satisfying, and developmentally appropriate interest of young children—is a good illustration of how the most ordinary of activities can be transformed when adults think carefully about the materials needed for an activity. For example, throwing a bean bag at a variety of objects and targets may, for some young children, be easier than handling a ball. When adults do provide balls, there should be a variety. Balls with different levels of inflation facilitate different types of play. A slightly under-inflated ball is good for throwing, because it doesn't roll away after landing. However, a fully inflated ball is needed if children are to approach success with **dribbling,** an activity of high interest for many children. If children are interested in **catching,** a stuffed cloth ball will allow for a higher degree of success than will a less flexible ball. **Striking** or **punching** are also movements that children can explore with soft balls and other large, soft objects. A pillowcase filled with quilt batting and suspended from a play structure can serve as a very adequate punching bag.

In planning for a wide range of movement experiences, adults should also **remember that young children are developing not only physical skills but also basic movement concepts,** such as awareness of what the body is doing and of how language is used in connection with movement. Designing obstacle courses for children is a creative and inexpensive way adults can promote the development of a wide range of movement skills and concepts. Courses can be engineered to foster specific movement experiences, such as balancing, "walking low" or "walking high," changing direction, hopping, climbing, or creeping. Many materials can be used for obstacle courses—role-play props, rope, chalk lines on the pavement, blocks, tires, logs, low sawhorses, boxes to tunnel through, balance beams made from planks laid flat on the ground. Obstacle courses also provide good opportunities for follow-the-leader games in which children imitate or demonstrate movements.

Moving the Daily Routine Outdoors

A final suggestion for bringing the curriculum outdoors is to literally **transplant to your outdoor classroom some segments of the daily routine that are ordinarily conducted inside.** For example, on a sunny day, materials for a limited number of the indoor areas can be brought outside, and working outdoors can then be one option children choose at work time. Circle activities are also easily transplanted. A tape recorder can be brought outside to use for movement and beat experiences.

Clearly, when adults realize that any part of the curriculum can be conducted outdoors, the possibilities for program activities expand dramatically.

Developing a
Creative Art Area

By Mark Tompkins

· ·

Does the art area in your classroom or center encourage creativity? Since self-chosen activities are the essence of meaningful, process-oriented art for children, your art area should make it possible for children to select from a wide variety of materials and a wide variety of ways to use those materials. The area should include **traditional art materials,** like paint, paper, crayons, and markers; **materials that can be used in many ways,** like yarn, string, cotton, plastic-foam pieces, soda straws, and corks; **discarded materials,** like wood scraps, old magazines, and rags; and **tools,** like paintbrushes, staplers, scissors, and toothbrushes. How the materials and tools are presented, configured, or prepared can often determine whether they attract children's interest or inspire creativity.

Some New Ideas

To generate more interest, excitement, and creativity in your art area, try these ideas for introducing children to some new materials or some new ways to use familiar materials:

• **Pop-bottle yarn feeder.** Put yarn in a two-liter plastic soda bottle for easier (and less messy) access for children. Take the black bottom off the pop container by twisting it off or by melting the glue with a blow dryer. Then put the yarn ball in the container, leaving the end of the yarn hanging out of the bottle top. Tuck the bottom back on—it should fit snugly, like a lid. You can also use an old margarine tub or oatmeal box in the same way, but the yarn is not as visible as it is in a clear bottle.

• **Marker-top saver.** Isn't it frustrating to lose the tops of the markers all the time? One solution is to get a foot-long piece of two-by-four lumber and drill holes in the wood the exact size of the marker tops. Insert and glue the marker tops into the holes. Now you have a permanent storage place for the markers, and you can't lose the tops.

To liven up children's painting activities, provide a wide range of paintbrushes, including a variety of conventional brushes as well as nontraditional "brushes"—sponges, string, crumpled-up paper, and other found objects.

• **Beyond white paper.** Providing only white paper on easels for children's painting efforts can be limiting. Make painting a three-dimensional experience by encouraging children to paint on old shoes, small boxes, wood scraps, or other objects. To attach objects to the easel, try fastening them on with clothespins or double-sided tape. Children will also enjoy painting on cardboard, cloth, plastic wrap, grocery bags, and foil.

• **Paintbrushes revisited.** Another way to liven up children's painting activities is to provide a wider range of paintbrushes, including a variety of conventional brushes as well as nontraditional "brushes"—sponges, string, crumpled-up paper, and other found objects. Children also will love using real paintbrushes and cans filled with water to "paint" the playground, the school building, climbing structures, and other outside objects.

• **Custom-textured paints.** Want to change the texture of your paints? Try adding evaporated milk or soap flakes to paint to give it a creamier consistency and a glossy look. Use coffee grounds, salt, or sand—along with white glue—to give paint a rough, coarse, gritty texture. Adding sugar will give paint a sparkling appearance when dry.

• **Computer leftovers.** For a great source of inexpensive paper that children love to use, go to any business or school that uses computers and ask for computer paper that they were planning to recycle or throw away. Children enjoy painting on and working with long sheets of continuous-feed paper, as well as tearing the paper along the perforated borders. You may be able to get computer paper in several sizes.

Children can use lots of materials for creative artwork. For example, using a real pumpkin as the starting point, these children are creating their own versions of "Mr. Pumpkin."

• **Foam chalk-holder.** Like crayons, chalk will quickly break if stored loose in boxes. A piece of plastic foam can make a useful chalk-holder. Use a closed pair of scissors or a screwdriver to carefully bore small holes into the foam. Insert one piece of chalk into each hole.

• **Tile tricks.** Floor tiles, pieces of sheet-vinyl flooring, and Formica scraps make good individual boards for working with Play-Doh. Some tiles have interesting colors, lines, and designs. Children can sculpt on the tiles or use them as bases for their completed creations.

• **The congenial easel.** Painting at the easel can be an isolating experience for children. One way to make painting more of a group activity is to build a large easel on a wall. Use a long sheet of plywood, angle it out from the wall, and add a storage tray for paint. With this arrangement, more children will choose to paint together.

• **Table-top easel.** Another type of homemade drawing surface is the table-top easel. Find a large wallpaper sample book—one book makes a double-sided easel. Remove the pages (reserving the paper samples for art projects). Find a shallow carton lid to serve as the base for the easel, and set the book cover up in it. (Cut notches in the sides of the carton lid, if necessary, to hold the easel to the angle you want.) To hold paper, use clothespins or clips at the top of the easel.

• **Light table.** Made of heavy clouded glass with a lightbulb underneath, the table's hard, shiny surface is ideal for working with translucent paper and paints and adds a new dimension to children's painting and drawing.

A Materials Checklist

To evaluate your art area, here's a checklist that identifies a wide range of materials that children can use for creative artwork. While you probably would not make all these materials available at the same time, this list of open-ended materials should provide you with many ideas to plan from.

Paper of different sizes, textures, and colors
- ❑ construction paper, many colors
- ❑ white drawing paper
- ❑ newsprint
- ❑ finger-paint paper
- ❑ large roll of wrapping, butcher, or shelving paper
- ❑ discarded computer paper (used only on one side; comes in rolls or sheets)
- ❑ paper scraps, various sizes, textures, and colors (available from printers)
- ❑ tissue paper
- ❑ graph paper, lined paper
- ❑ foil
- ❑ scraps of adhesive-backed paper
- ❑ paper plates
- ❑ cardboard or mat-board pieces
- ❑ wallpaper samples or scraps
- ❑ paper napkins
- ❑ coffee filters
- ❑ crepe paper
- ❑ old magazines and catalogs
- ❑ used greeting cards
- ❑ postcards, stationery, envelopes
- ❑ gift wrap

Materials for painting and printing
- ❑ tempera paints
- ❑ liquid starch (for mixing with finger-paints)
- ❑ soap flakes (for thickening paint)
- ❑ watercolor paints
- ❑ plastic squeeze bottles, jars with lids for mixing and storing paints
- ❑ brushes of different types and sizes
- ❑ muffin tins, frozen-food tins, margarine tubs, saucers (for holding paints)
- ❑ screening
- ❑ easels
- ❑ nontraditional paintbrushes or printing materials: sticks, string, feathers, rope, rags, dish scrapers, toothpicks, cotton swabs, toothbrushes, leaves, cut fruits and vegetables
- ❑ cleaning-up materials: rags, sponges, towels, newspaper
- ❑ smocks or paint shirts

Materials for fastening things together and taking them apart
- ❑ scissors
- ❑ yarn
- ❑ shoestrings

- ❑ string
- ❑ ribbon
- ❑ rubber bands
- ❑ elastic
- ❑ paper clips
- ❑ chenille stems (pipe cleaners)
- ❑ clear tape
- ❑ masking tape
- ❑ tape dispenser (heavy-duty)
- ❑ rubber cement
- ❑ white glue
- ❑ glue sticks
- ❑ paste
- ❑ paper punch
- ❑ staples and staplers (heavy-duty)

Materials for making two-dimensional art

- ❑ pencils
- ❑ colored pencils
- ❑ crayons
- ❑ chalk and chalkboard
- ❑ markers
- ❑ ink pads and stamps
- ❑ aluminum foil
- ❑ wax paper
- ❑ tissue paper
- ❑ paper plates
- ❑ wallpaper samples
- ❑ cardboard pieces
- ❑ scissors

Materials for making three-dimensional art

- ❑ clay
- ❑ Play-Doh
- ❑ modeling and molding tools: rolling pins, cookie cutters, plastic knives, hamburger or tortilla press, Play-Doh press, wooden dowels
- ❑ beeswax
- ❑ plaster of Paris
- ❑ buttons
- ❑ straws
- ❑ egg cartons
- ❑ small boxes
- ❑ ice-cream tubs
- ❑ empty thread-spools
- ❑ pipe cleaners
- ❑ clothespins
- ❑ bits of wood
- ❑ sequins
- ❑ cardboard tubes
- ❑ paper bags
- ❑ cloth, felt, rug, vinyl scraps
- ❑ feathers
- ❑ plastic-foam pieces

The traditional easel is a trustworthy companion for children in the art area. Notice how this child has used clothespins to attach her drawing to the easel.

- ❏ macaroni
- ❏ cotton balls
- ❏ old stockings and socks
- ❏ scissors
- ❏ shoeboxes

Materials that support learning about cultural diversity

- ❏ crayons and paints that mirror the skin colors of people in the school community (special skin-tone crayons in a range of shades may be ordered from school suppliers)
- ❏ art materials representing the arts and crafts of the community (e.g., weaving supplies, clay)
- ❏ old magazines and catalogs (for collage-making) with pictures of people from the cultures represented in the school community

The Book Area:
From Beginning to End

By Susan M. Terdan

• •

Effective reading experiences in the High/Scope program depend on a well-planned stock of books. Whether your books are housed in the book area, the toy area, or some other area of the room, you'll need to replenish your bookshelf throughout the year.

At the beginning of the year, as you choose your books, consider what you know about the children entering and returning to your program. Be sure to provide a wide selection of books to support a range of developmental levels and interests. Include some books with simple stories as well as some books that have hard cardboard pages, no words, and large pictures.

Besides purchasing books, program staff may select books from a variety of sources. Some programs already have books in storage that teachers can choose from on a rotating basis; public-school-based programs usually have access to the books in the school library; other programs make use of the public library.

You'll need to put at least as many books on the bookshelves as you have children in the classroom. When we first started the program at the High/Scope Demonstration Preschool, our book supply was low, so we obtained most of our books from the public library. Once a month, we'd check out 20 books to allow at least one book per child. Children enjoyed exploring our new selection of books each month. We kept the books long enough for the stories to become familiar to the children; they knew some of the stories so well they would recite lines as the adult read. We kept track of children's favorites, often checking them out again on our next trip to the library.

As the year progresses and you observe children's changing interests and abilities, add books accordingly. Throughout the year, you will continue to have a wide range of developmental levels in your group, and these differences will be reflected in children's reading behaviors. You'll observe children "reading" in various ways: pretending to read, "reading" to friends by reciting familiar stories they have memorized, telling

Young children love a good story. To sustain children's enjoyment of reading, keep them in the "driver's seat." These teachers are listening to children who are "reading" to friends by reciting familiar stories they have memorized.

a story, or picking out some letters or some words as they listen to or "talk through" a story. To support children's emerging reading abilities, keep the child in the "driver's seat"; that is, encourage each child to develop his or her preferred ways of reading. Listening to children as they "read," encouraging them to help tell the story as you read it, and supporting them as they talk about and explore books with their playmates are all ways to support children's developing interest in books and other print materials.

At year's end, as you look at your book area, consider how your book selection has changed. In addition, as you observe children using and talking about books, notice how their language and social abilities have expanded over time.

In the Elementary School—
A New Activity Area Develops

By Charles Hohmann

. . . .

In High/Scope elementary classrooms, just as at the preschool level, adults planning the arrangement of the classroom are responsive to children's interests and experiences. Here is an anecdote about a first-grade classroom activity area that grew out of an interest expressed by children. The classroom depicted is in a New Mexico public school in a community near an Indian reservation, so children's interest in beadwork was a natural outgrowth of their experiences in their community:

During math time one morning, Sarah, a first-grader, displayed her new necklace made of colorful beads strung on rawhide. One of the other children noted that the beads were similar to ones worn by her mother, who had made her own beads. Another child noticed that the beads followed a red/blue/red/blue pattern, similar to the patterns they had recently been working on in math workshops (two-unit, ABAB patterns). Several children expressed interest in making beaded necklaces. At this point, the teacher (seeing an opportunity for an excellent patterning activity) suggested that those interested in making some beads like Sarah's should plan to meet with him during work time.

During work time, the children, led by Sarah, formed a "committee" to create an area for beadwork. They first agreed on a name for it—the "beading area." As the children talked, they generated a list of questions about the beading area: What do we have in the room now to make necklaces (string, leather strips, wooden beads)? Where could we get different kinds of beads? Are there particular groups of people in different cultures who wear beads?

The group first decided to look around the classroom and collect already-available materials for making necklaces and beading. They collected different kinds of stringing materials: string, yarn, thread, plastic lacing, macramé cord, and wire. Next, the search began for things to string. They were able to find some glass beads in the art area and also collected macaroni, wooden beads, bits of wood, and buttons.

Next, they discussed where the materials should be stored. It was decided that a special table in the math area would be established as a beading area. The children went about organizing, arranging, and labeling the materials. The teacher suggested that the children add graph paper, plain paper, markers, and crayons, so the beaders could plan their designs.

The next day during review time, the children who had made plans to work in the beading area mentioned that the beading area could use more supplies. The class worked together to find a solution.

That night, all the children went home with a note asking parents to donate beads of any kind and other materials. Donations from families added a rich variety of materials.

Over the course of several months, a variety of art, math, and social studies activities grew out of the beading area. Children made many different kinds of jewelry by stringing the beads and also attempted more complicated styles depicted in books that the teacher checked out of the library. During this period, the teacher invited an elderly Native-American woman to visit the class and demonstrate various forms of Indian beadwork.

The beading area was initially very popular. Many children took part in setting up the area and used it to execute various plans. Later in the year, as the interests of the group changed, the teacher dismantled the beading area.

Classrooms That Reflect Family Experiences

By Beth Marshall

• •

Every day at work time, Efrat gets out the tape recorder and pops in a cassette of music to accompany her work on whatever plan she has made for the morning.

Kenneth and Callie are busy with screwdrivers and pliers, taking apart an old clock in the take-apart-and-put-together area. Kenneth tells Callie, "Sometimes my dad lets me help him when he fixes stuff. He fixes stuff all the time."

Jessica zooms the toy bus across the floor in the block area. "Rrrrrrummm. Rrrrrrummm. Let's pick up the people," she says.

Bradley is pushing the modeling dough with the heels of his hands. He adds some flour and pushes some more. "This is what I help my Grandpa do at his bakery," he says.

Corrin adds her name to her painting by tracing around some wooden letters. She tells her teacher, "We have some special letters at my house. They are really fun 'cause you just rub 'em and there they are! You don't even have to write!"

In the examples above, each of the children has brought something very special to the school or center: *a wealth of experience and knowledge that reflects his or her culture.* When we recognize that parents are children's first teachers, we are also acknowledging that their homes and communities are their first classrooms.

In classrooms, centers, and day care homes using the High/Scope approach, we strive to accept, value, and build on what children bring from their home cultures. Our goals are to **make children feel comfortable** in the program, to **strengthen the positive impressions they have of their own cultures,** and to **help them see the linkages** between their homes, their communities, and their schools or day care settings. We also hope to **broaden children's cultural experiences,** helping them learn about other cultures that are both similar to and different from their own and helping them recognize the connections between their lives and those of their classmates.

Every child has a culture. While culture is partly defined by a child's membership in broad groups—religious, regional, economic, racial—it is much more than this. Each family has a unique culture that can only be described by many small details—the books, records, toys, and other materials in the home; the ways family members spend their work and leisure time; the foods prepared and eaten; the style of speech the child hears.

Preschoolers learn about their own cultures, and those of their classmates, in terms of concrete details like these. They are too young to understand abstract concepts of culture that may focus on the history, artistic achievements, or national origins of a group of people. To help reach the goals for cultural learning that we have described, we must strive to **see culture from the child's point of view.**

Keeping the child's perspective in mind, we can take steps like the following to create classrooms that offer many cultural learning opportunities.

Learning About Our Own Backgrounds

First, before we can help children understand and appreciate the cultures of others, **we as adults must develop an awareness of our own cultures.** We are all transmitters of culture. When adults understand and are comfortable with their personal culture, they can bring important resources to the classroom or center. In "Bringing Your Home Culture Into the Classroom or Center" (on facing page), we describe two programs whose materials and activities reflect the personal experiences of the teacher or caregiver. Each of these adults is sharing a part of herself with her group of children, and the result in each case is a rich and stimulating environment.

As adults, bringing a part of our home culture to work makes us feel comfortable, proud of our roots, and more connected to family and community. This kind of sharing also helps us see and appreciate the similarities and differences between our own backgrounds and those of co-workers and program families.

You'll note that the outcomes of cultural sharing we've just described for *adults* are much the same as the goals we've listed for *children's* cultural learning! Similarly, to enable children to reach these goals, we need to **bring children's home cultures into the early childhood setting.** Once we have looked at ourselves and our own cultures, we next need to **identify the cultures of the children** in our classrooms, so we can add materials to the setting that reflect children's home and community experiences. We can only do this by learning from **parents,** the **community,** and **children.**

Identifying Children's Cultures

Let's return to the examples at the opening of this article to see how teachers learned about children's home experiences and then incorporated what they learned into their early childhood settings.

Parents are an invaluable source of information about their home cultures. Making a home visit is an excellent way to learn about a child's family setting and experiences. Later, after you've talked with the parents, you may want to note the information you've gathered on a family information sheet like the one on p. 140.

For example, when the teaching team visited Efrat's home, they discovered that although her mom is now a chemist, she used to be a concert pianist. Jazz was playing in the background while they talked, and when the recording ended, Efrat went over to the stereo and expertly put in another tape. After the visit, the team decided to add a tape recorder and cassettes of music to the music and movement area. They made a note to ask Efrat's mom if they could borrow some of Efrat's favorite selections.

Talking with parents informally as they drop off and pick up their child is another way of keeping in touch with what's happening in the family. When the child care director told Kenneth's mom that he had been using the tools in the construction area regularly, she found out that Kenneth's dad likes to tinker in his workshop. He often fixes broken appliances for friends and finds ways for

Bringing Your Home Culture Into the Classroom or Center

Here are some observations we made at two early childhood programs. In each case, the teaching adult's own family experiences are reflected in the setting:

- *Lakeisha learned to sew from her grandmother and has fond memories of sitting on the porch, doing patchwork and listening to Grandma's stories. The pleasure Lakeisha takes in working with fabrics and fibers is also reflected in the child care home she operates. The children in her care love to lounge on her large homemade pillows, which are covered with a patchwork of different textures and colors. They also can be seen playing with new beanbags they made in a small-group activity and weaving with yarn on a small loom Lakeisha has made from wood scraps and nails.*

- *Brenda's family spent their summers in a cabin. She vividly remembers playing with her brothers in the woods, and she enjoys camping with her own children now. Brenda frequently takes the children in her preschool on field trips to the nearby woods, and the evidence of these outdoor excursions can be seen throughout her classroom: slugs in a bowl; baskets of rocks, shells, pinecones, seeds, and sticks; an aquarium with tadpoles. Arranged on a shelf next to the door are bug cages, magnifying glasses, and butterfly nets.*

Family Information Sheet

Adult's name: _____   Adult's name: _____

Relationship to child: _____   Relationship to child: _____

Place of birth: _____   Place of birth: _____

Occupation: _____   Occupation: _____

Hobbies/special interests: _____   Hobbies/special interests: _____

_____   _____

_____   _____

Child's name: _____   Place of birth: _____

Special interests (*What does the child like to do? What kinds of outings does he/she enjoy? What toys or play materials does he/she enjoy?*): _____

_____

_____

Other family members living in the household (*please list names, ages, and relationship to the child*): _____

_____

Family lives at _____

Family has lived there for (*length of time*) _____

Other places they have lived: _____

_____

Ways the family celebrates special events (*please list the event and the way it is celebrated*): _____

_____

_____

_____

Things in family's home that are special to the family and that they would be willing to share with the class (*for example, Grandma's potato pancake recipe, Mom's rock collection, Dad's conga drum*): _____

_____

_____

_____

Possible additions to classroom: _____

_____

_____

_____

Kenneth to help him with this. In a daily planning session, the teaching team decided to change the construction area to a "take-apart-and-put-together area," to build on Kenneth's interests and support his home culture.

In this area they placed small used appliances, like toasters and hairdryers, along with screwdrivers, pliers, and safety goggles. Kenneth and the other children enjoyed taking the appliances apart and looking at what was inside.

The **community** can also give us many insights into children's cultures. Take a look at the community from the children's viewpoint. If you don't live in the community around your school or center, visit it often. What are the neighborhood's colors, sounds, and smells? What are people wearing? What types of goods are sold in the area stores? What occupations seem to be common? What types of vehicles do you see? (For example, in a rural area, tractors and farm equipment are common.) Are there special events or celebrations in the community (such as a street fair or food festival)? Looking and listening as you visit the community will give you ideas for materials to add to your classroom. The teacher in Jessica's program, for example, knew that many of the children in her group lived in an urban area and sometimes rode busses around town; so she placed toy busses in the block area.

We can also learn about culture from **children**. Adults can watch what children are doing with materials and listen to their comments about them. Hearing about Bradley's interest in imitating his grandfather, the teachers decided to add additional baking tools to the house area of their classroom. After hearing Corrin talk about the special letters in her home, one of the teachers relayed the anecdote to her mom. Her mom laughed and said yes, there were lots of press-on letters lying around the house right then. She had just started back to work as an architect and was able to do most of her work out of her home. The teachers decided to add some press-on letters to the art area—Corrin loved using them and demonstrating them to the other children.

The experiences of Efrat, Kenneth, Jessica, Bradley, and Corrin illustrate how adding materials and making changes in the classroom can encourage children to build on and exchange the experiences they bring from their families and communities. When these materials are available among the many choices open for children's play, learning about cultural diversity becomes a natural part of classroom life.

In addition, as illustrated by the example of Katie and Paul in "Learning From Each Other" on p. 142, the process of exploring differences

Learning From Each Other

On the first day of school, Katie and Paul are each rocking a baby doll to sleep. Katie, who is white, looks at Paul's (dark-skinned) doll and says, "You have a chocolate baby."

Paul, who is African-American, looks at his doll and answers, "It's not choco-late—it's my baby brother."

Katie asks him, "Your baby? Is he coming when you get picked up?"

Uh huh," Paul replies. "You wanna see him?" Katie nods, and Paul prom-ises to show her the infant when Paul's dad comes to get him.

When Paul's dad comes, they spend a little time playing together with the baby. Katie notices that Paul's brother is a lot like an infant cousin she enjoys playing with. Like her cousin, Paul's brother reaches for things with his hands and sticks his tongue out to imitate her.

Katie had just moved from a homo-geneous rural area, where most of the people have light skin like her own. She had never seen a baby doll that wasn't light-skinned. The brown-skinned doll was a vehicle that enabled her to explore some differences between herself and Paul. In the process of recognizing and exploring these differ-ences, she also began to see her own relatedness to Paul. She recognized that Paul's family life was in many ways similar to her own.

often leads children to realize they have much in common with people who at first seem "different." As children develop an appreciation of home and family experiences that are different from their own, they also begin to understand the many ways all families are alike. This helps them see their relatedness to people who may look different and have a different set of experiences.

Family Diversity
Classroom Checklist

By Beth Marshall

· ·

How well does your classroom or center reflect the diversity of children's home cultures? To evaluate your setting, here's a checklist that is organized by play area.

Art Area

❑ Paint, crayons, and paper mirror the skin colors of people in the school community. (Note: crayons designed to reflect actual skin tones are now available.)

❑ Other art materials representing the art and crafts of the community are available (e.g., weaving supplies, clay).

Block Area

❑ Toy people are multiracial and without sex-role stereotyping.

❑ Animal figures simulate animals found in your area (e.g., house pets).

❑ Toy vehicles represent vehicles found in the community.

Book Area

❑ Books written in children's home languages are included.

❑ Books depict a variety of racial, ethnic, and cultural groups, focusing on modern lifestyles and including natural-looking illustrations of people.

❑ References to color in books are nonstereotypic (avoid books that associate black with evil, white with purity and goodness).

❑ Books represent a variety of family situations, including single-parent families, two-parent families, biracial couples, stepparents, children cared for by extended-family members.

❑ Books portray women and men in realistic situations, with both girls and boys playing active roles, both women and men seen as independent problem-solvers.

❑ Books show children and adults with various disabilities. Disabled characters are portrayed as real people who happen to have handicaps rather than as objects of pity who struggle hard to overcome handicaps.

House Area

❑ There are multiracial girl and boy dolls with appropriate skin colors, hair textures and styles, and facial features.

❑ Contents and arrangement of house area mirror homes found in community (e.g., patio area in Southwest).

❑ Kitchen utensils, empty food containers reflect what children see their family members using.

❑ Dress-up clothing is reflective of the community, including occupations of the children's parents.
❑ Whenever possible, child-sized wheelchairs, crutches, glasses with lenses removed, etc., are available for children's role play.

Music and Movement Area

❑ Music tapes and instruments are reflective of children's cultures.
❑ A variety of instruments are available for children's use.
❑ Movement games that are characteristic of children's cultures are played.

Toy Area

❑ Puzzles reflect the community atmosphere (e.g., rural or urban).
❑ Puzzles represent occupations of the parents and others in the community.
❑ Toy figures, puzzles, depict multiracial people and avoid sex-role stereotypes.

Chapter Four

The Family Connection
· ·

*W*hen children come to preschool, they bring with them a wide range of family experiences. This chapter deals with the connection between those experiences and children's growth and learning. The selections explore the effects family experiences have on children's development and offer suggestions for working more effectively with parents and developing closer ties between home and school.

In the chapter's first article, "Parent-Child Relationships: A Foundation for Learning," David Weikart writes again about his experiences driving his grandson Brian to the High/Scope Demonstration Preschool (see also " 'Driving Master Brian': Supporting Children's Thinking," in Chapter 1). This time Weikart's theme is Brian's strong relationship with his father and the impact of this relationship on challenges Brian undertakes, both at school and at home. In describing his experiences with and thoughts about Brian and his dad, Weikart seeks to make early childhood educators more aware of "how much can be learned about children and the important adults in their lives by listening to their conversations, observing their play, and talking with their parents."

In the next article, Susan M. Terdan discusses home visiting, an important educational component of many early childhood programs. Terdan explores the barriers to effective home visits that often arise when parents feel threatened or pressured by the presence of the home visitor. To overcome these barriers, she recommends a "parent-first" approach, in which the home visitor focuses initially on the needs and feelings of the parents. She describes simple steps for developing trusting relationships with parents, steps that can become part of any efforts by program staff to improve communication with parents, whether or not home visits are involved.

While preschool teachers usually have frequent contacts with program parents, such contacts tend to dwindle as children reach elementary school, according to Barbara Carmody, who addresses this issue in the next selection, "Elementary School—When the Parent Is No Longer Apparent." In her article Carmody recommends strategies for strengthening home-school ties in the elementary years. Her suggestions, like those proposed by Terdan, place the primary emphasis on responding to the needs and interests of parents.

The next article, also by Barbara Carmody, deals with a sensitive issue: how early childhood staff can encourage parents to interact more effectively with their children. She suggests that staff first make efforts to get parents involved in the program, and then, when parents are present, subtly model appropriate strategies for interacting with children. She also suggests that staff create opportunities for parents to interact supportively with children in the school setting.

The last two articles are designed to help teachers respond when parents complain that they are seeing "too much play and not enough learning" in their child's school program. In the first of the selections, Linda Weikel discusses the role of play and learning at the preschool level, while in the final article, Charles Hohmann explains how playfulness is also a component of effective learning experiences for older children.

Parent-Child Relationships:
A Foundation for Learning

By David P. Weikart

. . . .

Every weekday morning, I drive my grandson Brian to the High/Scope Preschool in Ypsilanti, Michigan. This is the second article inspired by my daily trips with him—I've learned a great deal from them. The 25-mile drive takes about 45 minutes. In the confines of the car, Brian and I have a chance to look about the changing countryside ("Oh, 'Pa! Look at the little pigs!"), observe the weather ("It's so misty we can't even see the telephone poles!"), talk about family and school events ("What are you planning to do today at work time with that bag of wood?"), or sing songs. The radio is always off, because it takes my attention away from what Brian and I are doing.

One late fall morning, as we drove over a bridge that passes over an expressway, Brian jolted me with this comment: "My daddy goes down there to work." I asked him what he meant. He pointed to the expressway and said, "My daddy goes that way to work." True, each day his father, Dale, drives on that highway to his job in Detroit. I was surprised that Brian knew the way, but then I realized that Brian is very conscious of what his father does all the time. Indeed, Brian always mentions things about his dad as we drive to preschool.

When Brian was only 2 years old, I observed him taking a walk with his father around their yard. As they returned, I noticed that Dale, hands clasped behind his back, was walking with his head tilted forward as he studied the ground. Two steps to the left and to the rear was Brian, hands clasped behind his back and head tilted forward as he also studied the ground. While Brian's imitative posture was comical, the emotional point was made. I realized that Brian's awareness of his dad, even at this very early age, was very powerful in directing his behavior.

On another morning in midwinter, Brian and I left for preschool at the usual time. That morning Brian's father was late getting started, and he left for work shortly after I picked up Brian. As we passed through one of the towns along the way, Brian, looking in the right-hand mirror of the truck, spotted Dale pulling up behind us. He announced with some excitement that his dad was there. When the roadway opened to four lanes, his father drew alongside of us, waved, and passed on in the line of traffic. Brian waved back and proudly told me, "That's my dad."

I was impressed that he had recognized the car, so I asked him if he waved because he is Dale's son. Brian answered, "No, I'm his father." Confused, I asked Brian several times about the relationship, and he stoutly maintained that Dale was his father while also maintaining that *he* was Dale's father.

The closeness of this father-son relationship, expressed unknowingly in Brian's misstatement, is of extraordinary importance to his development. It affects the activities he undertakes, his behavior, and his perceptions of his role in the world.

Transfer of Learning

Brian and his dad are often busy working outside around their house, planting and tending the lawn and shrubbery and doing other seasonal chores. In late May, Brian worked with his dad planting a number of small evergreens and shrubs about the lawn. Dale would dig a hole to prepare the space for the planting, and together he and Brian would place the small tree or shrub in the ground, push the dirt around the roots, and carefully pack the earth. About a week later, Brian announced that he had found a mulberry tree that he wanted to plant. When his dad arrived home from work, Brian was waiting with his "tree" (a 6-foot branch, no roots, no leaves) and the shovel his dad had used. Dale asked Brian where he wanted to plant the tree, accepted Brian's choice of location (near another tree planted earlier in the week). Dale then suggested that Brian begin while he changed his clothes. When he came out about 20 minutes later, Brian had dug a fairly large hole, 12 inches deep and about 18 inches across. They planted the "tree." Later, Brian explained to me that the tree needed time to grow.

The next week at preschool, the children turned a large racing tire on its side and, led by Brian, proceeded to fill it with the pea gravel that surrounds the play equipment. It took Brian, who stayed at the task the longest, all of outdoor time to fill the tire (25 inches in diameter and 15 inches deep). As he shoveled the gravel, Brian used the shoveling technique he

Teachers, parents, grandparents, and caregivers can all learn a great deal about young children's views of the world by listening attentively as they talk about their experiences.

had learned when planting trees with his dad—placing both hands on the shovel handle and using his foot to push the shovel into the gravel. Brian's transfer of this father-taught shoveling technique to the school setting and his ability to focus on the task for an extended period of time reflect the strength of the relationship with his father as well as the duration and power of skills learned in that relationship.

The influence of Brian's experiences with his dad can also be seen when Brian plays by himself at home. Brian has a plastic building-set consisting of large tubes and elbow connectors that can be used to build child-sized chairs, wheeled toys, and other moveable objects. Strong enough to hold an active boy, these structures are also light enough to be managed easily by a child. With his father, Brian has used this set to build a desk, a four-wheel scooter, a short-run slide, and other toys. One day when his dad was not there, Brian used the loose-fitting collar joints that permit the tubes to rotate to build a "backhoe tractor" with moving parts (he is very interested in construction equipment). While not elaborate, this project illustrates again how, even when the parent is not present, interests and skills nurtured in parent-child experiences continue to develop.

Taking the Child's Perspective

Toward the end of May, on our ride to school one morning, Brian suddenly announced that his father was "disappointed." Not knowing what to expect, I said, "Oh, your dad is disappointed?" "Yes," said Brian. "He is disappointed because he can't play with me tonight." "And why is that?" I inquired. "Well," said Brian, "Dad has to take four men to the baseball game in Detroit because he is working and he can't come home to be with me." I must admit, I laughed a little at this, knowing that for Dale, who had been captain of his college baseball team and is very active in many sports, attending the Detroit Tigers game would be no hardship! Yet this incident again brought home to me the importance a child places on what a parent says and does.

Adults deal with a wide range of problems, experiences, and issues on a daily basis, but a child's world is so much more narrow. As we interact with children, we may forget to see things from the child's point of view. We walk through our yards and see the work to be done, contemplating the trees to be planted, the stones to be removed, the grass to be mowed. Though children are aware of the physical reality around them (as Brian surely was when he walked through the yard with his dad), it is often the actions and reactions of adults (for Brian, his dad's gestures while walking) that capture children's attention. In attempting to understand a child, then, we must try to see events and experiences from the child's perspective. Dale managed to do this when he explained to Brian why he would be late that evening. He phrased his explanation in terms of the egocentric view of the world that children normally have. He expressed his disappointment that he couldn't be home with Brian. Although he was disappointed, he also knew that he had work to do and that he would enjoy it. But he explained the situation to Brian in *Brian's* terms.

The important things for teachers and parents to learn from these observations are the following:

1. **We often think of a role model as an abstraction, but in fact, adults become role models for children in a series of concrete interactions and events.** Planting trees and building large toys with his father are events that link Brian's emotions to his developing skills and interests. When it's time for the child to work alone, the influence of the adult is still there, and the skills learned during the joint activity have special value for the child. Distant sports figures or popular television stars are of little use to children as role models, because there has been no personal interaction.

2. **When explaining an unexpected change to a child, use the child's frame of reference for the explanation,** as Brian's dad did when he explained his absence from home in terms of his relationship with Brian.

3. **The words a child uses are often a realistic expression of his or her emotions.** They need to be accepted as such and not corrected. To me, Brian's statement that he was Dale's father was his way of talking about their close relationship. I realized that understanding who is father and who is son was not the important issue.

For early childhood educators, these observations about Brian illustrate how much can be learned about children and the important adults in their lives by listening to children's conversations, observing their play, and talking with their parents. In Brian's case, his chosen activities—using the shovel, planting the "tree," and making the "backhoe tractor"—all show how powerful direct experiences are for the child's growth and learning. Their power for Brian is enhanced because his "teacher" is his father, with whom he has such a close relationship.

The "Parent-First" Approach to Home Visits

By Susan M. Terdan

. . . .

Visits to children's homes by teachers and program staff are a part of many early childhood programs; in some home-based programs, they are the primary activity. Because the home environment is so central to a child's development, the idea that home visits by teachers and other program staff can benefit both parents and their children seems natural.

Yet many early childhood staff report that home visiting doesn't live up to their expectations. They wonder why their home visits aren't going smoothly or why some parents resist home visits altogether.

We believe that home visits by early childhood teachers and caregivers can be a valuable source of support for families and a communication channel that improves the program experience for all concerned. But these positive outcomes of home visiting depend heavily on the home visitor's attitude and approach.

To better understand some of the problems of home visiting, let's look at a scenario from a typical home visit that was part of a center-based preschool program for at-risk children:

A Typical Home Visit

1. Teacher arrives with an armful of toys and a folder full of paper. She greets the family.

2. Teacher and parent do the paperwork: Teacher collects the filled-out chart from last week (the day-by-day chart records when parent and child did the week's learning activity), explains the goals of this week's activity, and shows parent the new chart. Teacher collects the toys from last week's visit.

3. Teacher introduces the new toys and explains the cognitive value of each one.

4. Teacher describes and models ways to use the new toys with the child.

Home visits by early childhood teachers and caregivers can be a valuable source of support for families and a communication channel that improves the program experience for all concerned.

5. Teacher does some sample charting of children's responses and successes.

6. Teacher gives parent a chance to try out the activities with the child; she assumes parent will feel more comfortable doing the activity after she has gone.

7. Teacher and parent clean up the toys.

8. Teacher says goodbye and confirms date and time of the next visit.

Let's take a closer look at the needs and desires of the parties in this scenario. The teacher's agenda for the home visit is clear, but what the family hoped to get out of it is much harder to define—the home visitor's plan leaves little opportunity for the parent to help the teacher understand the family's goals, needs, and culture. In cases like this, parents often respond by telling the teacher what they think she wants to hear, rather than by honestly sharing their expectations. The result is a home visit that quickly becomes a mechanical routine for all involved.

What are some of the barriers to effective home visits? Teachers often launch into a home visit without understanding the parents' expectations and needs. Here are some concerns parents may have about home visiting:

• They are afraid the home visitor will judge them.

• They are afraid the home visitor will tell them what to do and give them "homework."

• They feel they don't have the right toys.

- They can't afford educational materials.

- They are ashamed of their homes.

- They don't want their childrearing methods questioned.

- It's an inconvenience to have someone over regularly.

- They don't need home visits.

- They have a demanding job or social life that takes all their time.

- They can't focus on childrearing issues because they have pressing problems (finances, health, job loss, a family member's substance abuse) that sap their energy.

Letting Parents Take Center Stage

While teachers and caregivers don't create all these concerns, they confirm them when they conduct home visits that are unresponsive to parents' needs. To overcome these barriers, we suggest a "parent-first" approach to home visiting. This approach puts the focus of initial visits on the needs and interests of the parent, *not* of the child; working with both parent and child together comes later. As educators, we want to help parents take an interest in their child's development and progress, to recognize developmental milestones more easily, and to learn appropriate strategies for supporting children's development. While these are appropriate *long-range* goals for home visiting, in the early visits it's often more effective to focus on the more immediate goal of building a trusting relationship with parents. The home visitor must communicate that he or she is there for the parent "first."

So, if you are making your first home visit to preschooler Tanya's home, view this as an opportunity to get to know Tanya's

Focusing on Parents' Needs and Strengths

Rather than assume that a home visit should center around preplanned learning activities for the child, be responsive to the parents' needs and interests in planning home visit activities. For example:

In making initial home visits to a mother and her small children in their rural home, the home visitor focused primarily on getting to know the mother. In talking with the mother, she found out that the father, a truck driver, was gone most of the day. Even though the family had a car the mother could use, she was usually stranded without transportation, since she had no driver's license (the family had recently moved from another state). The home visitor offered to help the mother obtain her license, and this became the focus of the next three visits. During the next visit, the home visitor drove the mother to town, so she could get a booklet she needed to study for her driver's exam. The following week the home visitor drove her to take her written exam (which she passed), and the next week the visitor took her to town again, so she could take the road test (she was successful). With a driver's license, the woman was able to break out of the isolation and helplessness created by her lack of transportation. With this barrier removed, her self-confidence improved. Gradually the home visits became more centered around activities that involved both the mother and her children.

parents—as *people*, not just as Tanya's parents. In turn, this is her parents' chance to get to know you as more than Tanya's teacher. When you arrive at the home for the first visit, skip the parcel of toys and the "lessons" for Tanya. Focus on the needs, interests, and routines of the adults in the home. Spend time just talking with the parents. Get to know them and their interests (a good opener for discussions with parents: "What do you like to do when you are child-free?").

Your observation skills are essential here. Look around during your initial visits and note the materials in the home and the language being used. Find out about the family's daily routine, their hobbies, interests, and chores. Encourage the parents to tell you about their interests—raising livestock, farming, sewing, reading, gardening, remodeling, watching television.

Become an interested and appropriately involved friend of the family. This leads to a natural and positive interchange with parents. Use the family's home as the backdrop and existing materials as the things to manipulate, choose from, and talk about.

Let the parents "train" you. Remember, they are the experts on their family; you are the expert on education and child development. Parents will become more effective in their interactions with their children when someone takes an interest in interacting with *them* and helping *them* meet some of their needs or share some of their interests or skills. When you take an interest in the parents, the result is a widening circle that increasingly involves the children. Parents become interested in offering ideas for the next visit that are based on their own and their family's interests and abilities. Usually they suggest activities that involve the whole family.

When teaching in a Minnesota preschool program for special needs children aged 3 to 6, I applied this approach in my home visits. Although my initial focus was on the parents, children were never ignored. Encouraged to contribute their own ideas, parents usually planned home visits with me around their family's special interests: snow-sliding, taking long walks in the woods, canning, making cookies, playing all kinds of board games. Most of these were activities that the whole family could do together. They offered many opportunities in which, spontaneously and naturally, I could model strategies for supporting children (such as offering choices, using language to help children wait for attention, sharing control, and encouraging planning and problem solving). While modeling such strategies, though, I was careful never to take over the parents' role as primary caregivers. When parents saw that I had some useful ideas for interacting with children, they often adopted them automatically or asked for further suggestions.

When Parents Want
Numbers, Colors, and Shapes

I am a teacher in a center-based preschool program with a home visit component. During home visits, some of our parents make it clear to us that they expect the home visitor to teach the child such things as numbers, colors, and shapes, using very directive methods. They think the home visitors are not doing their job if they don't give "lessons" to the child. When I'm face to face with a parent whose point of view about education is completely different from mine, I don't know where to begin.
   —*A preschool teacher/home visitor*

Start by explaining that the home visits are designed primarily for the parents: "Your child *has* a program already—these visits are for *you*." Explain that the visits give you and the parents an opportunity to get to know each other better and for the parents to find out things about the program.

Then ask the parent what they hope the child will gain from the program and about their general goals for the child's education. Acknowledge and validate these goals; you'll probably find plenty of common ground here, because most parents will list goals—like learning to read and count, developing independence and self-esteem, and learning appropriate social behavior—that most educators share.

As you talk with the parents about their goals, note them down. Explain that many of the activities and materials in your classroom/center will help their child achieve these goals, and that throughout the school year, you'll be explaining how things happen in your classroom that contribute to these goals. In short, convey information about your curriculum or educational approach in small doses, always making reference to the parent's goals and expectations and the specific things the child is doing at home or in school.

It's helpful for the home visitor to think of the visit as a form of *teacher* rather than *parent* involvement. Your primary goal is not to teach the parents or their children, but to become involved in their home-life and to let them teach you about their strengths and interests. All parents have strengths on which you can build. In home visits with a family that enjoyed taking long walks, for example, I learned a great deal about the family's strengths in the course of my walks with them. For this family, walking offered the opportunity for relaxed conversations with the children, conversations in which the adults often pointed out new things to children and expanded on the observations children made when they saw something that interested them.

In addition to making the parents' interests the focus of home visits, we recommend giving parents many opportunities to shape the home visit schedule. Even if your program is planned around one visit a week, ask the families how many visits *they* want—provide options: once a

Offering Choices to Parents

Offering choices is central to our philosophy of working with children, and the same philosophy should extend to parents—especially if you are trying to promote parent involvement in your early childhood school or center.

Parent involvement can take many forms, and teachers and caregivers should accept this variety. One parent may wish to have a phone conversation with the teacher once a month; another may come in for her child's birthday. This is the level of involvement each of these parents is comfortable with.

Parents may resist involvement with the school or center for many reasons: They may have had negative school experiences as children; they may have had an unpleasant experience with an older child's teacher; they may feel they are too busy to help out. However, by letting parents know that they are free to choose from many forms of involvement (and that not being involved is also a legitimate choice), you help them feel a sense of control over their relationship with the school and stimulate their interest in participating.

To communicate to parents that their level of involvement with the school is their choice, distribute a checklist of parent involvement options, leaving open space for the parents' additions to it. It's also important for you to "take the pressure off" by including "No involvement right now—ask again in three months" as one of the options. Distribute the list to parents, and have them indicate the ways they wish to be involved.

Your checklist might look something like this (these are just *some* of the ways parents can be involved):

Parent Involvement Options

- ❏ Scheduled phone calls from teacher
- ❏ Unscheduled call from parent
- ❏ Scheduled call from parent
- ❏ Drop-in visit by parent
- ❏ Scheduled visit to home by teacher
- ❏ Notes back and forth between parent and teacher
- ❏ Weekly/monthly notes from teacher
- ❏ Helping with field trips
- ❏ Helping with parties
- ❏ Volunteering regularly in the classroom
- ❏ Sharing a special interest/hobby with children in the classroom
- ❏ Helping out with parties
- ❏ Helping gather classroom materials (old clothes, household tools, empty food containers, extra mittens and scarves)
- ❏ Taking out library books for classroom use
- ❏ No formal contact (ask again in three months)
- ❏ Other (explain)

Let the parents "train" you. They are the experts on their family; you are the expert on education and child development.

week, once a month, twice a month, no home visits at all. In the program described here, most families opted for two visits a month, and we made it clear that the frequency of visits could change at any time, at the parents' convenience.

Occasionally parents will indicate they don't want home visits. When that happens, we suggest trying the following approach: First, explain that the home visit is part of the child's preschool program. Say that although some parents eventually opt not to have ongoing home visits, you are requesting that the family take part in three initial home visits. Point out that during the visits, you will all have an opportunity to become better acquainted and that the parents can help you understand the family's needs, schedules, and interests. Assure parents that the visits will be informal. If the parents consent to these trial visits, follow the "parent-first" approach in those trial visits. At the end of the third visit, evaluate with the parents the possibility of more visits, and if they agree to them, set up a schedule that meets the family's needs.

In this article, we've focused on parents rather than children. However, this isn't meant to suggest that children's needs aren't just as important as parents'. If we as trainers, caregivers, and teachers can develop and use effective strategies for recognizing and supporting parents' strengths, we often set in motion a ripple effect that eventually will benefit their children.

It's much easier for parents to offer appropriate support to others when they've been supported themselves. Home visits enable us to offer parents this experience. Think of the visits as a way to improve your relationship with the family rather than as a vehicle to get the parents involved with the school. These are some of the positive outcomes of home visits of this type:

• The home visit is an event that both children and parent look forward to.

• Communication between home and school improves.

• The teacher becomes a friend to the family.

• The teacher gets to know the parents' interests, needs, strengths.

• Parents improve the interaction strategies they are using with their children.

• Parent-child communication improves.

• Parents use strategies with their child at home that are similar to those used at school by the teachers.

• Parents develop a lasting interest in children's school progress that will enhance their children's future school experiences.

Elementary School—
When the Parent Is
No Longer Apparent

By Barbara Carmody

· ·

In preschool, we as teachers *know* the parents. We see many parents every day, peering through the windows or lingering awhile in the classroom as they drop off or pick up their children. Parents tell us stories about their children and have many opportunities to observe their children in the school setting.

But when children reach the primary grades, something happens. Children arrive at school by bus or come directly from child care—we rarely see their parents face to face. While there are occasional conferences or phone contacts with parents, these often focus on negative news, creating an emotional barrier between parent and teacher. Back-to-school nights and other special functions are attended by many parents but offer little direct teacher-parent contact and provide parents with only a glimpse of a child's actual school life.

Thus, in so many ways, by the elementary years the parent has become the "inapparent parent" in the child's school. To reestablish the parent-school connection, we need to tune-in to families and establish a "parent-appropriate" environment. Some ideas:

• **Start by considering this question:** *What are the needs of the parents?* Before setting in motion any parent activities, **assess parents' practical needs**—Which evenings work best? Is child care needed? Do notes that are sent home need translation? One school that served a large population of migrant workers, for example, provided child care, healthful snacks, and bus transportation for families for all parent functions. Once these basic needs were met, parent meetings were well attended.

Teachers also need to **address parents' emotional needs.** Parents may bring negative attitudes from previous school experiences—attitudes that create a barrier to good relationships with teachers. Or parents may feel uncomfortable with the curriculum or the use of technology in the classroom. Teachers can counter such attitudes by striving for *positive*

Parent Involvement Ideas

Nurturing the connection between parents and the child's school is vital to our role as educators. Here are some strategies for strengthening this bond:

- **Provide a range of avenues for possible parent participation** (journal-keeping, class socials, opportunities to provide materials or assist in the classroom). Every parent is different. Inviting involvement at any level provides needed support for the child as well as for the classroom.

- **Offer information on your curriculum that will make parent involve-** ment more meaningful. For example, a parent who enjoys helping out in the classroom during work time may appreciate having information on and examples of open-ended questions.

- **Find out which parenting and educational topics are of interest to parents, and foster their continued learning.** For example, parents in one classroom often expressed an interest in discipline strategies, so the teacher invited a counselor to a parent meeting to discuss this topic.

contacts with parents. For example, one teacher sent home an individual journal on each child each weekend, adding a new anecdote each time about something the child did that week. The teacher invited parents to reciprocate by returning the journals with their own anecdotes added. This kind of effort to communicate in a positive way not only informs parents of what is going on in school but also sends a subtle message of support, saying to parents, "I want you to feel a part of your child's school day."

• **Another important question to consider is this:** *What are the strengths and interests of parents?* You can use parent conferences, socials, or questionnaires to find out about parents' work, hobbies, and preferences for participation. This can open up a potential gold mine of learning experiences. Often parents, like children, do not recognize in themselves a special skill or quality. In one such instance, a lawyer agreed to talk about his career to his son's second-grade class, even though he feared his job might sound boring. The children ended up discussing conflict resolution and expressed eagerness to know more. The father returned and held a mock court.

Thus, by focusing on the *parents'* needs and interests and providing encouragement for parent participation, you can lay the groundwork for effective parent involvement at the elementary-school level.

Modeling to the
Role Model

By Barbara Carmody

• •

The following incidents were recently observed in a preschool house area:

Two stuffed animals cradle 3-year-old Evan's head on a pillow. His feet stick out from beneath a too-short blanket. Soon his playmate, 4-year-old Megan, returns to his side with a wet paper towel and applies it to his forehead. "This will help your tem'ture," she says. "Now what book would you like me to read to you?"

Lori, aged 5, jerks a doll out of its highchair. "Look at the mess you made," she yells. *"Now go to your room and don't come out."*

These contrasting examples of Megan and Lori illustrate the impact of adult role models. Preschoolers tend to identify with and imitate the important adults in their lives. Knowing this, preschool teachers are sometimes disturbed by play such as Lori's and the negative interactions it reflects.

Children come to our early childhood programs from a wide range of situations, and we do our best to interact supportively with them while they are in our care. But remembering that the parent is the first teacher, the question often becomes, How can we as teachers have an impact on those other important relationships in children's lives?

Modeling positive, developmentally appropriate interactions is the most subtle and least threatening way we can impact the relationship between parent and child. But for modeling to occur, we need the presence of the child's parents or guardians. Attempting to involve the family in the preschool program, then, is a vital step in encouraging optimal support for the child.

Arrival and departure times often offer excellent opportunities to build closer ties with families. Encourage parents to allow ten minutes for both dropping off and picking up their child. This helps parents understand the child's need for a relaxed transition, enables parents and teachers to discuss the child's developing skills, and gives teachers opportunities to subtly model verbal and physical support.

For example, a parent witnessing a child cleaning up some water that he has spilled at the art table might just see a mess. But a teacher can model appropriate interactions, guiding the parent to see the problem solving that can result from such situations.

Teacher: *It looks like there's a lot of water on the table.*
Child: *I'm washing it real clean.*
Teacher: *It does look clean. I wonder about the water on the floor.*
Child: *Oh, I'm cleaning that too.* (The teacher steps back and observes with the child's parent as the child first attempts to wipe water off the floor with the sponge, which is already soaked. Having little luck with the sponge, the child then gets paper towels and wipes dry both table and floor.)

Planning casual, social gatherings for families is another way to strengthen home-school relationships and offer opportunities for parents to observe teachers interacting supportively with children. One preschool class held a Saturday potluck. The teachers, knowing that many of the parents did not often play with their children or understand the significance of play, attempted to create an atmosphere that encouraged adult-child play by setting up several activity areas for child and parent to visit together. These included spaces for bubble-blowing, ball play, and digging for pretend dinosaur bones, as well as a "big foot-little foot" obstacle course in which adult and child paired up, tied together at the leg, to venture through the course. On completion of the course with his son, one father exclaimed, "I don't remember when I've had such fun!"

As children leave the classroom each day, we as teachers are aware that they are involved in many interactions that we may never hear about. But if we can encourage Mom, before going home, to watch her child as he shows her the five ways he can come down the slide—or if we can provide Dad with the opportunity to dig for "dinosaur bones" with his daughter—then we know we have assisted the parent-child relationship. And this is the relationship that has the greatest power and the most far-reaching impact of all.

Talking With Parents
About Play and Learning

By Linda Weikel

• •

*"Why do you let them just **play** all day? I'm sending Lindsey to preschool so she'll **learn,** so she'll be ready for kindergarten next year. Why aren't you **teaching** her anything? All this play seems like a waste of time."*

Preschool teachers working in programs based on an active learning approach frequently hear complaints like this from worried parents who don't understand the value of play in an early childhood program. As professionals, we can understand the concern such parents must feel. These parents want their children to be happy, healthy, and successful in school, and they know (from their own experiences) how schools work. They understand the importance of reading, writing, and number skills for school success, and they know that their children will probably be tested on these skills and labeled according to the results—often before kindergarten even begins.

Who can blame these parents for being worried? They probably expected that the preschool experience would be preparation for formal schooling. As a result, they may wonder why the preschool doesn't look like a "real" school, where the teachers drill on letters, numbers, colors, and shapes and where play occurs only at recess.

How can you answer these parents' concerns? This article suggests some steps you can take to help parents understand how much children are learning when they seem to be "just playing." These strategies will also help you explain how High/Scope's active learning curriculum is designed to encourage the kinds of play and exploration that form the foundation for academic learning.

Believing That Play Is Valuable

First, before we can help parents see the value of play, we ourselves, as early childhood teachers and administrators, must be convinced of its value. Of course, by embracing High/Scope's active learning approach, you have already indicated that you recognize the value of play in the early years. To learn even more about how play relates to learning, consult any of the books listed in the partial bibliography on p. 165. Also spend some time each day observing and listening to the children in your classroom as they play, and make a conscious effort to notice which of High/Scope's *key experiences in early childhood development* are occurring. (As you observe, you may also use the High/Scope Child Observation Record assessment system to help you identify the learning experiences that occur during play.) These **reading and observational experiences** will reinforce your belief in the value of play and give you concrete examples to use in your discussions with parents.

Responding to Parents' Concerns

The next step is to find time for **open discussion with parents** about issues surrounding play and learning. Support parents as they express their concerns about a play-based active learning program. Let them know that as an educator, you share their goals. Just as they do, you want their children to grow, to learn, and to be successful throughout their school years. With these shared goals as common ground, you can begin to work with parents as *partners.*

In beginning to explain the lack of "school-like" activities in your program, you might remind parents how much their children have already learned without any direct teaching. For example, say something like this: "Just look at all the things Lindsey learned during her first four years, long before she ever set foot in any classroom." Point out that Lindsey learned to walk, talk, sing, move to music, put most of her clothes on, use the toilet, feed herself, recognize friends and relatives, interact with other people, and so forth, all *before* she entered preschool. Remind Lindsey's parents that while they supported and guided her throughout this learning process, they did not directly "teach" her.

Communicate to parents that learning is a process that happens *naturally*—children learn to talk not from formal lessons, but from having parents and others converse with them frequently during everyday activities. Through these experiences, children learn that they can use speech to communicate and to get their needs met. Point out to parents that children *want* to be able to do what adults can do—they are *intrinsically* motivated to talk, to walk, and to use other basic life skills. As a result, they will learn these skills without adults directly teaching them—and mostly through play, exploration, and interaction with others. Stress that whether playing at home, in the park, at their friends' houses, or at school, children are learning *all the time* from the people, objects, and ideas they encounter. How

For More About Play and Learning . . .

Bergen, D. (Ed.). (1988). *Play as a medium for learning and development.* Portsmouth, NH: Heinemann Educational Books.

Bredekamp, S. (1987). *Developmentally appropriate practice in early childhood programs serving children from birth through age 8.* Washington, DC: National Association for the Education of Young Children.

Caplan, F., & Caplan, T. (1974). *The power of play.* Garden City, NY: Anchor Books.

Chance, P. (1979). *Learning through play.* New York: Gardner Press.

Cherry, C. (1976). *Creative play for the developing child.* Belmont, CA: David S. Lake Publishers.

Frede, E. (1984). *Getting involved: Workshops for parents.* Ypsilanti, MI: High/Scope Press.

Garvey, C. (1990). *Play (The developing child series).* Cambridge, MA: Harvard University Press.

Hendrick, J. (1986). *Total learning.* Columbus, OH: Merrill.

Hohmann, M., & Weikart, D. (1995). *Educating young children.* Ypsilanti, MI: High/Scope Press.

Holt, J. (1989). *Learning all the time.* Reading, MA: Addison-Wesley.

Isenberg, J., & Quisenberry, N. L. (1988, February). Play: A necessity for all children (Position paper of the Association for Childhood Education International). *Childhood Education, 64,* 138–145.

Johnson, J. E., Christie, J. F., & Yawkey, T. D. (1987). *Play and early childhood development.* Glenview, IL: Scott, Foresman and Co.

Klugman, E., & Smilansky, S. (Eds.). (1990). *Children's play and learning.* New York: Teachers College Press.

Piers, M. W., & Landau, G. M. (1980). *The gift of play.* New York: Walker and Company.

Rogers, C. S., & Sawyers, J. K. (1988). *Play in the lives of children.* Washington, DC: National Association for the Education of Young Children.

Segal, M., & Adcock, D. (1986). *Your child at play: Three to five years.* New York: Newmarket Press.

Sponseller, D. B., David, J., Levadi, B., & von Hippel, C. S. *Getting involved: Your child and play* [Pamphlet]. Belmont, MA: Administration for Children, Youth and Families.

Stipek, D., Rosenblatt, L., & DiRocco, L. (1994, March). Making parents your allies. *Young Children, 49*(3) 4–9.

Stone, S. (1995, September). Wanted: Advocates for play in the primary grades. *Young Children, 50*(6), 45–54.

Van Hoorn, J., Nourot, P., Scales, B., & Alward, K. (1993). *Play at the center of the curriculum.* New York: Macmillan.

Wasserman, S. (1990). *Serious players in the primary classroom.* New York: Teachers College Press.

much they learn depends on the richness of the materials and experiences in their environment and the kinds of interactions they have with peers and adults. Explain that an active learning preschool program enhances this natural learning-process by providing a wide range of materials and experiences, plentiful opportunities to make choices, and support from attentive adults.

Foundations for Academic Skills

Once parents grasp the basic principle that learning can result from play and exploration, you can begin to educate them about how your preschool program paves the way for later academic learning. Below we list some of the traditional curriculum areas in the early primary grades, followed by the specific ways High/Scope preschools prepare children in these areas:

• **Reading:** In High/Scope early childhood settings we encourage children to work with many "real" materials—blocks, dress-up clothes, household objects, art materials, small toy figures, and so forth, as well as photos, pictures, drawings, and symbols of these things. Thus, when children encounter the *word* for an object, the word is anchored in an actual experience. We also expose children to many forms of print (books, magazines, signs, labels, lists, charts, letter blocks, ticket stubs, and so forth). Throughout the preschool's daily routine, children often see adults reading, both to entertain the group and to obtain information. Surrounded

What We Know About Young Children . . .		Influences How We Interact With Them
Children *construct* knowledge by acting on objects and discovering relationships between objects (rather than by being told facts by adults).		Our role as teachers, then, is to facilitate their "learning how to learn" (development of intelligence) rather than to directly teach them specific facts.
For young children, there is no distinction between "play" and "work," there is only *doing*—experiencing and learning. And they are intrinsically motivated to discover things about their world by interacting with people, things, and ideas.		We need to provide a large portion of time during the day for children to *play*—to pursue activities of their own choosing. During this time, they will be clarifying and extending their understanding of their social and physical world.

by print materials and seeing the significant adults in their lives reading, children in High/Scope settings naturally aspire to read. So their first reading occurs just as their first speaking did—as a result of their own explorations.

Similarly, High/Scope teachers provide experiences and materials that help to lay the foundation for letter learning, even though they do not directly teach writing or reciting the alphabet. Before children can make sense of the random lines and squiggles that make up the letters of the alphabet, they must learn to decode simple, recognizable symbols. To encourage this decoding process, teachers give each child a personal symbol (for example, a flower, plane, turtle, or bear). Children's symbols, along with their written names, are then used on their personal cubbies, their artwork, the message board, and so forth. Other kinds of symbols—photos, drawings, outlines of objects—label the materials and areas of the room, and children use these labels as they get out and put away materials, thus gaining additional experience with symbols.

• **Writing:** To develop the small-muscle coordination needed to hold writing tools, the preschool setting offers a wide range of interesting objects that children can manipulate with their hands and fingers. For drawing or making marks on paper, there are tools such as paintbrushes, markers, crayons, chalk, and pencils. Children will have the urge to write—and this often comes before the urge to read—when they see the significant adults in their lives communicating through writing. In High/Scope settings, children see writing used throughout the day: Teachers write brief anecdotal notes while playing with and observing children; they write down children's words upon request; and they encourage children to write in their own way. They accept whatever form this early writing takes, including scribbles or letter-like forms that children identify as "writing." Some children, on their own, are able to write real letters and real words either with invented or conventional spelling.

• **Numbers:** Because of the wide variety of materials and experiences available in a High/Scope active learning setting, there are plenty of opportunities for children to notice quantities and number symbols and to count; number "talk" and number skills frequently enter into their play. For example, James and Addie compare the number of blocks they have; Jamal matches one plate to each person as he pretends to serve dinner; and Mei-Mei counts the number of pegs she has on her pegboard. Teachers regard such incidents as natural opportunities for supporting emerging skills; they encourage individual children to continue to work with number concepts at their own developmental levels.

Other Benefits of Play

It's also helpful to point out to parents that cognitive and intellectual skills are not the only skills that contribute to young children's school success; **social, emotional, and physical skills and abilities** are just as important and are also strengthened through play.

Explain that High/Scope settings are alive with the buzz of conversation and social play. These frequent opportunities for **social interaction** help children expand their social and emotional abilities. Some of the important skills that develop through social interaction are negotiating, resolving conflicts, solving problems, getting along with others, expressing feelings, understanding the feelings of others, taking turns, being patient, cooperating, sharing, and making friends. Give parents many specific examples of how you see these skills developing in your program. Point out that High/Scope teachers are trained to assist and support children as they extend their social abilities during play. Most parents will agree that for lifelong success, developing social competence is as important as developing academic abilities.

When parents express concern about a play-based active learning program, let them know that as an educator, you share their goals. Just as they do, you want their children to grow, to learn, and to be successful throughout their school years. With these shared goals as common ground, you can begin to work with parents as partners in the active learning approach.

In addition, in active learning settings children are free to move about the setting—to sit on floors or at a table, to play with both small and large materials, to jump and climb, to play actively both indoors and outdoors, and to move to music. Point out to parents how this wide range of activities enhances children's physical skills and abilities, including their fine- and gross-motor development, bodily control, eye-hand coordination, and spatial understanding.

Ideas for Sharing Information

So far, we have discussed most of the basic ideas about play and learning that you will want to discuss with parents. Although we've presented these ideas in just a few pages, it may not be effective for *you* to present them all at one time. Since these ideas will be new to many parents, you may want to present them in a variety of contexts, focusing on just a few ideas at a time. As parents have more experiences with your program

*For young children, there is no distinction between "play" and "work," there is only **doing**— experiencing and learning. And they are intrinsically motivated to discover things about their world by interacting with people, things, and ideas. When parents understand this, they will support their children's discoveries and help them take advantage of the multitude of learning experiences that occur throughout the day.*

and see its impact on their children, they will gradually become more and more convinced of the value of play. Meanwhile, here are some creative suggestions for keeping parents interested in learning-through-play issues:

• In each area of the room, put a sign listing the kinds of learning that typically occur there (see "Signs of Learning" on pp. 170–171).

• Talk to individual parents when they drop off or pick up their children, pointing out the ways their children are learning from their specific play activities.

• Send home articles (translated, if necessary) on how play supports children's learning, growth, and development.

• Keep a lending library of books, brochures, and copies of magazine and journal articles that may be of interest to parents.

• Invite parents to come in and observe the children during work time.

• Hold parent workshops dealing with the value of play, and include time for parents to actually play with the materials in the classroom.

Signs of Learning

One strategy for helping parents understand the value of play is to post in each classroom interest area a sign listing things children typically do and learn there. Parents who are volunteering in the classroom, attending a parent meeting, or dropping off or picking up their children will notice and read the signs. You might also post a list of the High/Scope key experiences on a parent bulletin board or somewhere else in the room, at adult eye-level. Here are some lists to use in making your own signs.

In the block area, children . . .

- Explore: They take blocks off the shelves, heap them in piles, line them up, stack them, load them into cartons and trucks, dump them out, carry them, fit them back on the shelf.

- Build and make models, creating all kinds of block structures. As they work, they experiment with balance, enclosure, patterns, and symmetry.

- Imitate and pretend, combining blocks with little people, animals, and vehicles and creating play scenarios with houses, barns, hospitals, roads, and fences.

- Play games with their own made-up rules.

- Make plans and carry them out. They solve problems that arise with materials or with other children.

- Learn spatial relations, logic, and number concepts: They sort and compare; they notice similarities and differences; they learn about colors, shapes, and other attributes of things.

In the house area, children . . .

- Explore: They stir, fill, empty, pour, shake, mix, roll, fold, zip, button, snap, brush, and try on and remove dress-up clothes.

- Imitate and pretend: They cook, serve, and eat "meals"; care for babies; go shopping or go to work; dress up; have parties; go to "weddings" and "movies."

- Make plans and carry them out. Children solve problems that arise with materials or with other children.

- Learn social skills: They work with others, express their feelings, and use increasingly elaborate language.

- Learn to make sense of their immediate world by acting out familiar roles and re-enacting events they have experienced or heard about.

In the art area, children . . .

- Explore: They stir, roll, cut, twist, fold, flatten, drip, blot; they fit things together and take them apart; they combine and transform materials; and they fill up surfaces with color, paste, or paper scraps.

- Make things: They create pictures, books, weavings, movie tickets, menus, cards, hats, robots, birthday cakes, cameras, fire trucks.

- Make plans and carry them out. They solve problems that arise with materials or with other children.

- Learn to be creative and imaginative. They make pictures, models, and other kinds of artwork and express their ideas using symbols and sometimes even letters and words.

In the toy area, children . . .

- Explore materials; fill and empty containers; take apart and put together puzzles, nuts-and-bolts, and interlocking squares; make patterns with beads, parquetry blocks, and other small toys; sort and match. They use magnets, magnifying glasses, and balance scales.

- Make things out of Legos, Tinkertoys, small blocks, pegs and pegboards, and other building materials.

- Imitate and pretend using small toys and the structures they've built with them.

- Play games, sometimes with their own made-up rules.

- Make plans and carry them out. They solve problems that arise either with materials or with other children.

- Learn spatial relations, logic, and number concepts: They sort and compare; they notice similarities and differences. They learn about colors, shapes, and other attributes of things.

In the sand and water area, children . . .

- Explore materials (water, sand, pebbles, leaves, snow, shaving cream, Styrofoam pieces, and so forth): They mix, stir, heap, dump, dig, fill, empty, pour, pat, sift, mold, and splash. This provides children with a sensory, repeatable, comfortable activity.

- Make things and pretend with them: cakes, houses, roads, lakes for floating boats.

- Make plans and carry them out. They solve problems that arise with materials or with other children.

- Learn spatial concepts, discover the properties of tactile and malleable materials and improve their pouring skills. They learn to work together.

In the book and writing area, children . . .

- Explore print materials: picture books, wordless books, folk stories, predictable storybooks, poetry books, concept books, alphabet books, homemade and child-made books, photo books. They use magazines, story props, and writing materials.

- Look at and read books and magazines, simulate reading using their memories and picture cues, and listen to others read and tell stories.

- Create and write their own notes, stories, pictures, and books.

- Make plans and carry them out.

- Learn to enjoy books and stories, the foundation for reading. They begin to understand that words have meaning, and they often begin writing and reading words on their own.

How Can Parents Get a Daily Update?

If they had a better picture of what their children actually do in the classroom and on the playground each day, parents would be more likely to see the importance of play. However, parents often complain to me that when they ask their preschoolers what they did in school, they get vague answers like "Nothing" or "I just played." Are there any suggestions I can give to parents to help them find out more about their children's play?

—A preschool teacher

Suggest to parents that instead of asking children "What did you do today?" they should try open-ended questions or comments like these:

I wonder who was playing with you today.

Tell me about the block area—what was happening there this morning?

I wonder what the story was about today.

What kinds of things were on the art shelf today?

I wonder what happened outside on the playground today.

Show me how people moved at circle time today.

What did you like best about school today?

You might also start a small notebook for each child, one that can be sent back and forth between home and school each day. In the notebook, try to record daily at least one anecdote or personal comment about the child's play and learning. This gives parents information that they can use as they discuss school experiences with their children. After parents have been receiving the notebooks for a while, they often begin to look for examples of children's learning at home, so they can add their own comments to the notebooks.

• Send home a monthly newsletter with suggestions for appropriate play activities that parents can do at home with their children.

• To encourage play at home, send home "play kits." For example, one kit may contain art materials, books, or small toys, as well as ideas for activities that use household materials. This strategy is useful when parents ask for "homework."

• Throughout the year, but especially at parent conferences, share with parents your anecdotal notes illustrating children's learning.

In the Elementary School—
Play Sparks Learning

By Charles Hohmann

• •

For many elementary educators and parents, the word *play* has a negative meaning. For example, we might say to a child, "You're not getting anything done—you're just playing" or "Don't play with your neighbor when you're waiting in line." Used in this negative sense, *play* implies idleness, silliness, or laxity. And play can even be seen as destructive, as in "playing with someone's emotions." Many of us, then, see play as something that impedes a person's efforts to achieve a goal. In fact, the more goal-directed an activity becomes, the more we think of it as work, not play.

Yet play can be viewed more positively—as a path to the unexpected, the unplanned, the spontaneous. When we "play with" an object or an idea, we are exploring it, and we are open to surprise discoveries. Asking "Let me play with this for a while" is asking permission to experiment with new solutions or new ways of framing a problem. When we permit ourselves this kind of playfulness, we are entering a trial-and-error or "let's see what happens" mode.

It is play in this exploratory, creative sense that we want to encourage in learning experiences for elementary-aged children. Yes, we do want older children to apply their energy in goal-directed tasks; yet we also want them, as they pursue a goal, to explore new materials, use what they know in new ways, and be open to discoveries.

Since openness to discovery is necessary for constructing knowledge, at least some degree of playfulness is essential to creating the conditions for learning. Even when children are told or shown exactly how to do something, they have to try out the procedure themselves to internalize it. Play-like situations, in which we encourage children to try out and experiment with new ideas, techniques, and strategies, are more likely to lead to the internalization of knowledge than are direct-imitation or rote-repetition situations.

Elementary-level learning experiences can easily be designed to contain an element of play. In the following two **classroom examples,** note how children's playfulness contributes to learning:

• **A first-grade plan-do-review session.** Several first-graders together make a plan to use the ink pads and letter stamps in the writing area. They state their plans in very general terms, without specifying which stamps they will use or what they intend to make. The children start by "just playing" with the stamps. They experiment randomly with the materials available, trying various stamps, colors, and amounts of ink. Gradually, however, their efforts become focused. They make a variety of signs announcing various commands, for example, "NO TALKING," "NO BOYS A LOUD" [their own invented spelling], and "KEEP OFF." Throughout the activity, there is an ongoing sense of play—both with words and with feelings of being powerful.

• **A second-grade math workshop.** At the workshop station, the teacher has provided three jars of different-sized beads, about 100 or more per jar. The assigned task for the small group is to estimate the number of beads in each jar, record the estimate, and then count the beads to determine accuracy. The teacher has not specified a counting method. Each small group goes about the task of counting the beads in a different way. In one of the groups, the children can't agree about the best way to do the counting: Several children start counting the beads in one jar in the conventional way (counting one by one); meanwhile, another child counts a second jar's beads by making groups of 10 and then counting the number of groups. In another group, children line up the beads along the edge of a ruler, discovering that 30 beads are needed to span the ruler's length. They then use the ruler to measure out groups of 30 and add these to find a result. Still another group divides the task of counting among three children; the children then combine their results to get a total. Given the freedom to "play" at finding a solution in their own way, each group successfully uses a different set of mathematical concepts to devise a counting method that makes sense to them.

All of the principles and strategies of the High/Scope elementary approach are designed to foster this kind of play within task-oriented situations. For example, we encourage experimentation and creative problem solving by having children work in small, cooperative groups; engage in a daily plan-do-review sequence; work with real materials and objects; and produce tangible products. If play is an essential element of the High/Scope elementary approach—and it is—the rest of the approach consists of the tools and strategies that inspire and guide this play toward important learning outcomes.

Play on!

Chapter Five

Key Experiences in Child Development
· ·

Lights, Camera, Action! Spotlight onPretend Play
Beth Marshall

A Partnership With Young Artists
Mark Tompkins

Science: Here, There, and Everywhere
Jackie Post

Science: Our "Basic Four"
Frank Blackwell and Charles Hohmann

Science in the Elementary Grades: Beyond Dinosaurs and Volcanoes
Charles Hohmann

Classification: Collecting, Sorting, and Organizing
Michelle Graves

Spatial Learning: Beyond Circles, Squares, and Triangles
Mark Tompkins

It's About Time!
Mark Tompkins

Alternatives to "Calendar Time"
Mark Tompkins

High/Scope's Key Experiences for Infants and Toddlers
Jackie Post

The Infant and Toddler Key Experiences—Anecdotal Examples
Jackie Post

*W*hat kinds of learning experiences are important for young children? In the High/Scope approach, questions like this one—questions about the nature and content of appropriate educational experiences— are answered by the High/Scope key experiences in child development.

At the preschool level, the key experiences consist of 58 statements describing developmentally important activities for young children aged 2½ to 5 years. Teachers and caregivers use this list as a framework that guides them in interpreting their observations of children, arranging and equipping the classroom environment, planning activities, and devising ways to support children's interests and emerging abilities. The preschool key experiences are divided into these categories: creative representation; language and literacy; initiative and social relations; movement; music; classification; seriation; number; space; and time.

The High/Scope approach also includes a related list of 38 infant and toddler key experiences, which are divided into the following categories: social relations; sense of self; communication; movement; exploring objects; exploring attributes of objects; comparing and counting; space; and time. The key experiences extend to the elementary level as well. The High/Scope elementary key experiences are more specific in focus than the key experiences for younger children. Together they provide a detailed list of educationally important skills, behaviors, concepts, and processes in the content areas of language and literacy; math; science; music; and movement.

This chapter is not intended to provide a comprehensive treatment of all the High/Scope key experiences. Instead it looks in depth at a few groups of key experiences and some ways teachers can use them to support children's development.

In the opening article, "Lights, Camera, Action! Spotlight on Pretend Play," Beth Marshall explores a preschool **creative representation** key experience, **pretending and role playing.** She explains how children develop a range of important abilities as they create their own play "dramas." To illustrate her discussion, Marshall follows a group of children in the High/Scope Demonstration Preschool as they pretend to operate a barbershop. She describes how they develop a series of barbershop play episodes over the course of several months. This extended example demonstrates how, by providing related materials and experiences and joining in children's play, adults can support children in developing the complexity of their pretend play.

In the next article, "A Partnership With Young Artists," Mark Tompkins suggests ways adults can support preschool children as they engage in the **creative representation** key experiences that involve such activities as drawing, painting, and making models. Tompkins points out that adults can best support children's development as artists by avoiding praise or other evaluative statements and instead encouraging children to reflect on and describe their own work. Tompkins also suggests that adults can support children's artwork by creating alongside of and with children.

Children's beginning science experiences are the subject of the next three articles. In "Science: Here, There, and Everywhere," Jackie Post explores preschool science experiences, showing how scientific thinking develops as children strive to make sense of the world around them. Post observes that young children are natural scientists: They make observations, explore and experiment with materials, draw conclusions, and communicate their findings during the course of the normal activities of the preschool. Post points out that preschoolers use a wide range of key experiences during their scientific explorations (for example, key experiences in **classification, space, time,** and **language and literacy**) and suggests some steps adults can take to encourage, recognize, and support children's spontaneous science experiences. In "Science: Our 'Basic Four' " Frank Blackwell and Charles Hohmann turn to science in the elementary school, describing four basic kinds of activities—making collections, building, analyzing and testing, and taking surveys—that provide opportunities for elementary **science** key experiences. The theme of appropriate science activities for the elementary level is continued in "Science in the Elementary Grades: Beyond Dinosaurs and Volcanoes" by Charles Hohmann. Hohmann urges elementary science educators to move away from descriptive, second-hand science activities, replacing them with hands-on activities in which children gain opportunities to explore and solve problems with real materials.

Michelle Graves explores the preschool **classification** key experiences in the next article, "Classification: Collecting, Sorting, and Organizing." She points out that whereas many teachers understand classification only as sorting, the actual classification experiences occurring in the preschool classroom involve a much broader range of activities. Graves points out how classification occurs throughout the day, both indoors and outdoors, not only when children are playing with small, easily sorted toys, but also when children are pretending, engaging in movement experiences, and doing artwork. She provides teachers with many suggestions for recognizing and supporting classification.

In the next three articles, Mark Tompkins looks at two areas in the development of children's logical thinking, the **space** and **time** key experiences. In "Spatial Learning: Beyond Circles, Squares, and Triangles," Tompkins explains that preschoolers are developing an understanding of spatial concepts such as **proximity, separation, location, direction, nearness, and enclosure** as they work directly with objects in their world. He explains why the block area is a "laboratory for spatial thinking" and offers adult strategies for interacting with children as they construct with blocks. His next two articles, "It's About Time!" and "Alternatives to 'Calendar Time,'" explain why concepts of time are so difficult for preschoolers to grasp, then discuss ways adults can encourage the development of a more mature understanding of time. Tompkins explains why time activities centered on clocks and calendars are inappropriate for preschoolers; he recommends instead that adults support children in concrete, time-related experiences—experiencing and noticing consistent routines and time sequences, participating in "stop-and-start" play, working with egg and sand timers, and comparing and talking about simple time-intervals ("a short time," "a long time").

The last two articles in this chapter, by Jackie Post, introduce High/Scope's key experiences for infants and toddlers and explain their use in group care settings. This list of key experiences was developed in part by using information gathered from 21 infant and toddler program sites throughout the country. The infant and toddler key experiences are intended to be used in tandem with the preschool key experiences, so program staff can see children's development from birth to school age as a continuum.

Lights, Camera, Action!
Spotlight on Pretend Play

By Beth Marshall

• •

It's the beginning of a work time experience involving several preschool children. Callie, Martin, and Douglas are bringing large hollow blocks over from the block area to the toy area as Chelsea provides directions: "Yeah, that's good. . . . Make 'em all go in one line." The children work at lining up the blocks until they have made a satisfactory "waiting bench" for their pretend barbershop.

Meanwhile Corrin collects a chair and a tub holding dull scissors and clippers from the house area, and a large scarf from the music and movement area. She carefully arranges them in the toy area near the "waiting bench." Callie brings the large floor mirror over and sets it in front of the chair. Chelsea gets the phone from the house area and sets it down. She finds a clipboard, paper, and pencil in the reading and writing area. Survey-ing the scene, she announces, "We will be ready to cut hair at nine five two." Douglas adds some magazines and books to the waiting bench and sits down.

Corrin and Callie are negotiating about who gets to cut hair first:

"I should be the haircutter 'cause I got the clippers," says Corrin.

"Well, I got the mirror," replies Callie.

"I already have the clippers, though," says Corrin.

Finally they agree to take turns, with Corrin going first. Martin sits in the chair, and Corrin tucks the scarf around his neck, saying, "You want your hair cut, Martin?" Martin nods yes. "A little or a lot?" asks Corrin.

"A little," replies Martin.

Meanwhile, Chelsea tells Douglas he can be next and makes a mark on her clipboard. "Wait Douglas, this is prob'ly another one," she says,

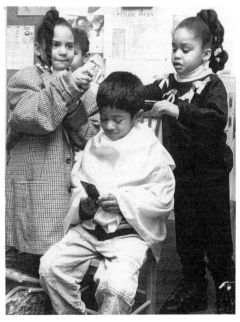

A pretend haircut offers a multitude of learning opportunities for these children. Through pretend play experiences like this one, children develop both social and cognitive skills.

picking up the phone receiver. "Hello?" she says. "Yes, you can get your hair cut. No, not now. How about seven-five-six? It's good? Then that's your time."

Corrin has finished Martin's haircut. Martin looks at himself in the large mirror. "Good," he says, satisfied, "a little haircut." He goes to Chelsea and pays her price of "14 bucks" in cut paper strips. She consults her clipboard and tells Douglas that it's his turn. Callie assumes the haircutter's spot as Douglas sits down.

Through pretend-play experiences like this one observed in the High/Scope Demonstration Preschool (and pictured on the previous page), children develop both social and cognitive skills. As they pretend, children use what they know from their own experiences and apply it to the play situation—a form of symbolic or representational thinking. And when pretend play involves more than one child, it helps children become aware of the points of view of others and gain experience in cooperating and negotiating.

A complex role-play experience, then, offers many opportunities for learning. You may be surprised that such a detailed, realistic "drama" was created spontaneously by a group of 3- and 4-year-olds. Yet this play situation, as complex as it was, had humble beginnings. It all started more than a month before with three children, a chair, and a pair of scissors. And the children's play developed as it did partly because of the support provided by classroom adults.

From this example, what can we learn about how complex representational play develops and how adults can encourage this process?

The First Step: Observing

The first step for adults who wish to help children expand the complexity of their role play is to **observe what children are interested in, what they are already depicting in their play.** Five weeks before the incident just described, the adults noticed a few children repeatedly acting out a simple play scene in which one child would sit in a chair as another pretended to cut her hair with a pair of scissors. During their planning session that day, the adults noted that this haircutting play had been occurring for about a week and that it involved the same three children and the same objects and activities each time.

Providing Related Experiences and Materials

Once you've observed children expressing an interest by re-enacting a role play scene, you can encourage them to extend this interest by **planning a related "hands-on" experience.** In this case, teachers scheduled

The first step for adults who wish to help children expand the complexity of their role play is to observe what children are interested in, what they are already depicting in their play.

a class trip to a neighborhood barbershop. At the barbershop, the children were able to sit in the barber's chair, feel the vibrations of the electric clippers and blow dryer, sit on the bench in the waiting area, and watch as one of their classmates got a haircut.

After a field trip or other related experience, children's interest in a topic is likely to increase. Once back in the classroom, adults can **provide follow-up support** that will enable children to build on this heightened interest. First, **consider the materials that are available to support the play topic.** To support pretend play, the classroom should be stocked with many **real-life tools and other props** and a plentiful supply of **open-ended materials** that children can use in a variety of ways. The teachers in this example added dull scissors (that wouldn't cut hair) and real hair clippers (with the cord cut off) to the variety of hair-care materials in the house area. Their classroom was already stocked with many materials that had open-ended applications, which children used imaginatively as the haircutting play expanded. Half-circle blocks became combs; scarves were used for clothing drapes; large, hollow blocks became a "waiting bench"; and paper strips and poker chips served as money.

Accessibility of materials is another thing to consider. Can children gather and use things from all parts of the classroom in their play? Are the materials in the classroom arranged and labeled in a way that makes it easy for children to find what they need for a play scenario? Do the children know where to find scarves they can use to drape over their clothing when they get a haircut? Do they have access to the magazines in the art area, so they can use them to complete their barbershop waiting room?

It's also important for adults to **be flexible and accept children's unexpected uses of materials.** In the pretend barbershop activity, the adults were initially nervous about children using scissors to pretend to cut hair. The teachers watched closely as the children used the scissors, and though they found that the children *were* very careful not to actually cut anyone's hair, they were still concerned because the safety scissors from the art area were fairly sharp. The teachers decided to look for some different kinds of scissors that were less likely to result in an "accident." They found some old safety scissors that were extremely dull, and these were the ones they put in the "haircut tub" in the house area. The next morning at greeting circle they talked with the children about using these scissors carefully for pretend haircuts. They continued to monitor the use of scissors and were relieved to see that no children went home with less hair than they came with!

Entering Children's Play

In addition to providing stimulating materials, adults can encourage the development of play by **taking part themselves in the play scenarios children create.**

When entering a play situation, be mindful of the need to **allow children to retain control of their play.** Children will often invite you to play with them if you **first observe what they are doing** and then **imitate their actions,** waiting for further cues.

When considering how to enter a play situation, it's helpful to be aware of the stages children typically go through as they develop a pretend-play scene. Psychologist Catherine Garvey (1990, p. 41) has observed a process that often occurs when children come in contact with new materials: "For the child an unfamiliar object tends to set up a chain of exploration, familiarization, and eventual understanding: an often-repeated sequence that will eventually lead to more mature concepts of the properties of the physical world."

Children go through a similar cycle as they repeat a pretend-play situation, exploring the situation in depth before they add new props and activities to their scenarios. First, children tend to **investigate physical properties of the play setting**—spending lots of time setting up the barbershop, for example. Next, children **become familiar with a sequence of events.**

In the barbershop example, the teachers initially observed children "cutting" the doll's hair over and over with little variation and repeatedly taking turns "cutting" one another's hair. The repetitive quality of these activities suggested to teachers that children were assimilating their newly acquired roles. After spending much time in this exploratory play, children eventually came to an understanding of the situation. At this point, they were ready to expand the play sequence, incorporating additional ideas and variations—washing the doll's hair, taking phone appointments. One of the adults, knowing that children first needed to explore the materials and roles, joined them by exploring in a similar way. The adult noticed that Martin and Audie were "cutting" dolls' hair by moving scissors over the dolls' head and saying "Bzzzz, bzzzz, bzzzz." So the adult got a doll and copied their actions and sounds. Martin and Audie responded to this by grinning at the adult and continuing with the doll's "haircut." Eventually Martin said, "Hey, you want to get your hair

Supporting the "Wannabe" Player

Sometimes the younger children in my center want to be involved in pretend play with the older children, but it just doesn't work out—the older children want players who are as adept as they are. Any suggestions?

—Child care teacher

One thing you can try involves joining in the pretending yourself. Once you've been accepted by the skilled players, you can invite a younger, less-skilled child to join in the pretend play. Then, give cues to that child about how he or she might take part in a way that is acceptable to the more skillful players. For example, in our preschool, several children had built a car out of blocks and were "driving to Georgia." An adult was invited to join them as the "teenage sister," and she did. The drivers decided they were tired and stopped at a pretend motel (the other side of a block shelf). The adult noticed

Chris eagerly watching this—he had tried unsuccessfully to join the players on several previous occasions. So the adult extended an invitation: "Chris, we're sleeping in a motel—want to sleep with us?" He nodded and came over. The adult told him they were trying to find something to cover up with, and Chris got an armful of scarves to use as covers. As the other children began to "get ready for bed," the adult said to Chris, "Now we're going to pretend to sleep." The other players were tolerant of Chris, because at this point, they really had limited contact with him—the adult was doing most of the interacting with Chris. As the play went on, the adult continued in her minor role and continued to give Chris hints about what he might do. She also tried to involve Chris more with the other children. Once Chris seemed to be on a fairly secure footing with the other children, the adult found a reason to withdraw, and the children continued on their own.

cut?" When the adult nodded, Audie said, "You can sit here," pointing to his chair. Bingo, she was in!

Once you have been invited to join children's pretend play, be careful to tread lightly, remembering how easily children's ideas are trampled, how easy it is for an adult to take charge of the play. **The adult should enter the child's play in a supporting role, as a co-player rather than as the "star."** Co-playing adults take minor or less critical roles in dramatic play—the patient rather than the doctor, the teenager of the family, the person getting a haircut. Children are the decision-makers and pivotal players—the doctors, the moms and dads, the haircutters. Early childhood researchers David Wood, Linnet McMahon, and Yvonne Cranstoun (1980) relate the advantages of adult co-playing; they see it as an effective means of building rapport, modeling play behaviors, engaging in play-related conversations, and drawing other children into the play.

Helping Children Add Complexity to a Play Scene

As you observe and imitate children and participate in their pretend play, they may give you cues that show they need some help in adding variations. Subtly, without stepping out of your play role, you could in this situation

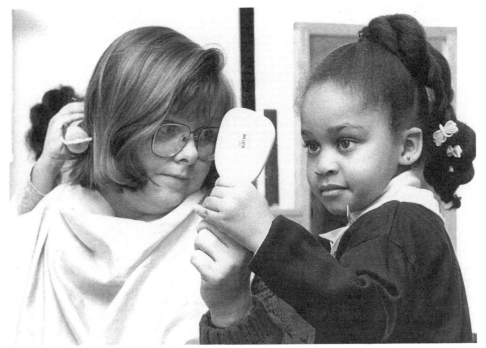

Once you have been invited to join children's pretend play, be careful to tread lightly, remembering how easily children's ideas are trampled, how easy it is for an adult to take charge of the play. The adult should enter the child's play in a supporting role, as a co-player rather than as the "star."

Time to Pretend

Time—to explore, to struggle with problems, to question, discover, and practice—is an essential element of all active learning experiences. This is especially true of children's pretending. Children may stay with a particular pretend topic for days, weeks, or months, eventually acting out detailed scenarios like the barbershop play described in this article.

Adults are best able to encourage children to expand a pretend-play activity when they are aware of the long time-frame that is typical of complex dramatic play. As part of a study of the development of children's play, the evolution of the barbershop play was documented in anecdotal records, video footage, and photographs (Marshall, 1992). Data from this study provide us with many insights about how complex role play evolves over time and about why patience is such a necessary ingredient in providing adult support.

From the study data, here is a week-by-week account of the development of the barbershop play scene:

Weeks 1 and 2: The repeated theme of haircutting first surfaces in fairly simple play. In this phase, only 3 children play at haircutting; they use just 2 props, scissors and a chair; and they enact a single activity, cutting hair. Responding to the children's interest in haircutting, the adults plan a class trip to the barbershop.

Weeks 3 and 4: Following the trip to the barbershop, the number of children playing at cutting hair doubles to 6, and the number of play elements (props used and activities depicted) increases dramatically from 3 to 11. As well as adding new props and activities, the children also add

details to ongoing activities. The props now include scarves (used for clothing drapes), a floor mirror, clippers, and blocks (used for combs). Haircutting becomes more realistic, including both clipping and cutting movements and sounds. Children now give pretend haircuts to dolls as well as to one another, and they act out the opening and closing of the shop.

Weeks 5 and 6: To the adults' surprise, new effects of the field trip are still surfacing during this phase of play, in the third and fourth weeks after the trip to the barbershop. The adults note yet another jump (from 6 to 13) in the number of children consistently playing barbershop; the complexity of their play also continues to increase, with children incorporating several new activities and accompanying props. They begin charging money for the haircuts, using paper strips and poker chips to represent money, and they now take appointments with the help of a phone they added. They also now pretend to wash as well as cut their dolls' hair, and they construct a "waiting bench" complete with books, magazines, and numbers for those waiting. It appears, then, that for some children, the observations made on the field trip need to "percolate" for several weeks before they can re-enact them.

This documentation of the unfolding of a richly detailed play scenario suggests both the potential complexity of long-term play in young children and the need for adults to pace themselves to the young child's slower timetable. Adults who wish to support complex play may want to ask themselves, "Are we allowing enough time for children's play to blossom and develop?"

pose a problem or make a comment that extends children's ideas or stimulates them to expand their play. In the example, an adult who one day was playing "haircut" with the children made such a comment to her co-players: "I wonder what I could do while I'm waiting for my turn to get my hair cut?" This gently reminded children about the waiting area they had seen at the neighborhood barbershop, stimulating them to create one themselves with classroom materials. Remember, however, that children may or may not pick up on a suggestion like this. If they don't, respect their choice, and look to them for further cues.

Adults, then, can support children's representational play by looking for interests that children already have, planning hands-on experiences related to those interests, providing the kinds of materials that will enable children to expand on a play topic, and participating themselves in the children's dramatic play. "Time to Pretend" on p. 185 makes clear the need for a final ingredient: Supporting children's complex play experiences like those in the barbershop example requires **patience.** It may take weeks or even months for children to develop a play scenario to this extent.

REFERENCES

Garvey, C. (1990). *Play.* Cambridge, MA: Harvard University Press.

Marshall, B. (1992). *"Want your hair cut?": Strategies for increasing children's representational play.* Unpublished master's thesis, Oakland University, Rochester, MI.

Weininger, O. (1988). What if and as if: Imagination and pretend play in early childhood. In K. Egan & D. Nadaner (Eds.), *Imagination and education.* New York: Teachers College Press.

Wood, D., McMahon, L., & Cranstoun, Y. (1980). *Working with under fives* (Vol. 5, Oxford Preschool Research Project series). Ypsilanti, MI: High/Scope Press.

A Partnership With Young Artists

By Mark Tompkins

• •

Martin is painting at the easel. His painting is an array of colors and unrecognizable forms. As the teacher approaches Martin, she pauses, unsure of what to do or say. Should she praise his effort by saying something like "Very beautiful, Martin, you've worked hard on your painting"? Should she ask questions about the colors and shapes she sees on his painting? Should she ask Martin if he wants to talk to her, or should she wait for him to initiate a discussion about his work?

Like Martin's teacher, many adults wonder how to communicate effectively with children who are engaged in artwork. Some teachers avoid interacting with children who are doing art—"They're working quietly and don't need me; anyway, what would I say?" Other teachers recognize the need to offer support to children working with art materials but are uncertain about how to proceed. Too unsure of themselves to interact spontaneously with children, these teachers often fall into rigid patterns—always asking the same kinds of questions or mechanically praising everything children make. As one teacher commented, "It feels as if I'm always following the same script. I'm never quite sure what to say and do when children are involved in art."

In traditional, teacher-directed art instruction, adults instruct children in what to make and how to make it; in fact, they often provide a

As they participate in children's art activities, teachers in High/Scope classrooms and centers think about how best to interact with individual children to support and perhaps extend the creative explorations they have initiated.

model for the child to copy, or cut-up pieces of paper or other materials for the child to assemble into some preordained product such as a paper snowman or bunny. In activities like these, communicating effectively with children is relatively straightforward. Telling children how to cut out circles to make a snowman's body or specifying where they should glue on a cotton ball to make the bunny's tail is one-way communication. Martin's teacher, on the other hand, is struggling with *two-way* communication: She wonders how best to interact with Martin to support and perhaps extend the creative explorations he has initiated.

In the High/Scope Curriculum, we have moved away from the traditional adult-directed model of art instruction, because we believe it stifles creativity and reduces children's problem solving, independence, and experimentation. Our goal is *creativity*, not conformity. When the product is valued over the process, opportunities for creative exploration are often lost.

In the High/Scope approach, we encourage children to create and experiment with a wide range of art materials. Because the adult is less concerned with the quality of the child's *product* than with the *process* used in making it, we call this *process-oriented art*. As Martin's teacher discovered, however, the adult who has made a shift to this new approach may often wonder, "What now? What can I do to make the most of this experience for children?"

Indeed, an adult's support can make an important contribution to early artistic development, nurturing the child's capacity for creative expression. Studies summarized by Donaldson (1978) lend support to the belief that young children working on art projects respond positively to the adult's presence, are eager to discuss their work, and can reflect on the artistic process. Effective involvement of adults in children's art activities

Planning for Young Artists

To spark creativity in children's art, **choose materials that reflect their interests**. Observe children and note what they enjoy doing, and then build on these interests in stocking the art area and in planning activities. For example:

Douglas, a 4-year-old in the High/Scope Demonstration Preschool, has played "airplane" in a variety of ways since the beginning of the school year. Other children have also become interested in Douglas's airplane play. This has led the teachers to add to the art area some materials for making airplanes and to plan ways to build on children's interest in airplanes.

The first thing the teachers did was to lead a small-group time in which they encouraged the children to make airplanes with any of the materials in the art area. The children produced several airplanes ranging from simple ones made from single sheets of folded paper to more complicated creations, such as an "18-seater with four wings" made from glue, tape, Kleenex, construction paper, plastic foam, and cardboard.

Following this experience, the teachers provided additional airplane-making materials for the art-area: rubber bands, popsicle sticks, and a set of small black plastic wheels. These materials enriched the airplane play even further.

depends, as Brittain (1979) has stated, "on exceptional tact and [should be] clearly geared toward the purpose and direction of the child himself."

In this article we define several adult communication strategies that may support children who engage in process-oriented art. To understand these strategies, let's begin by examining some of the ways adults commonly talk with children during art activities.

The Compliment Approach to Art

Probably the most common approach adults take to communicating with children about their art is to compliment, or praise, the children's work: "I really like the way you used the chalk." "That's a beautiful painting." Though such statements are in-

In the High/Scope Curriculum, we have moved away from the traditional adult-directed model of art instruction, because we believe it stifles creativity and reduces children's problem solving, independence, and experimentation. Our goal is creativity, not conformity.

tended to be supportive and encouraging, they can actually have a negative impact on children's work. Praise, though positive, is still judgmental, giving the message that it is the adult's role to evaluate the child's artwork. As a result, the child may grow inhibited, afraid to explore or to be creative. The result is a climate in which children become "praise junkies," who only feel good about their work when an adult tells them that it is good, beautiful, or nice.

Take Martin, for example. If the teacher had walked up and praised Martin's painting, what would Martin have said? Typically, nothing. Dispensing praise like this does not encourage a rich dialogue or interaction—in fact, it often stops a conversation in its tracks. Also, what about the child painting next to Martin? He or she will probably be quick to ask "What about my painting, Teacher, isn't it nice?" Thus a simple compliment may lead to a competition for adult favor.

Another problem with the compliment approach is its vagueness. "That's great, Martin" is a typical praising comment. Most of us don't want to rank children's art along a continuum of good, better, or best, so we simply tell children that all their art is "great." Before long, these terms become overworked and meaningless, and we lose our credibility with the children.

For many teachers, the alternative to mechanical compliments is to engage in a dialogue with children that encourages them to reflect on and discuss their work. Such a dialogue develops naturally when adults interact *as partners* with children.

The Partnership Approach to Art

In a partnership approach, adults participate in children's art activities— they truly become "part of" children's art experiences. This can lead to a sustained dialogue with children.

To become a partner in children's art, a good first step is to **stop talking so much or thinking so much about what to say. Instead, observe children closely when they are busy in art.** Sit or kneel next to children and simply watch what they are doing. Many times, observation is the best way to start a conversation—the child will begin talking to you about what he or she is doing. The dialogue that grows out of this approach is natural, and the questions the adult asks are related to the child's actions and how the child sees and thinks about his or her artwork. (For more on adult questioning, see "Artful Questioning.")

Using the art materials the same way the children do is another effective strategy for helping you form a partnership with the children. Because of the abundance of materials in the art area, it is often easiest to use this strategy there. If a child is making holes in clay, get another piece of clay and do the same. By imitating, you are telling the child nonverbally that you accept and value what she is doing. This type of encouragement often prompts the child to start a conversation.

The conversations that occur during art partnerships are free-flowing and offer the adult many opportunities to talk with children not only about the *process* of making something—the materials, how the child is using them, and the sequence of activities—but also about the *elements of art*—color, line, pattern, shape, space, and texture. Because the adult is discussing these concepts within the context of the child's project, they are more meaningful to children than they would be if taught directly.

A recent example from the High/Scope Demonstration Preschool illustrates how adult participation in children's art can enrich the experience. This incident also shows how an adult who interacts with children as a *real participant* in their activities—not as an outsider looking in— can sensitively introduce new ideas that broaden the scope of the experience:

Artful Questioning

What is the role of adult questioning in children's art experiences?

Many adults who are moving away from a product-oriented approach to children's artwork are experimenting with **questioning** as a technique for encouraging dialogue. These adults are usually aware that *convergent* questions (questions that have only one right answer—What color is this? What shape is this?) do little to stimulate reflection or conversation. For many adults, the alternative is to ask many *open-ended* questions—What are you making? Could you tell me about your picture?

While much preferable to "quiz questions" about colors and shapes, open-ended questions like these may not stimulate discussion for all children and can quickly become overused and tedious, especially if they are not asked in a conversational context. For example, a teacher recently shared with us the story of a first-grader who cautioned other children to conceal their drawings from the student teacher because "she'll make you tell her a real long story about it."

Thus, we recommend that you **use questions sparingly, and only as part of an ongoing conversation.** Too often the questioning approach can be intrusive, interrupting the child who is deeply involved in working, especially if an adult simply walks over and begins asking questions. Often young children's art is personal, not intended to be shared with others. Remember that children's art speaks for itself—it does not always need language to sanction it.

The developmental level of the child is an important consideration when asking questions during artwork. When a child's art is exploratory (for example, making a mass of scribbles or smearing glue on construction paper), you will probably find it difficult to have a meaningful conversation about it with the child, especially if you are primarily asking questions. Asking "What are you making?" assumes that the child's art is representational, and your questions may seem intrusive to the child whose artwork is exploratory. Chapman (1978) recommends that adults ask questions only when children's art is clearly representational. She explains that "about 30% of all 4-year-olds and about 80% of all 5-year-olds have something in mind before they begin to create a work. With these children, adult questions can be a meaningful part of the process."

Questions work best when the children have approached you about their art and you are responding to *them*. For example, we observed a preschool teacher working alongside a 4-year-old girl who was gluing wrapping paper on a box. The teacher picked up another box and began wrapping it. Soon the child opened a conversation, saying "I'm making a present for my mom." Reflecting what the child had just said, the teacher commented, "You're making a present for your mom." Before long, the two began to converse, and during the conversation the teacher was able to ask the child questions about what the present was and how the child had made it. These were questions that grew out of the teacher's genuine interest in what the child was doing.

By asking questions as part of a meaningful conversation like this, adults can help children reflect on their actions. Clearly such "artful" questions do play an important role in children's creative art activities.

One day, one of the teachers went over to the art table, where three children were playing with soap bubbles and straws. They had poured small amounts of dishwashing liquid into margarine tubs and were blowing into the soap with straws, causing bubbles to pour out over the tops of the tubs. Coming over to the group, the teacher observed briefly what was going on, then got a container, some bubble mixture, and a straw, and began blowing bubbles as well. By this action, the teacher had become a partner in the children's play and had earned the right to engage in a conversation with them and extend this play.

After a period of bubble blowing, the teacher could sense that the group was losing interest in their play, so she suggested they put some food coloring into the bubble mixture to see what would happen. This idea brought the children's interest back, and soon they were experimenting with mixing the colors. Two of them also got the idea of putting a small amount of colored bubble mixture on paper and using paintbrushes to paint with it.

When children are engaged with adults in cooperative art experiences such as this one, you rarely hear children making comments like "I'm not good at drawing [painting, cutting]." Instead of children copying adults, adults do artwork with children, following children's lead and occasionally making suggestions. Some teachers are concerned that if they "partner" with children in this way—using an active-learning, process-oriented approach that emphasizes child-chosen art activities—children will never achieve technical competence in using art materials or tools. Actually, children often learn such art skills more quickly because they are motivated by the opportunity to create things that are meaningful to them. For example, making a sword for a favorite superhero or making a pet paper snake will require the child to hold the scissors, handle the glue and tape, hold the marker steady, and so on. Self-confidence, technical proficiency, and a sense of accomplishment all develop simultaneously when teachers encourage children to approach artwork in their own way: to be creative, inventive, and unique.

BIBLIOGRAPHY

Brittain, W. L. (1979). *Creativity, art, and the young child*. New York: Macmillan.

Chapman, L. H. (1978). *Approaches to art in education*. New York: Harcourt Brace Jovanovich.

Donaldson, M. (1978). *Children's minds*. New York: Norton.

Gardner, H. (1980). *Artful scribbles: The significance of children's drawings*. New York: Basic Books.

Schirrmacher, R. (1986, July). Talking with young children about their art. *Young Children, 41*, 3–10.

Thompson, C. (1990). "I make a mark": The significance of talk in young children's artistic development. *Early Childhood Research Quarterly, 5*, 215–232.

Science:
Here, There, and Everywhere

By Jackie Post

. . . .

When you hear the word "science" used in relation to the early child-hood setting, what comes to mind? In many preschool programs, science is confined to a table in one corner of the classroom on which leaves, animal cages, shells, small fossils, magnets, magnifiers, "tornado bottles," and so forth are displayed. In these classrooms or centers, the only time science goes beyond the science table is when the class takes a field trip to a museum or a walk in the woods.

In the High/Scope approach, however, science takes place through-out the center and throughout the daily routine. Consider these entries from a science journal kept by Cara Miller, a preschool teacher at Corner Cottage Child Care Center in Ann Arbor, Michigan:

Aug. 7: We made "ooblick" [cornstarch and water mixture that changes consistency when handled] at small-group time today. The children stayed with the activity for a very long time. They talked about how the ooblick felt: "It is hard and then it melts," Ben said. "It's raining," Rayette said as she let it drip off her fingers.

Is this science? How about the following entry?

July 20: Several children were smelling, holding, looking at, and breaking apart seed pods in the backyard. This was initiated by Katie, who continued to collect and study the pods for about 15 minutes.

For adults working in High/Scope programs, science does not mean feeding static collections of facts to children—having children recite the names of planets or flower parts, for example. Instead, science is a messy, active process, full of false starts, incomplete conclusions, and trial-and-error discoveries. Adults encourage science learning by supporting children's natural curiosity about the materials and changes in their world. As these journal entries demonstrate, you can support science both formally—as in the first entry, by **planning specific activities** for children—and informally— as in the second entry, by **supporting the children's own investigations** of the world through the *materials* you provide, your use of *language,* and the *time* you give children to explore.

What Is Science?

Adults who have chosen some branch of science as their life's work are gathering information about how the world works by using certain basic processes: **observing, classifying, experimenting** to solve a problem or obtain answers to questions, **drawing conclusions** about why something is happening, and **communicating** their ideas to others.

Preschoolers, who are also gathering information about how the world works, use many of these same processes, but they take different forms in young children. The ways young children seek knowledge about their world are identified in the High/Scope preschool key experiences. Let's look at some of the basic science processes from the preschooler's point of view and in terms of the preschool key experiences:

Observation is perhaps the most basic of all science processes. For adults, observation is systematic. In the words of High/Scope science authors Frank Blackwell and Charles Hohmann (1991, p. 4), scientific observation is more than just looking, it is "looking with a purpose." For preschoolers, observation is a spontaneous process that involves all the senses and the entire body. Like the children who were exploring the seed pods, preschoolers typically observe by picking up the object, smelling it, listening to any sounds it may make, manipulating it, and possibly taking it apart or tasting it.

As they observe in this physically active, exploratory way, preschoolers engage in many of the key experiences. They may observe the object from many different viewpoints or take an object apart and put it back together to see what it consists of *(space key experiences)*. Or, they may notice and describe the attributes of materials and the similarities and differences among various objects *(classification key experiences)*. When 3-year-old Caitlin says, "This lemon tastes sour, but this sugar cube tastes sweet" or "All the paper clips stuck to the magnet, but none of the rocks did," she is using **classification** skills to organize her knowledge of the world. This is not unlike what adult scientists do when they seek to find categories to describe the materials, organisms, or phenomena they are studying.

Like adult scientists, children use **experimentation** to solve problems and find answers to questions. However, while the adult's experiments follow rigorous procedures and are carefully planned, the child's experiments involve a more random, trial-and-error process. For example, the

*Children use **experimentation** to solve problems and find answers to questions. However, while the adult's experiments follow rigorous procedures and are carefully planned, the child's experiments involve a more random, trial-and-error process.*

child might go around the room hitting different objects with a wooden rhythm stick, listening for the sound produced by each object (*music key experiences*).

For the child, as for all "scientists," observation and experimentation lead to **conclusions.** While the adult's conclusions are often stated in terms of abstract theories or unseen processes, the young child's conclusions are based on what he or she has directly experienced and are communicated in the child's simpler language. For example, a young child might conclude, "If we take this flower [a cut flower] outside and plant it in the garden, it will grow big" (*time key experiences, language and literacy key experiences*).

Supporting Children's Science Learning

In sum, investigating how the world works—science learning—is a natural process for young children that goes on all the time and involves many of the High/Scope key experiences. How can adults best support this process? Read on—

What's Wrong With My Science Table?

An administrator recently suggested that we add a science table to our preschool classroom. I tried setting one up with magnifiers, a balance scale, magnets, and a few plants. However, I've noticed that the children rarely spend any time there. What's wrong?
—*A preschool teacher*

Having just one spot for science in your classroom may be the problem. Children often want to use items such as those you've mentioned, but they need to be presented in a context that makes them useful and interesting to children. Unrelated materials that are on display on a science table may not capture children's interest unless it is clear how they can use the materials.

Can you think of ways to encourage children to use the materials elsewhere in the classroom? For example, for part of the day, you could take the magnifiers outdoors, where children could use them to look at insects, leaves, bark, the sidewalk, and so forth. You could take the scale to snack, where children could use it to see which is heavier, the juice or the crackers. Or perhaps the plants could live in the house area, where watering them could be part of the role-play activities that go on there on a daily basis. You might introduce the magnets in a small-group activity, encouraging children to discover which things around the classroom stick to them and which don't.

If you can find such ways to encourage science activities throughout the classroom, you will be more successful in supporting children's natural investigative interests than you will be by limiting science activities to one table.

First, create an environment that encourages exploration. Look at how your classroom is set up. Is it easy for children to explore there? Are open-ended materials available? Do children have the time to make observations and follow up on them? Consider this example: At work time, Alexander has planned to sort through some natural materials: pine cones, nuts, leaves, sticks, and rocks that the class picked up on a walk the day before. He spends almost all of work time sorting them into groups and then loading them on a small truck and driving them around the room, group by group. The next day, Alexander chooses to work with the same materials again. To promote this kind of experience with materials from nature, the pine cones, nuts, leaves, and so on must be arranged in a location where Alexander knows they are available for play—not in "don't touch" displays.

Second, create problem-solving situations for children. Use small-group times to give children a chance to solve science problems, do experiments, predict outcomes, and communicate their observations. Here are some examples of such small-group times:

1. Give children drinking straws and several different kinds of objects: pieces of paper, wooden blocks, Legos, paper clips, sponges, ping-pong balls, and so forth. After children have played with the objects for a while, ask them to predict which objects they can move by blowing on them. Encourage children to explore the classroom with the straws, testing various other objects.

2. Play a tape on which you have recorded sounds made by objects in the room, for example, water running, blocks being clicked together, a triangle playing. Ask children to guess the sounds, then make their own tape, using objects in the room.

3. Provide magnets in several sizes and shapes. Encourage children to experiment with them to see what sticks to the magnet and what doesn't.

Third, use active learning strategies as you interact with children. Strategies like the following assure that they will have hands-on experiences, choices, chances to discover and solve problems on their own, opportunities to talk with adults and with other children about what they are doing:

• *Begin with concrete experiences.* Most of children's investigations involve something they can touch or see or have had a hands-on encounter with in the recent past. Beginning with such concrete experiences isn't hard if we simply *observe what the children are doing, what their interests are, and what they are saying.* For example, suppose you notice that children are pretending to be spiders or observing spiders inside the center or on the playground. Some ways to encourage further learning about spiders are the following: You could *support children's interests by imitating them* (point out the spiders and spider webs you see, hunt for spiders yourself), *introduce related materials* (bring in spider-catching materials, read books on spiders), or *plan related small-group experiences that encourage problem solving* (plan a small-group time in which children make "spider webs" by weaving yarn or crepe paper around structures on the playground). All these strategies reach children at the concrete level, or close to it. These activities will be meaningful because they build on something children have experienced directly.

• *Follow up on children's intentions.* If children show an interest in some particular area, help them find a way to follow up on that interest (maybe they need materials, an informed adult, or time to try something out). Children are much more likely to remain with an activity if it was their choice. For example, Abby and Elizabeth want to try swinging with their two swings tied together. Having managed to tie the two swings together with a jump rope, they ask a nearby adult for a push. Initially hesitant (concerned that the swings will move too erratically to be safe), the adult agrees, after asking the children what they think might happen. The children are pleased when their prediction that the swings will "go bumpy" is confirmed by what happens.

• *Allow children to discover things and figure things out on their own.* Don't always provide answers. It would certainly be a lot faster to tell Jimmy that his toy car isn't running simply because he has put the batteries in backwards.

Accepting Children's Explanations

A child discusses an upcoming trip to the airport with her parent:

Child: *Are we going to see airplanes or helicopters?*

Adult: *Airplanes.*

Child: *I like helicopters better.*

Adult: *Why?*

Child: *Because helicopters go faster because the propeller goes around really fast.*

Adult: *Helicopters go faster than planes because the propeller goes around really fast?*

Child: *Yeah.*

Children use their own experiences to reach conclusions about how things work. This child has only seen planes flying from a distance, but when she was visiting a local hospital recently, she happened to be near the rescue-unit helicopter as it took off. So she has personally observed that a helicopter's propeller goes very fast and has noticed how the wind it creates blows the nearby shrubs and plants. Because she has witnessed up close the movement of a helicopter propeller, she has concluded that helicopters go faster than planes.

We, as adults, often feel the need to give our children facts to correct such inaccurate conclusions. But correcting their observations won't allow children's own reasoning powers to develop.

A Science Diary

Here are some examples of science activities—listed by time of day—that occurred throughout one week in a typical preschool classroom. In each of these activities, children are investigating the materials and relationships in the world around them. In parentheses we note the basic science processes being used by the children in each example.

Circle Time

The adult asks children to move around the room like their favorite animals as she plays some taped music. Some choose snakes and spend the whole song on their stomachs, crawling around the floor. (*communicating observations*)

Work Time

Sun-hee, who at home has seen a cat pick up and carry one of its kittens back to its sleeping box, acts out this observation with stuffed animals. (*communicating observations*)

Children build block towers, trying various sizes of blocks and various tower heights to see what will make the towers topple over. (*experimentation*)

Meena notices that pictures made with a lot of paint take longer to dry than those made with less paint. (*classifying, drawing conclusions*)

Cleanup Time

Gabe calls an adult over to the sink, where he is cleaning up painting materials, to show the adult how he can fill the empty paint cups by squeezing water out of the sponges. (*communicating observations*)

Outside Time

The children catch some grasshoppers in jars that have magnifiers in the covers. They spend several minutes watching each grasshopper before letting it go. (*observation*)

Philip observes that the bug in the sandbox looks smaller when he looks at it from the top of the climber. (*observation, drawing conclusions*)

Small-Group Time

The adult boils some red cabbage in water as children make predictions about what will happen. She takes the resulting red-tinted water, cools it, and encourages children to try mixing it with various combinations of materials—water and white vinegar, water and baking soda. Children notice and describe the color changes. Then the children decide to pour the different mixtures together. They enjoy the fizzing they get when they pour the vinegar water into the baking-soda water, and repeat the process to try to get this to happen again. (*observation, classification, experimentation*)

The teacher has planned a small-group time in which children learn to mix their own paints. Sara and Athi are mixing paints together and observing the color changes. (*observation, experimentation*)

However, letting him figure this out by trial and error will be a far more memorable "lesson."

• *Use supportive language.* As children talk about their discoveries, focus on listening—don't talk too much. *Keep your questions to a minimum, and when you do ask a question, make it open-ended.* Instead of "Who can tell me why the water changes color when we add the powdered drink mix?" you might ask "What do you think might happen if we mix the water and this drink mix together?" or phrase your question as a statement: "I wonder what might happen if we mix the water and the drink mix." Then, when children offer predictions or explanations, *accept what they say.* Refrain from correcting children when their explanations don't match what we know of the real world.

• *Remember that you don't have to have all the answers.* Don't feel that you must immediately provide children with answers to every question. *Keep good reference materials and resource books available.* If questions arise, consult these sources or another adult, or *refer children to other children for answers.* For example, Sue, a preschool teacher, refers Nick to Andy (another child) at work time, because Nick wants to know how to get his paper airplane to fly with a spiral motion, and she doesn't remember how to do it. Sue knows that this is something Andy has been shown by a visiting adult and has successfully repeated on his own.

When adults look for ways like this to support children's curiosity about the world, science learning can be "here, there, and everywhere" in programs for young children. As "A Science Diary" on p. 199 reveals, science can occur throughout the daily routine and in every area of the classroom.

REFERENCES

Althouse, R. (1988). *Investigating science with young children.* New York: Teachers College Press.

Blackwell, F., & Hohmann, C. (1991). *High/Scope K–3 Curriculum series: Science.* Ypsilanti, MI: High/Scope Press.

Holt, B. (1989). *Science with young children.* Washington, DC: National Association for the Education of Young Children.

Wasserman, S. (1990). *Serious players in the primary classroom.* New York: Teachers College Press.

Williams, R. A., Rockwell, R. E., & Sherwood, E. A. (1987). *Mudpies to magnets.* Mt. Rainier, MD: Gryphon House, Inc.

Williams, R. A., Rockwell, R. E., & Sherwood, E. A. (1990). *More mudpies to magnets.* Mt. Rainier, MD: Gryphon House, Inc.

Science:
Our "Basic Four"

By Frank Blackwell and Charles Hohmann

· ·

In the High/Scope approach to elementary school science, teachers encourage children to encounter facts and concepts directly as they work with hands-on science materials. The following four basic types of science activities are recommended for children in this age group because they build on children's natural interests and offer many opportunities for the elementary science key experiences:

• **Collecting activities** take advantage of the avid interest most young children take in hunting for natural treasures and then exploring what they collect. The wide range of natural materials suitable for collecting includes seeds, shells, locally grown plants, insects, sands, sea plants, soils, and rocks. Collecting encourages children to **sharpen observational skills,** to **notice attributes and patterns** and **classify materials** accordingly, and then to **communicate results** through displays, graphs, or other representations.

• **Building activities** are a natural extension of the building that goes on in young children's play. Experiences in designing, building, and modifying structures are valuable because they allow children to **explore simple physical causes.** As they build, they begin to understand how objects interact by pushing, pulling, holding, and bumping one another, and they begin to see how they can exert some control over these events by manipulating the factors involved. Building activities may center on projects of the child's own design (building a variety of structures out of rolled pieces of newspaper), or they may involve simple instructions provided by the adult (asking children to build a simple electrical device, for example).

• **Analyzing and testing activities** introduce children to scientific procedures for examining materials. Analyzing is an extension of sorting by attributes. When children **analyze** they **take apart a substance or collection; note the materials that compose it; if possible, count or measure**

Examples of the
Four Basic Activities

Collecting: Children collect a large number of leaves; then subgroups work on various tasks—ranking leaves by size, classifying leaves by shape, making leaf rubbings, using resource books to identify leaves.

Designing and building: An adult supplies various flexible plant materials (long plant stems, vines, grasses) and challenges children to make a strong fiber rope with the materials; children discuss ways to make strong ropes.

Analyzing and testing: *Analyzing*— Children compare the quantities of raisins in a cup of two different types of bran cereal. *Testing*—Children use an eyedropper, squares of cloth, and waterproofing materials like crayons, candlewax, and salad oil to explore how fabrics are waterproofed and then to test and compare the effectiveness of different waterproofing methods.

Making surveys: Children make counts of the animal life in a defined area and then graph the results.

each component; then discuss the implications of their findings. For example, children might conduct a quantitative analysis of a packet of dried fruit, a bag of bird seed, or even a bucket of litter collected from a block of city sidewalk. In **testing** activities, children **subject a material or an organism to a standard procedure and then assess in some systematic way the change that is produced.** For example, children could test the buoyancy of various materials (wood, cardboard, plastic foam, cork) by making small identical "rafts" of scraps of these materials and piling paper clips on them to see how many clips are needed to sink each type of raft.

• **Survey activities** are fascinating to most young children. In such activities, children **collect, tabulate, and report on statistics or observations about some facet of the immediate group or environment.** For example, they might tabulate the ages, heights, weights, hand spans, shoe sizes, distances from home to school, or preferred games of classmates; the roofing or siding materials observed in the town; the plant life seen in a given area. The value of survey activities lies in planning methods of tabulation, arriving at interpretations, and designing presentations of the data.

Science in the Elementary Grades: Beyond Dinosaurs and Volcanoes

By Charles Hohmann

· ·

W̲hat are your memories of your primary school science experiences? If you're like most of us, you might recall textbooks filled with pictures of the wonders of nature and the universe, posters depicting plant and animal families, and field trips to museums filled with "don't touch" exhibits. Aside from the occasional opportunity to play with magnets or peek into a microscope, you probably experienced few hands-on science activities, and most of the topics you studied were probably far removed from your everyday experiences.

Things haven't changed that much since the days when you watched your teacher point at a diagram of the solar system. Teaching primarily through words rather than through direct experience is still the prevailing approach to science education. Children still get most of their science instruction through lecture-style presentations, books, videos, and so forth. Though the idea of hands-on science has caught on in many children's museums, classroom teachers have been slower to adopt this approach.

This doesn't mean that it isn't an exciting and valuable experience for children to read books, view videos, and use other

Teachers use the High/Scope key experiences in science to assess how far children have developed in their scientific thinking and to plan experiences that will be developmentally appropriate for them.

prepared materials as a way of learning about such topics as space travel, dinosaurs, and volcanoes. After all, much of what we know about nature and the universe is accessible to children only through such "second-hand" sources. In High/Scope elementary classrooms, adults therefore offer a variety of books, tapes, videos, and other such resources that children can use to pursue their interests in a range of scientific topics.

But science in the High/Scope Elementary Curriculum is more than this. In the High/Scope approach, much of science instruction takes place in *workshop* sessions in which children break into small groups of six to eight to work on specific tasks. The emphasis in these sessions is not on the exotic and unusual but on content that can be discovered through firsthand experience.

In a typical science workshop, teachers assign a task or choice of tasks to children. The tasks are designed to give children opportunities to discover, invent, explore, and solve problems as they work directly with tools and raw materials. For example, children might be involved in any of the following as workshop activities: testing the absorbency of various kinds of paper; building bridges out of rolled and stacked newspapers and testing the loads borne by different designs; collecting and classifying different kinds of tree barks.

In planning and conducting science activities, teachers are guided by the elementary science key experiences, which are grouped in the following six categories:

Is There Any Place for Dinosaurs?

Recently I attended a High/Scope workshop on elementary science, and the presenter used dinosaurs as an example of a developmentally inappropriate science topic. My first-graders love the topic, so this is hard for me to accept. What's wrong with learning about dinosaurs, anyway?

—*An elementary teacher*

Nothing is wrong with supporting children's interest in dinosaurs. The problem comes in thinking of this as a *science* activity. In the High/Scope Curriculum, science is defined as the search for causes—the "whys" and "hows" that explain events in the physical world and the life cycles of living things. For a topic to be the basis of a developmentally appropriate science experience, we have to ask whether young children can directly observe and manipulate the causal factors that pertain to that topic

and whether they can reach at least a partial understanding of these key concepts through their own explorations.

Since young children are unable to work directly with most of the causal factors involved in the evolution and extinction of dinosaurs, we don't see this as an appropriate area for *science* experiences. However, since children are obviously fascinated by the topic, by all means provide them with plentiful opportunities to hear about, read about, write about, and make representations of dinosaurs. We would suggest, however, that you think of these as "literacy" or "natural history" activities, rather than science experiences.

And don't neglect to offer children many hands-on experiences with observable changes, everyday materials from nature, and simple machines and gadgets—experiences that are the basis for *developmentally appropriate* science in early childhood.

In the High/Scope approach, much of science instruction takes place in workshop sessions in which children break into small groups of six to eight to work on specific tasks. The emphasis in these sessions is not on the exotic and unusual, but on content that can be discovered through firsthand experience.

- **Observing,** looking with a purpose, collecting data

- **Classifying and ordering** materials according to their attributes and properties

- **Measuring, testing, and analyzing,** assessing the properties and composition of materials

- **Observing, predicting, and controlling change,** understanding causality

- **Designing, building, fabricating, and modifying** structures or materials

- **Reporting and interpreting** data and results

High/Scope Elementary Curriculum materials provide a detailed developmental sequence for each of these groups of key experiences. These sequences focus on general processes and activities through which children's scientific thinking develops. (For many examples of science activities in specific content areas and a complete list of elementary science key experiences presented in checklist form, see the *Science* volume of the High/Scope Elementary Curriculum Guides by Frank Blackwell and Charles Hohmann, available from High/Scope Press.)

Teachers use the key experiences to assess how far children have developed in their scientific thinking and which experiences will be developmentally appropriate for them. During the course of children's science activities, teachers also use the key experiences to help them recognize "teachable moments"—times when it is appropriate to offer support to children to help them extend their thinking or consolidate what they have learned.

Together, the *key experiences,* the *workshop framework,* and the availability of a wide variety of *manipulative materials* in the elementary classroom create an approach to science that builds on children's natural curiosity.

Classification:
Collecting, Sorting, and Organizing

By Michelle Graves

• •

Each day, we as adults use established criteria to systematically arrange materials and events into groups or categories. We do this when we decide what clothing to wear, what food to eat, which music to listen to, which job opportunities to consider, or which politicians to elect. To make such choices and decisions, we use our **classification abilities.** We must be able to notice, in detail, the characteristics of people, situations, and events; to weigh similarities and differences carefully; to determine how new objects, people, and events fit into established categories; and to re-define our categories when necessary to accommodate new experiences and knowledge.

Young children need to explore materials in a hands-on way to become aware of their characteristics.

Young children, when given the opportunity to explore and interact with an environment rich in materials, people, and events, are developing the classification skills needed to make such judgments and choices. Building on the actions and interests of children as they sort, organize, and describe the world around them is one challenge of teaching in a High/Scope classroom. Another is trusting that when this approach is used, children *will* learn to classify in ways that reflect their own interests and developmental levels—they do not need attribute cards, Lotto games, sorting drills, or other special exercises to develop classification skills.

Classification Throughout the Classroom

When choosing materials that encourage young children to classify, many adults think of small manipulatives—buttons, beads, Lego blocks, small toy figures, and animals. Such materials lend themselves to sorting activities, and teachers who are observing children usually find it easy to recognize these kinds of classification activities.

However, it's also important to be aware that sorting small, regular-sized objects is just one kind of classification experience. In settings organized around the High/Scope approach, classification occurs throughout the classroom and throughout the day, not just when children are sorting beads, Legos, and buttons. Indeed, classification happens when children are pretending, climbing on play structures, digging in the sand, doing artwork. By observing children's actions, participating in their play, and listening to their conversations, adults can gather many clues to children's classification abilities.

When we as teachers are able to use children's actions and language to recognize that they are classifying, we are better able to support and extend this thinking process. The High/Scope **key experiences in classification,** listed below, give adults a framework for recognizing and supporting the classification experiences that are typical for preschoolers:

• Exploring and describing similarities, differences, and the attributes of things

• Distinguishing and describing shapes

• Sorting and matching

• Using and describing something in several ways

• Holding more than one attribute in mind at a time

• Distinguishing between *some* and *all*

• Describing characteristics something does *not* possess or the class it does *not* belong to

As a teacher in the High/Scope Demonstration Preschool, I have been working with my team member to create a setting that supports classification in children. In this article,

Everyday Classification Stories

Can you identify the classification key experience(s) reflected in each story?

At **outside time,** James was pushing two children around the playground on the toy taxi. When the adult asked if she could have a ride, he said, "Sure." After going around two more times, he stopped the taxi and said, "Get off. You're too fat and I can't go fast."

During a turn-taking game at **large-group time,** Jordan picked Brianna, who was wearing a pink shirt, to be the next person to lead the group. To indicate his choice, he said, "She has pink."

At **outside time,** Audie sledded down the hill in various ways: sitting up, lying on his belly, standing up as on a snowboard, lying on his back so he could "see the clouds," and hanging on to a second sled that held his friend James.

At **work time,** when asked how drivers would know where the finish line was in a pretend stock-car race, Trey said he would make a sign. He cut white and black paper from the art area into little squares, pasted them, checkerboard-style, on white paper, and wrote the word "Finish" on his sign.

At **cleanup time,** Emma said to Keisha, "You pick up something furry and brown."

Classification occurs in a variety of settings and throughout the day, not just when children are sorting beads, Legos, and buttons indoors in the classroom or center. Here, children are noticing attributes, similarities, and differences as they explore nature on a field trip. By observing children's actions, participating in their explorations, and listening to their conversations, adults can gather many clues about children's classification abilities.

we describe the strategies we've used to encourage classification experiences, and we present the encouraging results we've observed in children. (Specific classification key experiences that relate to our classroom observations are highlighted in italic when they appear in this discussion.)

Strategies That Promote Classification

Because noticing the individual qualities of materials is the first step in grouping and classifying them, it's important for adults to **provide materials with a variety of qualities** (round, flat, soft, rough, smooth, light, dark). These kinds of materials give children opportunities to *explore and describe similarities, differences, and attributes of things.* As you select a range of such materials for the interest areas in your setting, keep in mind that young children need to explore materials in a hands-on way to become aware of their characteristics; just looking at materials is not enough. In the High/ Scope Demonstration classroom, therefore, we choose materials that children can handle freely—materials that they can pound, roll, throw, squish, glue, tape, twist, turn, fill, empty, push, and pull.

As we begin to know children better, we **add materials that support their interests**. Because digging among pebbles, stones, and dirt for "treasure" at outside time was a favorite activity last fall, we added various types of scoops (spoons, shovels, ladles, measuring cups) and containers (coffee cans, buckets, boxes, plastic tubing), so children could experience digging in additional ways *(using and describing something in several ways)*. To provide more ways for children to use the pebbles and stones they collected, we brought the materials indoors, where children could use them in combination with paint, glue, cardboard, Play-Doh, pots and pans, tea kettles, baskets, dump trucks, and carpet squares. As children played with these materials indoors, we observed many more examples of classification. For example, after one group of children decided to paint pebbles, we saw Marcia separate blue ones from green ones in her artwork. Other children used the pebbles for pretending in the house area, where we heard Frances say to Alex, "Don't use *all* of them for soup, we need *some* for the chicken nuggets," clearly demonstrating her ability to *distinguish between* **some** and **all.**

As children work with sorting and grouping materials in these various ways, we **support their classification thinking by our words and actions:**

• Sometimes we **simply sit down with a child and begin collecting or sorting in a similar way.** For example, JoJo was playing with sticks and tongue depressors at the sand table, standing them up in the sand as he sorted them into separate groups. An adult who was observing him sat down and began working in the same way with the sticks and tongue depressors.

• Sometimes, when imitating a child who is classifying, we **add a new dimension to our activity, then watch to see if the child will try something similar**. For example, Audie was pretending to "go fishing" at the sand table, using one of the sticks as a fishing pole and pulling out "fish" (shells) from the sand. After a while, his play expanded to include "cleaning the fish" at the washing machine in the house area. Observing this, one of the adults went over to Audie and imitated him as he caught fish and cleaned them. After adult and child had repeated this sequence several times, the adult pulled out a frying pan and said, "I'm kinda hungry—I think I'll cook my fish now." Audie, apparently ready to include another activity in the category of "going fishing," soon followed suit.

• Sometimes, when we observe a child making groupings, we **make a comment acknowledging that the child is classifying, then wait for the child to explain his or her thinking.** For example, Emma had cut out pictures of toys and was pasting them on a piece of paper. The adult said to her, "I notice you've pasted several things in this corner of the paper." This was enough to encourage Emma to explain her thinking. She replied:

In the High/Scope Demonstration Preschool, we choose materials that children can handle freely—materials that they can pound, roll, throw, squish, glue, tape, twist, turn, fill, empty, push, and pull.

"That's where I put the toys that I already have. Over here are the toys I want." As we comment on children's classifying activities, **we are careful not to impose our own ideas about the attributes or categories of materials.** Instead, we try to understand the child's ideas about collections and how they fit together. For example, if Colin is sorting buttons by a system that we don't understand, we might just observe him carefully or make a neutral comment to elicit his thinking ("You've made a big pile of buttons"). But we would avoid comments that might push him to sort the buttons according to our own categories: ("That's nice, Colin. Now why don't you try to separate all the buttons with two holes from all those with four holes.")

Adults in High/Scope classrooms also **support classification by planning for it during the adult-initiated parts of the routine,** such as group times, transition times, planning, and recall times. In so doing, adults take into consideration the individual interests and developmental levels of children as well as the classification key experiences.

*These teachers use cleanup time to provide children with important classification key experiences. The children obviously have many opportunities to **sort and match**, to **distinguish and describe shapes**, and to **explore and describe similarities, differences, and attributes of things!***

For example, we had observed that one child, Emma, enjoyed making collages with old catalogs and magazines and also enjoyed *sorting*. To build on these interests, we brought toy catalogs and newspaper advertisements to greeting circle and then to small-group time, along with scissors, glue, and paper. We found that Emma spontaneously sorted the toy pictures as she pasted them on the paper and that she readily described the *attributes* that were the basis of her selections. When Emma made a grouping of "toys I love," for example, she explained that she liked a certain toy because "it's cute" or "it snuggles." Over the course of several days, she grouped the pictures in a number of different ways. Some of her collections included "toys for girls to play with" and "toys only for boys." We accepted the explanation she gave for this grouping, "just because it's so," even though we didn't agree with it.

To expand on the interest in babies shown by Erica and her playmates, as well as to provide them with opportunities to describe some of the details of babies and baby care *(exploring and describing attributes)*, we made up action songs at large-group time. To the tune of "Early in the Morning," we sang, "This is the way we rock our babies, rock our babies . . ., so early in the morning," acting out the motion as we sang. We did this for a variety of other attributes of baby care suggested by children (including burping, changing diapers, and feeding).

When we plan such activities, we try to gear them to children's developmental levels. For example, we observed that Kacey (see "One Child's Classification Skills" on p. 214) had an exceptionally mature understanding of the attributes of materials and the alternate uses of materials. We wondered about her ability to *describe characteristics something does not possess or the class it does not belong to,* a key experience that is typically just emerging in older preschool-aged children. To see whether she understood the concept of *not,* as well as to offer additional opportunities to *use and describe something in several ways,* we brought art materials and symbols for the interest areas to planning and recall times. As Kacey planned and recalled, we encouraged her to use stencils, stickers, markers, a hole punch, and scissors to mark the area symbol sheets, first to show the areas she was going to or had been in and then to show those she would *not* go to or had *not* been in. Kacey's enjoyment of this activity confirmed for us that this was an experience well suited to her developmental level.

These are just a few examples of the many ways we've used our observations of children in planning experiences that encourage children to classify.

Recognizing that a new setting often stimulates children's thinking about *similarities and differences,* we **encourage classification experiences by scheduling events outside of the classroom.** Recently, a simple walk around the block resulted in conversation among children about the attributes of the houses and what was appealing to them: "I like this one because it has a curvy porch." "Well I like it because it has a refrigerator on it." "I like this porch because it has chairs you can sit on."

As in all aspects of learning, children's individual interests and developmental abilities are reflected in the way they approach classification. Four-year-old Erica's use of classification reflected her strong interest in dramatic play relating to the theme of baby care. Early in the year, we noticed that she would sort through the blocks to find a cylindrical one that she could use as a bottle to feed her baby *(distinguishing and describing shapes).* She would often label her bottle "Coke" or "orange juice," clearly demonstrating her understanding of the *attributes* of bottles and beverages. Her ability to *make finer sorting distinctions and describe attributes* increased over time. By January she was packing suitcases for overnight trips with her baby, *matching* the kind of clothing she selected with the event. She packed clothing and props into different suitcases for each activity:

One Child's Classification Skills

Children's use of classification skills is best understood when seen in the context of the child's personal interests and level of development. For example, we noticed early in the school year that 4-year-old Kacey had a strong interest in art materials and would often organize and sort them as she worked on art projects.

Initially, she displayed a simple understanding of categories and attributes, usually separating materials into groups with exactly the same characteristics. For example, early in the year, while using lacquered beans to make a collage, she sorted out three identical gold beans to paste on her cardboard.

As the year went on and her awareness of multiple attributes developed, she was able to make better use of the specific qualities of materials to meet her goals in her artwork. One day this winter, for example, she planned to "make a drawing for daddy." During work time, she used the shape stencils, felt-tip pens, and sequins to make a picture of a man with a triangular head, a rectangular body, and limbs and features drawn freehand. She sorted through the sequin container to find just the right colors, then surrounded her picture with a patterned sequin border. In this art project, Kacey demonstrated the ability to distinguish shapes and select materials with the particular attributes she needed. Her classification skills were clearly far more refined than those of most of the other children in our group.

Even more surprising to the adults, however, was what Kacey did with her work time picture later that day, at small-group time. The teacher had provided scissors and computer paper, and the rest of the children were cutting the paper in various ways. Kacey took her paper, folded it once, cut it in three places, then left the table to go to her cubby. She did not talk to anyone throughout this process, and the teacher watched in anticipation. Kacey came back from her cubby with the picture she had made at work time, went to the art area for tape, and then laid the cut-out computer paper on her pictured man to form a perfectly fitted shirt! Kacey's addition to her art project was remarkable to us not only because of her unexpected use of the computer paper *(using and describing something in several ways)* but also because she kept her work time project in mind even much later, when the project was out of sight.

"Pajamas for bed, rattles to play with, and dress-up clothes for when we go out to a restaurant."

In a classroom where children have many opportunities to classify and receive support from adults who understand their thinking, the progression we observed in Erica's classification abilities over the course of the year is a natural development.

Spatial Learning: Beyond Circles, Squares, and Triangles

By Mark Tompkins

. . . .

For most adults, spatial thinking is an everyday part of life. Every time we tie our shoes, line up the silverware to set the table, or draw a map to guide a friend to our home, we are solving spatial problems. All of these tasks require a basic understanding of spatial relationships.

Spatial knowledge is acquired through years of experience and intellectual maturation. Preschoolers are just beginning to develop an understanding of spatial concepts.

In this article, we'll suggest ways to support the development of children's spatial thinking. One aspect of spatial thinking that is emphasized in many preschool settings is the identification of shapes and patterns. Typically, adults teach about shapes by decorating the room with cutouts of different shapes, reading books about shapes, using shape flash cards, encouraging children to play lotto shape games, and asking children to identify the shapes of objects they are playing with.

Children learn about shapes by doing—by actually working with objects. Thus, it's important to provide lots of materials that encourage activities involving spatial thinking.

With enough practice, children *do* learn to identify circles, squares, and rectangles. But this skill makes only a small contribution to the overall development of children's spatial thinking. In High/Scope programs, we want children to do more than just *identify* shapes. We want them to acquire an *understanding* of how shapes work; how things fit together and can be taken apart; how things can be transformed, enclosed, and positioned.

When we watch children at play, we recognize that they learn about space (and shapes) by doing—by working with objects, not by talking about pictures or identifying cutout shapes. Thus, the best way adults can support children in learning about spatial relationships is to set up a play environment rich in materials that encourage spatial thinking. Within such an environment, the adults work alongside children and talk with them about what they are doing and discovering.

How Spatial Thinking Develops

Our perspective on how spatial thinking develops comes from two main sources: the work of child development theorists, like Piaget, who have documented the developmental changes in children's spatial thinking, and the findings of brain researchers who have identified the right hemisphere of the brain as the site for spatial processing. These theorists and researchers contend that spatial thinking is a largely nonverbal process that develops over time, primarily through children's active explorations and transformations of objects.

Preschoolers are in the process of mastering some of the spatial concepts that adults take for granted. For example, preschoolers don't fully understand the relationships of *proximity* and *separation*—how close together or far apart things are. A child may say that the sand table is close to the door, until someone places another object between the two; then the child may think that the sand table and door are farther apart. Preschoolers are also learning to recognize where things are *located* and the *directions in which things are moving*, although by adult standards their judgments are not always accurate.

Preschoolers are also learning to understand and use the *spatial language* that is attached to such concepts. Adults often don't realize that preschoolers are confused by the large number of spatial terms used in everyday conversation. Many children, for example, find it difficult to follow adult directions like these: "Put this in Luke's cubbie. . . That's the one in the second row, in the middle. Pull the cubbie all the way out, and put the toy in the back half of the container." Likewise, a child trying to fit a puzzle together is only confused by advice such as "Try turning that piece upside down" or "This piece goes at the top instead of the bottom."

To develop spatial thinking and language, children need opportunities to experience for themselves how things take up space, how they move, how they look and feel, how they fit together, how they may be transformed when they are reshaped or repositioned. The following list of **space key experiences** provides a summary of the important spatial activities through which preschoolers develop their spatial thinking.

• Filling and emptying

• Fitting things together and taking them apart

• Changing the shape and arrangement of objects (wrapping, twisting, stretching, stacking, enclosing)

• Observing people, places, and things from different spatial viewpoints

• Experiencing and describing positions, directions, and distances in the play space, building, and neighborhood

• Interpreting spatial relations in drawings, pictures, and photographs

These six key experiences, which have been derived from research on spatial thinking as well as from observations made by High/Scope teachers, can help you observe, assess, and support children's emerging spatial thinking. The block area, discussed in the remainder of the article, is a prime spot for this observation, assessment, and support.

Observing things from different spatial viewpoints! This child is thoroughly enjoying one of High/Scope's six space key experiences.

Save the Block Creations

Ben is in the block area, building a farm with unit blocks and the large, hollow blocks. Five minutes before the end of work time, a teacher comes over and begins to play with Ben, helping him build a fence to "keep the cattle in." The teacher then notices the time and reminds Ben it is almost time to clean up. After cleanup time is announced, the teacher helps Ben put away the blocks.

As teaching adults, most of us don't think twice about tearing down block creations like Ben's. We routinely dismantle children's constructions when we put away building sets, toy figures, and other reusable materials at the end of work time. By contrast, the creations children make from expendable materials—paintings, sculptures, and collages—are put on display or sent home to parents.

While it's obvious why we treat art projects differently, it's important to remember that Ben values his farm just as much as other children value their artwork. Yet the child whose work remains on display—at home or in the classroom—can't help but feel a greater sense of ownership of the creation. Since a child's painting or sculpture remains available for others to see, the child may also feel it has more value to others than the block creation that comes down immediately. In addition, the child who makes a permanent creation may find that recall experiences are more meaningful, because the object to be talked about is available to look at and touch.

While blocks do have to be put away eventually and can't be sent home with children, it is possible for adults to help children attach a greater sense of ownership and permanence to their temporary creations. Some ideas:

- **Reserve space for temporary displays of children's work with blocks (and other reusable materials)** on a tabletop, bookshelf, cabinet top, or section of the floor. If you have separate morning and afternoon programs each day, then have two small display tables/spaces. By displaying block structures, you show children that their creations are valued. Keep in mind that the more blocks you have in the block area, the longer a structure may be kept up. In most classrooms, two days is the normal limit for a block display.

- **Attach signs and names to products.** The sign may show the child's name or personal symbol or a short mes-

The Block Area

A laboratory for spatial thinking. As children work with blocks and other building materials in the block area, they encounter and experiment with many spatial concepts. Consider, for example, the spatial concepts (indicated by highlighted words) that Luke, Elle, and Wynn are working with in the following examples:

*Luke is playing with a set of six cloth blocks in the toddler room. A few days ago he was observed stuffing them **into** a box, taking them **out**, and repeating the process.*

sage: "Ben's farm." Such signs help children see the importance we place on their work. The sign is also a symbol of permanence that serves to protect the structure for a while.

- **Take photos, make videotapes, or have children draw pictures of things they have made.** Display photos and pictures on walls, send them home to parents, or organize them in albums. Children and parents love to look through these albums and often order reprints of particular pictures. Photos and drawings are also good "story starters" for encouraging children to describe orally or in writing what they have been doing.

An added advantage of "saving" block creations, particularly in pictures or photos, is this: For adults, the saved block creations can document the child's stage of development in understanding spatial relationships. Research on block play reveals that children progress through these stages as their understanding of spatial relationships increases:

1. Stacking, knocking stacks over, restacking.

2. Making block rows (often representing roads).

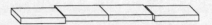

3. Combining stacking and row-making (structures usually lack interior spaces).

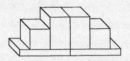

4. Making enclosures (usually designed to contain things or people).

5. Making enclosures that include arches and other forms (structures may represent a variety of objects).

*Today he has discovered that one block can be set **on top of** another. He tries to put yet another block on top, but the stack falls **over,** to his delight.*

*In the preschool, Elle and Wynn are using blocks to make a house that the doll family can live **in**. They use several **large** blocks to make the walls. Then they put **shorter** blocks **inside** the house to make rooms for the furniture and dolls. Later, **beside** the house, they build a garage that has a **long** ramp for the cars to use when they drive **up to** the house.*

Through experiences like these, children learn that blocks may be placed flat, on edge, or on end. They develop an understanding of how these block positions may be combined to produce different characteristics in their structure. As they experiment with different building methods and materials, children are also learning how variables of balance, weight, size, shape, thickness, width, and length affect the structures they are creating.

While this article focuses primarily on spatial thinking, it's important to note that block-area play is also rich in **creative representation** key experiences. Children use blocks to build representations of houses, stores, trains, bridges, offices, and boats. As they build these structures, children are not only working with construction problems; they are also exploring the roles of moms, dads, animals, drivers, farmers, and workers.

Block-area materials. To encourage productive play experiences like these, the block area must be well equipped and carefully planned. Many kinds of materials may be used for building, and a well-stocked block area includes as wide a variety as possible. Large hollow blocks may be your best block investment. Though the initial cost is high, they are very durable and promote a host of productive play and learning experiences. The size of the blocks enables young children to build structures that are life-sized (for them); these large structures often give rise to dramatic play that is very personal, physical, and compelling to a young child. Other children prefer unit blocks, which offer fewer physical challenges but allow children to create whole cities or farms.

In addition to a variety of blocks, props like steering wheels, carpet squares or pieces, bedspreads, sheets, tubes, rope, small trucks, and farm animals are also important to remember when stocking the block area. These props encourage creativity and add to the realism of the structures children construct. Once the blocks and other materials are selected, make sure all materials are stored in clearly labeled containers and shelves. To make a comfortable, sound-absorbing work surface, cover the floor of the block area with low-nap carpet.

Spacious, carefully designed, and well-stocked, the block area can be one of the most intensive learning areas in your room. A final ingredient for an effective block area is appropriate **adult support.**

The adult's role when children are building. Adults can support children's play in the block area by using the same nonintrusive strategies they use throughout the classroom, center, or home. That is, they **observe** what children are doing, **imitate** their actions, **wait to be invited** to join them, and then **participate** *as partners* rather than as leaders in the play.

Puzzled About Puzzles?

Several children in our group have gotten very frustrated recently when playing with the puzzles. I'm not sure what to do. Should I show them how the pieces fit, or should I ignore their frustration and let them figure it out for themselves?

—A preschool teacher

To prevent children from getting frustrated, first make sure you have available a wide variety of puzzles suited to all ability levels. These might range from knobbed, board-style puzzles of 4 or 5 pieces, to simple jigsaw puzzles with 15 or 16 pieces.

Once you are sure you have an appropriate range of puzzles, take your cue from the individual child as to how much help you should give. As a general rule, it's best to let children figure out problems for themselves. Providing too much help gives children the message that if they have a problem, adults can fix it for them. So if Callie is having a difficult time with a puzzle, don't intervene at first. Just observe and see if she comes to you for assistance. If she then asks you for help, ask her to describe or show you what she has done. If she is very frustrated, encourage her to talk about these feelings, and then suggest she try out some new strategies. Encourage her to come up with some ideas, but if she doesn't, you can make suggestions. The adult's role is one of observer and supporter—-not of puzzle problem-solver.

If after you go through this process, the child still can't make the pieces fit, that's okay. Sometimes it takes lots of practice or some help from a peer to solve a problem like this. To paraphrase Piaget, *thinking takes time*. The child who progresses the furthest is often the one who was most confused initially.

To understand the adult's role in children's block play, consider this recent example from the High/Scope Demonstration Preschool.

*Trey (whose father is a bus driver) had been building a "bus" with the large wooden blocks. This attracted other children, who began playing "bus" with Trey. Barbara (one of the teachers) had been observing this game and was soon invited to sit on the "bus." Once she and several other children were on board, they had lots of decisions to make—what kind of food to bring, where to sit, where to go. The group quickly decided that the "bus" was too **small**, so they made it **bigger** by adding many more seats. The children worked hard at **fitting** the big wooden blocks **end-to-end** to make the "bus" **longer**. They then made a "driver's seat" **up front** and made a "steering wheel" to fit **on top** of the "dashboard." They also decided to build a "refrigerator" in the **back** of the pretend bus. Trey said it needed to be "on the **back** wall, but in the **middle** of the aisle."*

Barbara did not make any of these decisions for the children; rather, she helped them work together to figure out solutions to the spatial problems that arose. Her primary role was that of a play partner who, through her understanding of the High/Scope key experiences, helped children engage in spatial thinking by the support she gave.

This extended play activity is typical of the spatial learning experiences that result when adults provide a stimulating environment and appropriate support for the development of children's ideas.

REFERENCES

Bender, J. (1979). Large hollow blocks—Relationship of quantity to block building behaviors. In L. Adams & B. Garlick (Eds.), *Ideas that work with young children* (pp. 140–146). Washington, DC: National Association for the Education of Young Children.

Cartwright, S. (1990, March). Learning with large blocks. *Young Children, 45*(3), 38–41.

Gardner, H. (1983). *Frames of mind: The theory of multiple intelligences.* New York: Basic Books.

Hirsch, E. S. (Ed.). (1984). *The block book.* Washington, DC: National Association for the Education of Young Children.

Hohmann, M., & Weikart, D. P. (1995). *Educating young children: Active learning practices for preschool and child care programs.* Ypsilanti, MI: High/Scope Press.

Kuschner, D. (1989, November). Put your name on your painting, but . . . the blocks go back on the shelves. *Young Children, 45*(1), 49–56.

Reiferl, S. (1984, November). Block construction: Children's developmental landmarks in representation of space. *Young Children, 40*(1), 61–67.

It's About Time!

By Mark Tompkins

• •

"My daddy is older than the teacher because he is much bigger."

❦

"Is yesterday my birthday?"

Any adult who has tried to explain to a preschooler what time it is or how long it will be till they arrive at a destination has discovered that young children do not understand time as adults do. While adults operate in a world of years, months, weeks, days, hours, and minutes, preschoolers understand only the simplest of time concepts. Typically, for example, preschoolers may use and understand such simple terms as *now, before, after,* and *morning;* however, they are usually confused about the days of the week and may have no idea what *ten minutes* or *half an hour* means.

Most adults recognize that young children's understanding of time is incomplete (and often humorous) but wonder just how they can encourage a more mature understanding of time in children. In this article, we explore why children are so perplexed by time concepts and what adults can do to make time language and concepts more meaningful for children.

How Preschoolers Think About Time

"Is it time yet for moving to our new house?"

❦

"When will it be tomorrow?"

The primary reason that concepts of time are confusing to young children is that they have difficulty holding more than one idea or concept in mind at a time. In 3- to 5-year-olds the ability to store or "conserve" information, which is essential to an understanding of time concepts, is in the early stages of development.

Preschoolers' thinking can be compared to a slide projector that processes just one slide (or idea) at a time. The ability to hold one "slide" in mind while other slides come into view is incompletely developed

Lacking the ability to use clocks and calendars, young children base their ideas about time on what they are seeing and experiencing—on concrete, observable events. For example, this child is about to break one of the balloons that mark the number of days until his teacher returns.

in preschoolers. While this "slide-projector thinking" is a hallmark of preschoolers' development, adult thinking, by contrast, is more like a split screen that allows several slides (ideas) to be viewed simultaneously. Adults can mentally juggle a number of concepts and ideas at once.

Because of their slide-projector thinking, preschoolers find it hard to see how *this morning* can be part of *today* or *Wednesday;* it is also difficult for them to know which unit of time is longer or when another Wednesday will occur.

This inability of preschoolers to hold more than one idea in mind at a time also makes it next to impossible for them to comprehend calendars. For us, a calendar provides a clear record of the year, month, week, and day, because we are able to conserve many ideas at once. We can see how each progressively smaller time-unit fits into the whole year. But to a young child, the calendar is an abstract chart filled with shapes, words, and letters that make no sense.

Lacking the ability to use clocks and calendars, young children base their ideas about time on what they are seeing and experiencing—on concrete, observable events. Given young children's need for concreteness, it is understandable that concepts of time—which cannot be seen, heard, or touched—are difficult for them to grasp.

Because their reasoning depends on concrete experiences, and also because they are self-centered in their view of the world, preschoolers experience time *subjectively*—they interpret time concepts in terms of their own experiences and emotions. To 4-year-old Ilana, who has been made to sit still, a five-minute wait is an eternity. By the same token, if Ilana is absorbed in a play activity, five minutes goes by in a flash.

Of course, adults also experience time subjectively. For us, too, "time flies when we're having fun." But as adults, we are also constantly checking our subjective experience of time against our *objective, abstract* understanding. Because we see time as a measurable entity divided into uniform units, we can use watches, clocks, and calendars to keep our lives organized.

However, because young children usually can't grasp the logic behind such timekeeping tools, we won't increase their understanding of time by instructing them in clock-reading or having them recite the days of the week. Instead, we need to **offer children opportunities to begin to use the language and logic of time** in connection with direct, concrete experiences.

The Time Key Experiences

The following four High/Scope key experiences in understanding time provide the basis for such developmentally appropriate experiences:

1. **Starting and stopping an action on signal.** Observing the beginnings and endings of time periods will help young children begin to see that time periods have a beginning, an end, and a specific duration.

2. **Experiencing and describing rates of movement.** Preschoolers are beginning to describe and recognize the relationship between speed and time. As they drum, hop, hammer, sing, build, dance, and run at different speeds and as they talk about what they are doing, they are developing their understanding of relationships between speed, time, and the distance traveled as they move.

3. **Experiencing and comparing time intervals.** Preschoolers often use such terms as *a long time,* or *a short time,* but since they haven't yet developed the concept that time passes at a uniform rate, they use these terms subjectively. Opportunities to compare and talk about time intervals will strengthen their objective reasoning.

4. Anticipating, remembering, and describing the sequences of events. Phenomena that involve cyclical continuity—morning turning into evening, days into weeks, one season into another—are very abstract and thus are difficult for preschoolers to grasp. On the first warm spring day, adults often look forward to seeing leaves on the trees, green grass, and the birds returning. For preschoolers, who are rooted in the here and now, it's simply a warm day. Preschoolers don't see the big picture—the seasonal cycle. If they are given opportunities to take note of simple sequences and cyclical changes, however, preschoolers gradually develop the ability to anticipate and describe such changes.

Activity Suggestions

Adults can use High/Scope's time key experiences to guide their observations of children's temporal thinking, to serve as a planning framework, and to guide interactions with children that will stimulate their developing understanding of time. Here are some activities and strategies that will involve children in using the time key experiences:

• **Make sure the daily routine is consistent.** A consistent daily routine is a key curriculum element that provides many natural opportunities each day for children to make connections between time concepts and their everyday experiences. Through the routine, children have opportunities to observe the beginning, ending, and duration of time periods; to notice the relationship of past to present to future; and to use the language of time in talking about these experiences. (For more about the daily routine and time concepts, see the article following this one.)

• **As children go through the plan-do-review process, encourage them to notice and talk about the passage of time.** For example, tape record the children's oral plans during planning time, and play them back during recall time. As you listen with the children, note their spontaneous comments about time and encourage them to compare time intervals: "Eleanor, you said your plan would take a little while to finish. *Did* it only take a little while?"

• **Make a variety of timers available for children's use,** for example, egg and sand timers. These give children a concrete way of measuring the time used in various activities. Such timers can be used when two children take turns, or just before children must make a transition.

Timely Ideas

Here are some materials/activities that help children learn time concepts:

Sand timers

You can make sand or water timers out of two clear plastic bottles of the same size. It's a good idea to have bottle pairs in different sizes, so you can make timers for different time-intervals.

To make a timer, take two bottles of the same size, and drill a small, clean hole in each bottle top. Fill one bottle with sand or water, and attach the top. Tape the other bottle, pointing down, to the top of the first bottle. (You can use dowels and a wood base to stabilize the timer.)

Musical Chairs and Simon Says

Children enjoy stop-and-start games like Musical Chairs and Simon Says, but we suggest altering the rules so there are no winners or losers.

For example, Simon Says could be transformed into a brief circle-time activity in which the teacher suggests that "we all move like snakes" (or bears, bunnies, dogs, and so forth), indicating when to start and stop new motions by saying "Teacher says . . ." Children could take turns leading the group.

Musical Chairs is another favorite game, but be sure you have enough chairs for everyone—don't play the game the traditional way in which chairs are eliminated one by one. Young children will find the game of stopping and starting to the music quite enjoyable without the element of competition.

• **Encourage "stop-and-start" play.** Play stop-and-start games like Simon Says or Musical Chairs (see "Timely Ideas" for modifications). Color-code buttons on tape players and computers with red and green tape, so children can stop and start them easily. Provide STOP and GO signs outdoors to encourage "traffic light" play.

• **Make sure you have available in your setting many items that can move or be moved at different rates of speed**—for example, balls, riding vehicles, pinwheels, trucks and cars, ropes, and swings.

• **Provide containers in the sand and water table that have different-sized holes in them,** so children can observe water and sand flowing out of them at different rates.

• **Don't correct children's mistaken statements about time intervals** (for example,"I've been waiting for my turn *all day*" [after a 5-minute wait] or "I'm really having to wait a long time for my dad today" [when

Dad is not late]). Instead, accept the child's judgment about how long something has taken, and then ask why it took that long. This helps children become aware of their reasoning and helps adults understand the preoperational point of view.

• **Adopt a tree in your neighborhood or playground.** At different times of the year, have the children take photos or draw pictures of the tree. Save the various pictures and, together with the children, compare them over time—they will easily see the changes that have occurred.

• **Offer cooking experiences.** They are wonderful opportunities for children to experience change and sequence. With children, make pudding, applesauce, popcorn, an omelet, or a fruit salad, and then use photos or drawings to make a chart that shows the steps in the recipe.

As you can see, opportunities to encourage children to develop a greater understanding of time are all around us, once we realize how abstract our adult notions of time are for the preschooler.

Alternatives to "Calendar Time"

By Mark Tompkins

. . . .

Calendars are a traditional part of many preschool classrooms, but they are usually not effective in helping young children understand the passage of time. The calendar's nonpictorial format and its reliance on standard time units—months, weeks, days—make it far too abstract and intangible to represent time understandably to young children.

If we wish to represent time in a form that young children can understand, we must consider how children think—not how adults think. For example, the daily routine is a time-organizing framework that young children can grasp, because it builds on a thinking capacity that is just emerging in the preschool years—the ability to notice and remember sequences of events. Because the routine is consistent from day to day, children develop the ability to predict which event will come next in the routine. To follow the routine independently, children do not need to understand how clocks work or what standard units of time mean—they simply need to become aware of a repeated sequence of events. While this is a challenge for many preschoolers, it is a one that is well within their abilities if the routine is kept simple and consistent.

If we start with the idea of the daily routine, then, it *is* possible to use charts and other graphic representations to help preschoolers understand the passage of time; in fact, this can be a valuable learning activity. A **daily routine chart** is a good strategy for introducing children to the idea of representing time graphically.

Typically, a daily routine chart is fairly large (at least 12 inches × 36 inches), sturdy, made from cardboard, and covered with Con-Tact paper. The chart depicts each element of the routine in sequence, from the top to the bottom of the chart. Each segment of the routine is represented with a photo, a drawing, and the word for that time of the day.

For such a chart to be understandable to children, make sure your routine is consistent from day to day and that the names of time periods are consistently used. Early in the school year, teachers find that review-

The daily routine chart depicts the segments of the routine in sequence, and each segment is represented with a photo, a drawing, and the word for that time of the day. The chart used in High/Scope's Demonstration Preschool is prominently displayed by the entrance, so children can see it as they arrive to start their preschool day.

ing the daily routine chart each day with children enables them to learn the routine in a short time.

Once children are comfortable with the daily routine chart, another idea to try is a **message board**. The message board extends on the idea of the daily routine chart, providing children with information about specific things happening "today" and a few days into the future. The message board can be a sheet of paper, a chalkboard, or a wipe-off board—anything a teacher can use to post daily messages. The messages are presented in pictorial form, with a few words and numbers. Teachers go over the messages with the children at opening circle.

The other day in the High/Scope Demonstration Preschool, the teachers had posted several messages on their board. The first message was that Sue was going to be the substitute teacher for three days. This was depicted by a picture of Sue with three circles next to it. Above this

Once children are comfortable with the daily routine chart, another idea to try is a message board. A message board provides children with information about specific things happening "today" and a few days into the future. This High/Scope's message board is an attention-getter as children eagerly check it at the beginning of the day to see "what's new."

message was a picture of Becki, the regular teacher, with a drawing of an airplane next to it and three circles. This let the children know that Becki was traveling and would be back in three days. (At the end of the day, the teachers crossed off the circle representing that day, so children could see how many days were left.)

The daily routine chart and message board are excellent vehicles for introducing the concept of a *day*. Once this concept is understood by children, the concept of a *week* may be introduced. A good way to represent a week for young children is to make a **circle chart.** Use a large cardboard circle divided into seven wedges (pizza stores will usually donate such circles). Title each section with the name of a day of the week, and use a pin to mount the wheel on another piece of cardboard, so it can rotate. Write the word "today" above the wheel, so the proper segment can be rotated to the "today" position to show which day it is. You can also use small

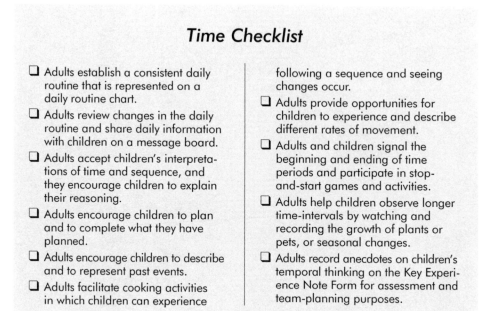

Time Checklist

- Adults establish a consistent daily routine that is represented on a daily routine chart.
- Adults review changes in the daily routine and share daily information with children on a message board.
- Adults accept children's interpretations of time and sequence, and they encourage children to explain their reasoning.
- Adults encourage children to plan and to complete what they have planned.
- Adults encourage children to describe and to represent past events.
- Adults facilitate cooking activities in which children can experience

following a sequence and seeing changes occur.
- Adults provide opportunities for children to experience and describe different rates of movement.
- Adults and children signal the beginning and ending of time periods and participate in stop-and-start games and activities.
- Adults help children observe longer time-intervals by watching and recording the growth of plants or pets, or seasonal changes.
- Adults record anecdotes on children's temporal thinking on the Key Experience Note Form for assessment and team-planning purposes.

pictures or symbols under the name of each day to indicate whether it is a "stay-at-home day" or a school day. For example, a house could stand for no-school days, a paintbrush for school days. The advantage of representing a week with a circle is that children can begin to see how the seven-day cycle is repeated. This is also a good format to refer to when talking about *yesterday, today,* and *tomorrow.* (Note: this kind of chart is most appropriate for older preschoolers or kindergartners.)

Because they represent and organize time in a way that is directly related to concrete, observable, meaningful experiences in children's lives, charts like these are effective alternatives to calendars.

High/Scope's Key Experiences
For Infants and Toddlers

By Jackie Post

• •

Infants, older babies, toddlers, older toddlers—how can adults best support the development of these very young children?

In this article, High/Scope introduces an up-to-date list of **infant and toddler key experiences** to help answer this question. These key experiences, which reflect a long history of High/Scope efforts in the infant and toddler area, are partially based on information first presented in *Good Beginnings*, High/Scope's manual on infant and toddler care, and on High/Scope's original list of sensorimotor key experiences for children 12 to 24 months old.

In developing this expanded list of key experiences for the infant and toddler years (birth to age 2½), High/Scope trainers and staff have also drawn on infant and toddler observations collected since September 1993 from 21 program sites around the country. These sites include both large and small early childhood centers, some in which infants and toddlers are served together in mixed-age groups and some in which young infants, toddlers, and 2-year-olds are grouped in various ways by age-range. The sites include center-based child care programs, family child care homes, and a college-based drop-in center.

We are presenting this resource on infant and toddler develop-ment because so many of the early childhood staff attending High/Scope training workshops have requested more information on these earlier years of development. These teachers, child care staff, and administrators often report that their centers are serving younger and younger children, as well as many older children who are still functioning at the infant and toddler level in some areas. In addi-tion, even adults who are working only with older preschoolers find that having information on where their 3- to 5-year-olds "have been" gives them a more complete perspective for understanding the children's current actions and interests.

In updating the infant and toddler key experiences, we've chosen a format similar to that used for the High/Scope preschool and elementary

High/Scope Infant and Toddler Key Experiences

Social Relations

- Bonding: building significant relationships with primary caregivers

- Building relationships with peers and other adults

- Expressing emotions toward others

- Responding to the needs of others

Sense of Self

- Distinguishing "me" from other people and things (for example, recognizing one's own image in a mirror)

- Asserting oneself—making and expressing choices, preferences, and decisions

- Solving problems encountered in exploration and play

Communication

- Listening and responding to sounds, voices, words, sensations, and facial expressions

- Communicating with movements, gestures, facial expressions, sounds, and words

- Participating in the give-and-take of communication—both verbal and nonverbal

- Using language to fulfill needs

- Enjoying speaking and being spoken to

- Listening to stories, rhymes, and songs, and exploring books and magazines

Movement

- Moving parts of one's body (reaching, grasping, pointing)

- Moving one's whole body (rolling, crawling, cruising, walking, running, balancing)

- Moving with objects

- Moving to music

Exploring Objects (Prerepresentation)

- Exploring objects with one's mouth, hands, feet, eyes, and ears

key experiences. By using these sets of key experiences in tandem, program staff are better able to see children's development as a continuum.

Infant and Toddler Key Experiences—What Are They?

The key experiences are statements that describe how infants and toddlers explore the environment, learn about themselves, and begin to interact with others in their world.

Staff of programs serving young children are sometimes unaware of the wide range of important learning experiences that occur during the first few years of life. While these adults may often observe and comment about milestones in babies' physical development—rolling over, crawling, and learning to walk—they may see children as doing nothing else worth noting until they learn to talk. The infant and toddler

- Searching for hidden objects and people—discovering object permanence
- Exploring building and art materials
- Imitating the actions of others
- Associating actions with objects
- Using one object to stand for another
- Responding to and identifying pictures

Exploring Attributes of Objects (Classification)

- Exploring and noticing the colors, shapes, sizes, textures, and other attributes of things
- Exploring and noticing how things are the same or different
- Exploring and noticing how things can be grouped together

Comparing and Counting

- Experiencing *more* and *less*

- Arranging objects in one-to-one correspondence
- Using number words

Space

- Noticing the location of objects in the environment
- Exploring and noticing the relationships of objects to other objects
- Observing objects and people from different perspectives
- Filling and emptying
- Taking things apart and fitting things together

Time

- Anticipating familiar events
- Noticing the beginnings and endings of time intervals
- Experiencing *fast* and *slow*

key experiences are intended to help program staff become more aware of the many areas of infant/toddler development.

You'll note that the infant and toddler key experiences, like the preschool and elementary key experiences, are presented in general categories rather than in a strict chronological sequence. Many other resources, by contrast, present information on infant and toddler development by looking at the typical behaviors of children at various chronological stages, for example, 0–3 months, 3–6 months, 6–12 months. While this sequential type of presentation can be very useful to parents and others who are focusing on one child at a time, we find that for adults working in group care settings (in which children are at many different levels of development), it is more helpful to first think in terms of a general area of development (such as communication or movement) and to then think in terms of the developmental sequences within that area. Thus, adults who are considering how to support the development of children's *movement* abilities may think of the key experience *moving one's whole body*, knowing that, of the children in their group, some will be walking, some cruising, some crawling, and some rolling, but all will be using *movement* as a way to get from place to place.

How to Use the Infant and Toddler Key Experiences

Like the High/Scope preschool and elementary key experiences, the infant and toddler key experiences provide adults with a framework for observing children and building plans for supporting, enhancing, and extending their play and discovery processes.

Let's look first at how the key experiences can help us in **observing** very young children. When adults are asked to "make observations of children," they often struggle to determine just *what* to observe—so much is occurring. Infants and toddlers need much individual attention from adults just to take care of their physical needs—frequent feedings and meals, diaper changes, clothing changes, routines associated with sleeping and waking. In addition, the range of development in the infant and toddler years is very wide. If we look at what children are doing at 2 months of age, for example, it will be very different from what they are doing at 26 months. When children are changing so quickly, we need to adjust our observational "lenses" much more frequently than we do when observing older children. It's not surprising, then, that busy adults may find it difficult to make meaningful observations of children in this age group. Having the infant and toddler key experiences available on a daily basis, however, will help these adults focus their observations.

Bonding: building significant relationships with primary caregivers— one of High/Scope's infant and toddler key experiences.

The infant and toddler key experiences give adults a context for their observations. For example, at snack time we may wish to look for the communication activities children are engaged in while they are eating and exploring

Adults in home-based programs use the High/Scope infant and toddler key experiences to organize their thoughts and observations about children's behavior at a time of life when children are changing rapidly. As caregivers continue to make careful observations, they become more aware of the child's needs and interests at the moment; this, in turn, enables them to provide appropriate support for each child in their care.

their food (**key experience:** *using language to fulfill needs*). Or we may want to focus on how the infants will react when they see snowsuits being brought into the room just before outside time (**key experience:** *anticipating familiar events*).

Rather than try to answer in a random way all the questions that arise in observing a very busy group of children, adults use the infant and toddler key experiences to organize their thoughts and observations about children's behavior and about what they should do to support children. For example, an adult without such a focus might wonder, "What are the babies doing with the floor toys?" But when the adult is familiar with the key experiences, the question becomes more focused—"Are the older infants still using the shape sorter as a fill-and-empty toy, or are they trying to put the shapes in through the matching holes?" (**Key experiences:** *filling and emptying; exploring and noticing the color, shapes, sizes, textures, and other attributes of things*).

Similarly, a question such as "Why does Sarah cry when Susan [a caregiver] leaves the room?" becomes "Has Sarah developed a strong attachment to Susan and is this why she cries when Susan leaves the room?" (**Key experience:** *bonding: building significant relationships with primary caregivers*). Likewise, the question "Doesn't Jeffrey know that isn't *his* cup he's picking up?" becomes, with the help of the key experiences, "Is J effrey exploring anything within reach, or has he chosen to pick up Michael's cup because he has noticed particular features of the cup?" (**Key experiences:** *moving parts of one's body: reaching, grasping, pointing; exploring and noticing the colors, shapes, sizes, textures, and other attributes of things*).

Accurate observations of children are important because **observation is an essential part of adult-child interaction.** The key experiences help us focus on what children *can* do rather than on what they cannot yet do or are not doing because they are not interested. Observation makes us more aware of the child's needs and interests at the moment; this, in turn, leads us to support the child more appropriately. Observation, then, does not remove the caregiver from the interaction; in fact, it increases the probability of a positive interaction. In the preceding example of baby Jeffrey, who has picked up another baby's cup at mealtime, the adult who lacks an observational framework may make an inappropriate response—by not allowing Jeffrey sufficient time to explore the cup or by taking the cup away and saying "That's not your cup!" However, if the adult is guided by the key experiences, he or she will probably interpret the observation in terms of Jeffrey's need to reach for objects or explore the attributes of the cup. As a result, the response will be more appropriate.

The observational framework provided by the infant and toddler key experiences helps adults support children appropriately. The insights gained from the key experiences lead not only to more effective on-the-spot interactions but also to more effective planning of learning experiences and more appropriate choices of materials.

The Infant and Toddler Key Experiences— Anecdotal Examples

By Jackie Post

. . . .

This article provides an anecdotal example of a child behavior to illustrate each of High/Scope's key experiences for the period from birth through age 2½. The anecdotes were collected from the field sites participating in High/Scope's effort to revise and expand its resources focusing on the infant and toddler years. Though each anecdote illustrates the key experience under which it is listed, the anecdote may also "fit" with additional key experiences on the list.

Social Relations

- Bonding: building significant relationships with primary caregivers

  Daniel goes over to Mindy (his caregiver) and sits down in her lap when she comes into the block area.

- Building relationships with peers and other adults

  Henry and John, laughing, play a brief game of peek-a-boo around the basketball pole at outside time.

- Expressing emotions toward others

  Matt goes over to Rebecca, who has just returned after a week's vacation, and gives her a kiss.

- Responding to the needs of others

  Matt hugs Christopher, who is crying because his mom has left.

Sense of Self

- Distinguishing "me" from other people and things (for example, recognizing one's own image in a mirror)

As he sits on the floor, Mitchell waves at his image in a mirror in front of him, touching first his face and then the reflection of his face in the mirror.

• Asserting oneself—making and expressing choices, preferences, and decisions

Kayla is playing with blocks spread out in front of her. When another child attempts to take two of the blocks, Kayla says "Mine" and moves the two blocks closer to herself.

• Solving problems encountered in exploration and play

Lizzie eats her dry cereal out of a paper cup at snack time, pouring the cereal into her mouth as if she were drinking it.

Communication

• Listening and responding to sounds, voices, words, sensations, and facial expressions

Kelly looks at Tracy (an adult) when Tracy speaks to her, and she smiles at the sound of Tracy's voice.

• Communicating with movements, gestures, facial expressions, sounds, and words

When Tejas's book falls to the floor from the chair in which he is sitting, he says "Uh-Oh."

• Participating in the give-and-take of communication—both verbal and nonverbal

Dee, an adult, is rocking Austin, while looking into his face and singing to him. She begins singing the sounds "La, la, la" instead of the regular words to the song. Austin looks up at her and says "La, la, ma, ma . . . "

• Using language to fulfill needs

Lyle says "Help me" as he brings his shoes over to an adult after naptime.

• Enjoying speaking and being spoken to

At circle time, Julia chimes in as the group sings a rhyming song:

Adult: One, two . . .
Julia: Buckle my shoe
Adult: Three, four . . .
Julia: Shut door

• Listening to stories, rhymes, and songs, and exploring books and magazines

> *Danielle looks through a familiar storybook, saying some words quietly to herself.*

Movement

• Moving parts of one's body (reaching, grasping, pointing)

> *Laying on his stomach, Matt reaches for and bats at a beach ball.*

• Moving one's whole body (rolling, crawling, cruising, walking, running, balancing)

> *At outside time, Jamie and three other children jump up and down in the empty plastic wading pools.*

• Moving with objects

> *Gina pushes a car on the floor and crawls after it.*

• Moving to music

> *When Blake's caregiver sings "Sally the Camel," Blake bobs up and down as the numbers are sung and moves his hips from side to side to the words "Boom, boom, boom."*

Exploring Objects (Prerepresentation)

• Exploring objects with one's mouth, hands, feet, eyes, and ears

> *Hope takes her pacifier out of her mouth, looks at it, changes its position, and puts it back in her mouth.*

• Searching for hidden objects and people—discovering object permanence

> *Lizzie continues to crawl toward a cup, even after her caregiver has put it behind a chair, out of Lizzie's sight.*

• Exploring building and art materials

> *Nick colors with chalk on a chalkboard that lies flat on the floor. He makes long, curved scribble lines on one edge and leaves the center of the board blank.*

• Imitating the actions of others

> *Cathy (an adult) is folding diapers for the infants, when Karlie comes over and starts folding diapers for her baby doll.*

Using the Infant and Toddler
Key Experiences in Team Planning

The High/Scope infant and toddler key experiences, like the preschool and elementary key experiences, are used in daily planning sessions by staff members of High/Scope child care programs. The following dialogue is an excerpt from two teachers' discussions in a typical daily team-planning session. The setting is a table in the toddler's art area in a large center-based child care program. Program staff members Linda and Maria are co-teachers for a group of eight toddlers. Linda is relatively new to this program. As you read this dialogue, consider how the team members use the infant and toddler key experiences in interpreting their observations and planning for the next day.

Linda: *That was really a busy morning! It's like being on roller skates—I feel like I'm still moving!*

Maria: *Yes, the group was extremely active today. I think they wished we could have spent more time outside, but the sprinkles turned to rain pretty fast. Linda, do you have any observations on the children from this morning? I can write them down on their Key Experience Note Forms as we talk.*

Linda: *Yes, I've got a note here about Sean. He was especially interested in climbing up the steps to the slide all by himself, and he had to work hard to pull his foot up each time he climbed another rung on the ladder.*

Maria: *I'm putting this down on Sean's form under "Sense of self—solving problems." You know, I saw you over at the slide with Sean and the others when I was in the sandbox. It seemed like the slide was crowded today.*

Linda: *Yes, and some children had a hard time waiting for the child before them to go down—especially when a child didn't go down right away. Some children tried crawling over the child in front of them, so they could go down first—a pretty unique way to approach problem solving!*

Maria: *I wonder if we can find some other ways to give children opportunities to climb and slide, since we have just one slide.*

Linda: *Well, where I worked before, we made an obstacle course outside for the toddlers. To make the course, we used some of the big wooden blocks from indoors, some cardboard boxes with the ends cut off, which the children liked to crawl through, and some of the stationary things in the play yard, like the trees and other equipment. We could do something similar here, by making some new things for children to climb on and crawl through. Because of their ages, of course, we wouldn't expect the children to explore the "stations" on the course in any particular order.*

Maria: *That's a great idea! An obstacle course might give children some other ways to move their whole bodies, something we are focusing on right now as these children become increasingly mobile. With some of the children busy on the new structures we'll set up, those who have chosen the slide will have more time to slide down without being rushed. The other thing I like about this idea is that it will shorten that waiting time at the slide, which is often difficult for these little guys.*

Linda: *Great—I'll see what else I can remember about the course we built before and start collecting some things for it. Maybe we could even try it out tomorrow—if it stops raining!*

Maria: *There might also be some children who would want to move with objects through the obstacle course. We could put some balls out alongside some stations on the course to see if they might try to throw or roll a ball ahead of them as they crawl through a box or climb over something. I noticed as I looked over the children's Key Experience Note Forms that we have quite a few examples of them moving with objects indoors, but very few examples outdoors. This might give them some new ways to move with objects while outside.*

- Associating actions with objects

  Julia rides around on a toy train, making the "choo-choo" sound over and over.

- Using one object to stand for another

  Daniel puts a pot from the house area on his head as if it were a hat.

- Responding to and identifying pictures

  Carlos sees a picture of a duck in his book and excitedly says "Quack, quack, quack."

Exploring Attributes of Objects (Classification)

- Exploring and noticing the colors, shapes, sizes, textures, and other attributes of things

  Marcus squeezes a soft ball at outside time and exclaims, "Look, I got a wiggly ball."

- Exploring and noticing how things are the same or different

  Jenny tries to take a blanket another child is using. Dee (an adult) offers Jenny another blanket that is almost identical but that has a hole in it. Jenny, refusing this blanket, says, "No, Dee, it's broken."

- Exploring and noticing how things can be grouped together

  Sam brings plastic animals—one by one, eight in all—from all different areas of the room and puts them on the tray in front of Michael. When he is done, he turns away from Michael and claps.

Comparing and Counting

- Experiencing **more** and **less**

  Playing with Play-Doh at small-group time, Kate observes, "Hey, there's some more" when she discovers that some Play-Doh is left in the container.

- Arranging objects in one-to-one correspondence

  Keith takes three play people out of a basket and puts each one in its own little car.

- Using number words

  While touching the pegs on the pegboard one by one, Tiara chants "One, two, three, five, nine, eight; one, two, three, five, nine, eight . . . "

Space

- Noticing the location of objects in the environment

Michael has finished his snack (which the class had outdoors). When Bonnie (an adult) asks him to throw his napkin away, Michael walks over to the trash can and puts his napkin in it.

- Exploring and noticing the relationships of objects to other objects

Alex comments to the adults who have come outside after him, "You're outside, too!"

- Observing objects and people from different perspectives

Jason looks at Jan (an adult) through his legs as he bends over with his hands touching the floor. Jan says "Upside down!" and Jason responds "Down."

- Filling and emptying

Samantha fills up her purse with small blocks and carries it around the room with her.

- Taking things apart and fitting things together

Zachary fits the small pegs into the pegboard, one at a time.

Time

- Anticipating familiar events

Sam brings his chair across the room to the lunch table and sits down, an hour before lunch occurs.

- Noticing the beginnings and endings of time intervals

Raoul is taking turns jumping on the mini-trampoline with Lyle. Raoul jumps several times, says, "One more minute," then immediately gets off the trampoline and says, "Your turn" to Lyle. They alternate turns for several minutes.

- Experiencing **fast** and **slow**

*John is pushing another child on the swing at outside time. John says to David (an adult), "I pushin' Henry **fast**!"*

Chapter Six

Special Events

· ·

Celebrating With Preschoolers
Susan M. Terdan
Primary-Grade Holiday Activities
Diana Jo Johnston
Field Trips: A New Definition
Michelle Graves
Primary-Grade Field Trips That Work
Diana Jo Johnston

*T*he selections in this chapter look at some special events common to most early childhood programs—holiday celebrations and field trips. The authors suggest new approaches to these commonplace events, approaches that take into consideration the developmental needs and emerging skills of young children.

In the High/Scope approach special-event activities are not viewed as a departure from the regular program. Instead they take place within the same active learning framework that guides all program activities.

In "Celebrating With Preschoolers," Susan M. Terdan suggests alternatives to the ways holidays are typically celebrated in preschools. Terdan recommends letting preschool holiday activities grow out of the interests children express in a holiday, rather than imposing highly structured holiday activities on children simply because a particular calendar date has arrived. She discusses the natural cycle of preschoolers' interest in holidays, suggesting that adults provide special holiday experiences and materials during the time when children's interests are highest (for preschoolers, this time usually begins just before the holiday and extends for some time afterward). In "Primary-Grade Holiday Activities," the next article, Diana Jo

Johnston describes the holiday-related projects that older children spontaneously initiate in High/Scope elementary classrooms. She points out that observers will not see 25 identical Christmas trees, Easter bunnies, or shamrocks in High/Scope classrooms, because children's holiday interests typically will lead to a more complex and varied range of holiday projects.

"Field Trips: A New Definition," by Michelle Graves, deals with another standard activity in early childhood classrooms. Graves urges preschool teachers to plan field trips from an active learning perspective. When field-trip experiences are planned to be simple, concrete, active, and geared to children's interests, both children and adults will find field trips to be fun and stimulating rather than exhausting and confusing, Graves says. In "Primary-Grade Field Trips That Work," Diana Jo Johnston provides field trip suggestions geared to the interests and abilities of older children. She suggests that elementary teachers restructure traditional outings to include more active experiences for children. She suggests some simple ways of varying standard field trip plans to make them more engaging for elementary school children.

Celebrating With
Preschoolers

By Susan M. Terdan

. . . .

Holiday activities and special-occasion celebrations are common in early childhood programs, probably because most adults enjoy sharing the fun of these traditional events with preschoolers.

In many preschools and centers, adults typically prepare extensively for a holiday. A month before the holiday, teachers hang up decorations—often purchased or adult-made. In subsequent weeks, there are many holiday lessons and projects, all planned to the last detail by the adults. Children learn holiday songs; they assemble centerpieces, decorations, or gifts from components laboriously prepared by the adults; and sometimes they rehearse for performances or pageants. Then, the day after the holiday, the decorations come down—soon to be replaced with those for the next holiday—and the cycle begins again.

Adults usually work very hard on such special-occasion activities. In all the excitement of getting ready for a big event, however, they may forget to consider the occasion from the young child's point of view. Holiday projects like these often aren't meaningful to preschoolers,

Instead of planning many holiday activities, art projects, and lessons for the month before a special event, a more developmentally appropriate approach is to let the special event or holiday emerge through the children's conversation and actions before planning related experiences.

who learn most from activities that grow from their own choices and that relate to their own interests and experiences.

In High/Scope programs, holiday experiences, like any other topic or content area, can provide a firm foundation for supporting children's development. In fact, because children acquire concepts most readily when they are excited about what they are doing, the holiday season is a wonderful opportunity for learning. But in considering when and how to incorporate a special occasion into preschool learning activities, early childhood staff should attend carefully to children's expressions of interest and subtle cues.

In contrast to the adult-oriented holiday activities seen in so many programs, let's consider these examples of *child-oriented* special-occasion activities:

Nov. 8: *At small-group time, Sharee and Christopher cover a large sheet of paper with purple paint. "Let's put these on and be Barney and go trick or treat," Sharee says to Christopher. Sharee tapes the purple paper onto her clothes and, going around to each child at the table, says "Trick or treat!"*

Feb. 5: *It is work time in the block area. Jamal builds a "sled" with the large wooden blocks, sits on it, and sings the chorus of "Jingle Bells" twice through by himself.*

June 21: *At work time in the house area, Jolissa places four dolls in chairs around the table. In the middle of the table is a large bowl of corks. "There's the cake," she says, pointing to the bowl. "We're having a birthday party, just like mine, with cake!" (Jolissa's birthday was in April.)*

These anecdotes describe children who are finding their own ways to recognize special events, with the support of adults who are attuned to their interests and developing abilities. In this article, we look at some ways to encourage child-oriented holiday and seasonal activities like these. To understand what's appropriate, however, we need to look first at the preschooler's sense of time.

How Preschoolers Experience Time

Most preschoolers find it difficult to think far into the future or to reflect on events that are long past. They lack an understanding of abstract time units. The concepts of days, weeks, months, seasons, and years, which adults use to organize their lives, are not meaningful to most young children. Young children operate on a much more concrete level—in the here and now. They are not oriented to the past or future; nothing is as important to young children as what they are doing "right now."

What If This Happens?

The mother of one of the children in my preschool program complained to me that because Santa was not a part of the family's religion, she didn't want any Santa Claus activities in the program. Some children in the program enjoy pretend play about Santa; in addition, we usually have a Santa at our end-of-year potluck, and children enjoy this. How can I remain sensitive to the needs of all the children without stifling their natural interest in Santa?
—*A preschool teacher*

Explain your philosophy of supporting and extending children's interests. Then simply say that while you will not introduce Santa play, you will not stop children who are playing Santa, just as you wouldn't stop children who are acting like bears or cats.

We would suggest, however, that you discuss with your parent committee your plan to have Santa at the potluck; in the case of organized holiday observances like this, it's important to consult parents.

What if I'm waiting for children to initiate ideas and activities related to a holiday or special event and they don't do so?
—*A child care provider*

When a particular holiday or special event does not emerge in children's play or conversation, it may mean that the event or holiday is too abstract to have relevance to children. Because of their basis in historical tradition, many of the special days marked on our calendars are really not understandable to young children. The preoperational child need not experience all of life's special events in the classroom or day care center. If something doesn't come from the children, let it go, and pay attention to the interests that children are expressing.

Yet, it's important for young children to develop the ability to plan for the future and reflect on the past. This is one reason why the High/ Scope approach includes the **plan-do-review sequence** in the child's daily routine. But the plan-do-review sequence is geared to the preschooler's way of understanding time: Because it is usually too difficult for preschoolers to anticipate or recall across a long time-period, *planning* comes right before *work time,* and *recalling* comes right after work time.

Suggestions for Adults

In consideration of preschoolers' undeveloped sense of time, we offer adults the following suggestions for promoting developmentally appropriate special-occasion activities.

The month before. Typically, adults who are planning special-occasion activities for early childhood programs are guided by the calendar: They

Before, During, and After

Here are some examples of how teachers may identify and support children's interest in two upcoming holidays.

Thanksgiving

Before and during the holiday: You will probably hear very little talk about Thanksgiving before the actual day. If the topic does come up, it will probably arise just before the actual day and center around children's excitement about visiting relatives or attending a parade.

Once Thanksgiving comes up in children's conversations, listen carefully and add materials that support their particular interests. Add food containers for Thanksgiving foods, suitcases, and a pumpkin to the house area. Have orange and brown paint and paper available in the art area.

After the holiday: Respond to children's conversations about their visitors, the parades they attended, or other activities they took part in during their weekend break. Keep the Thanksgiving food containers available in the house area, and add materials related to children's Thanksgiving experiences. For example, if children went apple-picking or helped make pies, add books and play materials related to apples and pie-making. Re-stock the orange and brown paper. Have pumpkin pie or pumpkin bread for snack.

December Holidays

Before and during the holidays: Christmas and Hanukkah may arise in children's talk and play in a variety of ways in the days before the holidays: Children may talk about visiting Santa, make and wrap pretend presents, pretend to get Christmas trees, talk about getting Christmas cards.

begin their special classroom activities about a month before the actual event. For children, however, anticipating an activity that is a month away—especially one that as yet has no relation to their daily experiences— may not be meaningful. Therefore, instead of planning many holiday activities, art projects, and lessons for the month before the event, a more developmentally appropriate approach is to **let the special event or holiday emerge through the children's conversation and actions.** Listen to children carefully, talk with them, and observe their play. What children know and understand about a special event or holiday will reveal itself. There can be many factors—the experiences of siblings, what their parents are doing, the displays they see in stores, holiday advertising on television— any of which can inspire children to talk and play-act about an approaching holiday. Most likely, young children will begin to show inter-

Support children's interest in the holidays by doing these things: participating in their conversations and role play about the festivities; adding related books to the bookshelf (along with titles on other subjects); adding green, red, yellow, and blue paint, paper, and old holiday cards to the art area; planning a small-group time around glue and glitter; adding holiday music to the tape collection; adding a variety of boxes and wrapping paper (recycled paper is fine) to the art area; adding "dressy" clothes, robes, and a tub of old decorations to the house area.

After the holidays: Except for those holiday projects that children took home before the break, keep all the holiday props available in their respective areas until children's interest in them dies down. Observe, listen to, and enter into children's conversations and play about the December holidays, supporting and extending the new ideas and interests that emerge. Re-stock the art area with holiday-related items that have been consumed. However, if you have had a long school break, don't be surprised if the holiday is over in the children's minds when they return to school. In this case, put the holiday materials away, and support the children's current interests, whatever they may be. But be alert—a holiday may resurface in children's play when you least expect it. For example, in the High/Scope Demonstration Preschool, present-wrapping (children's strong interest in December and January) emerged again in children's play in April—at which time adults set out a new tub of wrapping materials in the art area!

est in an event immediately before rather than weeks in advance of the event. When this occurs, it's time for adults to think of ways to build on children's interests.

Right before and during the event. Once children display an interest in an upcoming event, adults should listen, observe, and interact with them to discover what children know and to determine the extent of their interest. The team can then plan ways to support and extend children's ideas and interests by adding related materials to the areas; planning field trips, small-group times, or other special activities; and interacting with children as they re-enact and talk about the special occasion. You will probably note a wide variety of interest levels among the children in your group. Adults need to be attuned to such differences as they support and extend children's holiday-related activities. Adults should also recognize

When in Holland . . .

Active Learning at Tulip Time

Finding developmentally appropriate ways to share the fun of holidays and special events with young children is a concern of all early childhood providers. For **High/Scope Endorsed Trainer Kathie Spitzley**, director of the **Good Times Family Day Care Home** in **Holland, Michigan**, this issue becomes especially important every May, when local citizens celebrate their Dutch heritage in the biggest community event of the year, the Tulip Festival.

Kathie's approach to this event builds on the children's natural interest in re-enacting festival experiences. Kathie points out that nearly all the families in the community participate in the festival in all kinds of ways, so the event is a part of children's everyday lives that emerges naturally in children's conversation and role play.

On festival days, a series of parades is the biggest town event. On these days, Kathie keeps the sequence of the daily routine the same but shortens the time segments to allow the 3- to 5-year-olds in her program to at-

tend the parade in the afternoon with the teachers. Kathie carefully plans these expeditions so they are not too taxing for children. For example, she arranges with a shopkeeper to reserve a place on the parade route for children to sit and keeps a staff member standing by to take home children who get tired early.

At greeting circle on the morning of a parade, Kathie and the children talk about what the parade might be like. Since many parents and townspeople—including virtually all the town's school-aged children—march in the parades, Kathie and the children talk about which relatives or neighbors they can expect to see in the parade. Later, pointing out these familiar people as they march by is great fun for everyone.

Kathie reports that, once they are back in the center, children spontaneously represent the marching musicians and dancers they saw in the parades, as well as other festival experiences, through building, imitation, role play, and artwork. At work time, the day after a parade, many children choose

that in some children's eyes, other activities may be just as important as (or more important than) the special event.

After the event. One of the most dramatic changes that can be observed in many early childhood settings is the transition that occurs on the night after Halloween. One day the center looks like "Halloween Heaven," and the next, like "Plymouth Rock Feast." Overnight, it is as though Halloween has never been, and Pilgrims, turkeys, and cornucopias fill the setting.

Once a special event is over, adults can flip the page of a calendar or cross off the day, turning their attention to the next big event on the calendar. This doesn't work for young children, however. You'll often observe children living out a special event or holiday long past its actual date. This is because, once an event has occurred, it becomes concrete and real

to make musical instruments, banners, and hats like those they saw in the parades. For weeks afterward the children use these props both indoors and outdoors, creating their own parades and festival activities.

Another traditional activity that most children see at festival time is community members scrubbing down the streets. As a result, pretend street-scrubbing usually is another popular play activity; Kathie prepares for this by offering brooms and buckets of water when children are outdoors.

In these and many other ways, Kathie helps children build on their festival experiences. For these young children, tulip-time fun extends well beyond the actual festival dates.

Here Come the Brides

Recently, in Kathie Spitzley's day care home, there was much discussion of weddings, since three of the children had family members who had invited the children to be in their wedding parties. After the subject came up several times in the children's conversations and pretend play, Kathie decided to raise the subject of weddings at greeting circle. There was excited talk about wedding clothes, ceremonies, gifts, and foods, with the children showing great interest.

To build on children's interest in weddings, over time Kathie added the following materials to the interest areas: a wedding photo album in the book area; bride magazines, lace, and white fabric pieces in the art area; rings, fake flowers, and "dressy" clothes in the house area. By talking to one of the parents, Kathie found out that one of the upcoming weddings was a traditional Swedish candlelight ceremony, so Kathie also added some candles (no matches, of course) to the house area.

After the weddings were over, children's interest in weddings and wedding-related play continued to increase for several weeks. Children continued to play with the wedding materials, and Kathie brought in some additional materials related to topics children raised: white crepe paper for car decorating, boxes and wedding wrapping paper for pretend presents.

to the children. When an event is a part of their experience, it becomes something to come to terms with and relive. A special occasion that is fresh in children's minds will usually lead to a variety of play activities. Some children will re-enact an event through role play and imitation, others through building and art projects, and they will often build on one another's ideas as play develops and expands. Adults should observe the children's timetable for these play activities, continuing to support the play by offering relevant materials and interacting appropriately with children.

For example, in the High/Scope Demonstration Preschool, two weeks after Halloween, teachers noticed that there was still a high interest in Halloween-related play. They made plans to continue singing some Halloween songs at circle time, restocked the art area with glitter and other costume-making materials, kept the big black hats in the house area, and kept "Mask Parade"—a mask-making program—on the computer. Of course, Halloween was just one topic on teachers' minds as they planned; they also discussed children's strong interest in racing cars and castle-building, and they made plans for incorporating these interests as well.

In an environment where each child's interests and developmental levels are respected, children have many opportunities to make choices and act on them. Adults recognize and pay attention to holidays and special events as they are reflected in children's play, just as they do when children show an interest in race cars, baby dolls, or any other play topic. The adult's role is to validate, support, and build on children's ideas, always beginning at the *child's* level of understanding.

Primary-Grade
Holiday Activities

By Diana Jo Johnston

• •

In High/Scope elementary classrooms, you will not see a display of 25 identical Christmas trees, shamrocks, or bunnies. Instead, you will find a variety of student projects—some related to upcoming or past holidays and others completely unrelated.

Holiday and special-occasion celebrations and activities occur naturally in High/Scope elementary classrooms, because, like all other learning activities, they grow out of children's experiences. During the plan-do-review sequence, children plan and carry out projects that stem from personal interests. At this time, children often initiate activities related to what they are doing at home and in the community to prepare for family holiday gatherings, weddings, graduation parties, or other upcoming events.

Child-chosen projects take a variety of forms: invitations, greeting cards, poems, collages, decorations, special performances, gifts, costumes, and so forth. Such child-initiated holiday projects are often more elaborate and original—and require children to use a wider range of skills and resources—than the all-one-kind holiday projects planned by teachers in many elementary classrooms.

Teachers must use sensitivity when approaching any holiday that has religious or cultural significance. In general, High/Scope teachers do not initiate activities related to religious occasions. However, if a *child* initiates such an activity or conversation, this may be welcomed and supported. For example, permitting children to bring in photographs, special clothing, foods, greeting cards, and other items from the special-occasion celebrations they participate in at home is one way to show respect for the child's culture or religion. If another child's parent objects to this kind of sharing, the teacher explains that the activity was child-initiated and that all children are welcome to share aspects of their home cultures in the classroom.

However, when a holiday has historical significance—for example, Presidents' Day, Martin Luther King Day, or Thanksgiving—it's entirely

Holiday Experiences for Younger and Older Children

For many of the younger children in the primary grades, holidays are not real until they've experienced them. These children particularly enjoy representing special-occasion activities *after* they have taken place. Drawing pictures of a birthday cake, pretending to cook a turkey or Christmas cookies, writing stories, and singing festive songs are a few examples of the representational activities that are typical of 5-, 6-, and 7-year-olds. Adults support them by offering related music, storybooks, clothing, and art supplies.

Children who are developmentally more mature (typically, those in second and third grade) will often want to make special plans for upcoming events. Because a child remembers a previous birthday party, the *Cinco de Mayo* parade, or the fun of wrapping and unwrapping gifts during past holiday seasons, the child may initiate a preholiday activity during work time or a workshop time. For example, he or she may make decorations, mark on the calendar the number of days until an event is to occur, or make greeting cards or invitations. In each case, the teacher offers the encouragement or resources the child needs to extend those ideas.

appropriate for the *teacher* to introduce related activities and materials in a social studies context. In planning for such activities, though, it's important to keep children's developmental differences in mind. At kindergarten and first-grade levels, the focus might simply be on awareness of the holiday, with the teacher introducing the holiday at greeting circle and perhaps reading a related book to children. By second and third grade, children have greater ability to understand historical events remote from their experiences and can undertake projects requiring research and writing skills. During social studies or writing workshops in the week of Martin Luther King Day, for example, a teacher might ask older children to choose a famous African-American to learn more about. The child could then write a paper or do a poster presentation on that figure.

In holiday activities, the High/Scope teacher's role is to provide choices and to offer materials, resources, and other support, so children can develop their ideas. Teachers also support children who do not show an interest in a holiday or who choose not to participate in holiday activities.

Field Trips:
A New Definition

By Michelle Graves

. . . .

"It's field trip day!"

For some early childhood program staff, these words come with high expectations. These teachers or caregivers look forward to a refreshing change of scenery and the chance to experience new people and places with children.

But for others who work in programs for young children, field trips are a dreaded, twice-yearly occurrence. To these staff, the phrase "field trip" conjures up unpleasant memories: counting heads anxiously; dealing with confused children, public scenes, and transportation breakdowns; returning to the setting with exhausted children who wonder out loud when work time will be or why they didn't have snack at their regular tables.

My prior experience as an educational consultant and as a director of a full-day child care program and my current experience as a teacher in the High/Scope Demonstration Preschool have convinced me that field trips can play an important role in young children's educational development. They give children opportunities to explore the neighborhood and community *outside* the center. In addition, they often stimulate further learning *inside* the classroom or center after children return. After an outing, we often notice that children add details to their representations and role-play activities, use materials in new ways, and readily describe the new experiences they've had.

Planning Field Trips for Active Learning

Because we've seen the positive impact they can have on children, we view field trips as a regular and important part of our program rather than as an "add-on" that calls for a lot of extra planning and logistical support. Field trips don't have to be big, splashy affairs that require long bus rides and extensive volunteer help. Sometimes the best field trip ideas are simple. A regularly repeated visit to a neighborhood spot can be more valuable for children than a one-time trip to a famous tourist attraction that is unconnected to their everyday experiences. In addition to the field trip destinations that we describe throughout this article, some other good "active learning destinations" are these:

The school parking lot	The natural history museum
A local grocery store	A field with a hill for sledding or tumbling
A nearby construction site	A greenhouse, botanical garden, or flower shop
The school playgrounds and parks nearby	A street where city workers are chopping or shredding branches
The local laundromat	A recycling station
A fire department or police station	A curbside spot during garbage pickup
A nursing home during craft or music time	The post office
A baseball field	A service station
A pond	A pet store or petting zoo
The local high school during band rehearsal	A bakery
A city swimming pool	A pizza shop
A city bus on its usual route	The work sites of parents

The key to successful field trips to destinations such as these is to keep the guiding principles of the curriculum in mind as you plan and conduct an outing. Like other activities in High/Scope programs, field trips should provide children with concrete experiences and opportunities for active involvement, and they are most meaningful when they are geared to children's interests and developmental levels. Well-planned field trips are also smoothly integrated with the rest of the program and, as a result, they do not disrupt or exhaust children.

Following are some ideas and strategies for choosing a place to visit, planning the field trip, and following up on the experience in your regular classroom routine.

Strategies for Successful Field Trips

Careful preparation of all concerned prior to a field trip is required to insure success. Some tips:

- **Inform parents that regular outings are a part of your program** and explain why you think they will be important to their child's school experience. This can be done in a parent meeting or as written school policy in a parent handbook. Blank field-trip permission forms should be included in the child's initial enrollment packet, and individual permission forms should be signed before each outing.

- **Acquaint yourself with all licensing requirements regarding transportation for outings.** Check the local and state social service department recommendations for transporting children on foot, in private vehicles, by public transportation, or in school-owned vans.

- **Introduce outings slowly and within the context of the daily routine.** In the beginning of the school year, children need ample time to internalize the daily routine and all its components. Depending on the developmental ages of your children, this may take two to six weeks. Once children are familiar with the daily sequence of events, you can begin to build field trips into it. Here are some ideas for doing this:

> *Prepare* both parents and children beforehand. Send out permission slips at least a week before the field trip. As their parents return the forms, children will begin to be aware that a field trip is coming up.

> *Keep field trips short* enough so you can go through part of your classroom routine on the day of the field trip. Don't make the trip your very first activity.

> *At greeting circle* at the beginning of a field-trip day, use the language of the routine to explain the change in scheduling that a field trip brings: "At small-group time, we'll be walking to a flower shop." "Today at work time we'll be taking a trip to the apple orchard. We'll return before nap time." You should also explain which adult each child will be assigned to on the outing and what the transportation arrangements are.

> *Follow up* on field trips by planning related small- and large-group activities and strategies for planning and recall times and by providing related materials for children's use at work time.

> *Take pictures* of children's experiences on the trip, and have them available later in an album in the book area.

At the Demonstration Preschool, our first field trip this past school year was a walk around the school neighborhood. The day of the walk,

Disruption or Extension?

I recently attended an inservice workshop in which the consultant said that field trips are not part of their curriculum, because they are too disruptive to the children's daily routine. As a teacher in a full-day child care program I understand the importance of a consistent daily routine. But I also feel that visits outside the center are important opportunities for introducing children to new places, people, and ideas. Should I reconsider my thinking on this subject?

—A child care teacher

We believe that children learn best through direct experiences, and that field trips provide valuable direct experiences with the community that build on the learning that is taking place in the classroom. Parents who work full-time sometimes find it hard to introduce children to a wide range of community experiences, and this is another reason we agree with you that programs for young children should provide out-of-school activities.

We at High/Scope are also firm believers in taking cues from the children. If you notice that after outings children are disorganized, cry a lot, have trouble sleeping or eating, and don't often represent the trip in their conversations and role-play activities, it may be time—not to abandon all field trips—but to consider whether you are planning them around the needs and interests of young children. It's also helpful to think of field trips as a regularly occurring extension of your daily routine rather than as a disruption to it. If you prepare children adequately for field trips, making sure they know when and where they will be going, and if you integrate the field trip with the flow of your routine, then your outings and follow-up experiences will be more successful.

we gathered with children at their familiar small-group tables and then announced that for small-group time we would be taking a walk together around the block. Since small-group time is normally scheduled near the end of our school day, we had requested that parent volunteers come earlier than usual to pick up their children, so they could help us as children explored new territory. Once the volunteers arrived, to eliminate some of the head-counting worries and to insure that children would feel comfortable focusing on their surroundings, we assigned small groups of three or four children to adult "partners."

Our walk led us down an alley filled with sticks, stones, and an assortment of wild flowers. This stimulated much conversation about texture, weight, and smells. Further along we discovered a work crew, with all its equipment, building an upstairs addition to a one-story home. Over time, we repeated this walk, and children enjoyed noticing and talking about the changes in the house. They enjoyed making guesses about whether the roof or the windows would be in place and about who would be inside the rooms when they were finished. After these walks, the children's block-area structures became increasingly elaborate, often having window openings, or scarves and blankets draped and taped across the top to make a roof "to keep the rain outside."

• **Capitalize on the talents of your parents and the special features of your community.** Another successful fall field trip was a walk to the local farmers' market. After exploring the different stalls filled with fruits and vegetables, we gathered for a snack of apples and cider. We gave each child the opportunity to choose from spring bulbs that were for sale (the flowers were pictured on the labels). Following the trip, one child's father, a High/Scope employee whose job is to maintain the school grounds, helped children plant the bulbs at outside time in the following few days. He came equipped with wheelbarrow, digging tools, and flowerpots. Each child planted some of his or her bulbs in a communal spring flower garden and others in individual pots that we put away for the winter. In the spring, when the blooms began to be visible in the cooperative garden, children enjoyed watching the changes each day and had a variety of reactions. Erica questioned teachers about where the individual flowerpots were stored—she was the only child who remembered them without prompting. Maria, certain that she remembered exactly where she had planted her bulbs, plucked "her flowers" out of the communal garden.

• **Use your observations of children's activities as you plan special outings** that support and expand on their ideas. One year at a day care program I directed, we noticed lots of hair-fixing play in the classroom, so we scheduled a visit to a local beauty college. This turned out to be an excellent place for children to visit, since the college had numerous washing basins and work stations and many students eager to try out their skills. The students shampooed each child's hair and styled it with the blow-dryer. Once we were back in the classroom, children's role play soon incorporated these experiences.

• **As you prepare for a field trip, it's also important to talk with the people who are hosting you** about what children will be doing. Explain the children's need to actively experience the new setting, and plan specific ways to make this happen. For example, before visiting the local library with children in the Demonstration Preschool, we talked with the librarian about ways children could participate in the storytelling time. The librarian thoughtfully prepared action books, songs, flannelboard pieces,

An Outing Built on Children's Interests

One day as children snacked on yogurt at the High/Scope Demonstration Preschool, 3-year-old James said to another child, "You know, if this was frozen yogurt or ice cream, I would eat some." Several more children then joined in the conversation, eagerly sharing their views on the differences and similarities between yogurt and ice cream and the particular flavors that they wished we could have for snack. James's comment, together with the discussion it stirred up, was the seed for a successful field trip and a series of enriching follow-up activities. Here's how these activities developed and grew:

Noting children's lively interest in ice cream, we contacted a local ice cream store known for its homemade flavors and arranged a visit. As planned, we arrived 30 minutes before the store was open to the public. The store owners, who frequently hosted groups of young children, had planned a variety of hands-on activities for our group. After everyone had washed and dried their hands, children took turns stepping up on a milk crate to pour a cup of M & M's candies into the ice cream machine. While the machine was cranking the ice cream, we explored the walk-in refrigerator and freezer. Then everyone got a chance to help with lifting up the handle of the machine to let the ice cream flow into big, round containers, and we all took turns stirring the nearly finished ice cream with a huge spatula. These ice-cream-making activities took about 20 minutes, after which we all ate small cones of vanilla ice cream with M & M's.

To follow up on the field trip, the teachers planned a variety of activities for the next day. For planning time, they made ice-cream-cone cutouts and put the symbols for the interest areas on the scoops. By either coloring the appropriate area or putting a sticker on it, children indicated the areas they were planning to work in. We also planned a related small-group time around the following materials: homemade purple Play-Doh spiced with mint flavoring for an added smell experience, cone-shaped wooden spools (obtained from a local yarn shop), ice cream scoops, napkins, and paper ice-cream cups.

The next day we added the same materials to the house and art areas to support children's re-enactments at work time. Only a few minutes after work time began, we observed Julia "setting up shop" in the house area. A small table had become the ice cream counter, and Julia stood behind it, offering to sell ice cream to children on the other side: "Do you want a cup or a cone?" After several days we added notepads and paper to the house area, so large orders could be "written down." By this time the "store" had expanded its menu, and Julia was comfortable reeling off a variety of menu choices to her prospective customers: "Hot dogs, French fries, chili, or anything you want, really."

We also added a song to our circle time repertoire that recalled aspects of the field trip. Children suggested the words to the verses, each describing a remembered activity: washing their hands, stirring the ice cream, eating ice cream cones, walking around the flower beds outside the store, pushing buttons on the juke box.

As this example illustrates, field-trip ideas that start with children's expressed interests can lead to a range of active learning experiences.

A Simple Idea:
A Cemetery Visit

At a child care program operated for families of staff at a large medical center, the teachers often overheard children talking about health issues they'd heard their own family members discussing. These conversations sometimes touched on explanations of death and of where people went when they died.

When one child came to school with stories of the funeral of a close relative, teachers planned a field trip to a cemetery that was within walking distance of the school. As the year went on, this became a regular outing. Initially, children were fascinated with the different shapes and sizes of the tombstones, feeling them for smooth and rough places. Later, they wondered what the letters and numbers inscribed on the stones meant, and once, they discovered and talked about a freshly dug grave. During and after these trips, staff sometimes listened to children discuss their ideas about death and often referred children's questions to their peers. Some of the ideas they exchanged: "It's when you don't breathe anymore." "Your heart stops pumping blood." "Everybody cries and it's sad and then you eat a lot." As a result of these experiences, it seemed quite natural for children to openly discuss their feelings when they discovered a dead hamster in the center's cage one day.

and puppets. As a result, the stories came alive for children through their motions and language.

• **Finally, be prepared for the unexpected.** Take a backpack containing snack food, juice or water, a first-aid kit, and the children's information cards listing emergency phone numbers and insurance information. Also include a few small toys and books as options for children who may tire before others are ready to leave.

Once you've planned your field trip carefully, you're ready to reap the rewards of all your preparation. As you embark, however, **remember to keep an open mind, so you can respond to what individual children are seeing and learning.** If you avoid the pitfall of a predetermined agenda, you will broaden your opportunities to observe and record valuable anecdotes about each child's interests and developing abilities. For example, during our neighborhood walk, we noticed Audie using social and classification skills when he asked construction workers specific questions about the different types of equipment. We also observed that Mark was using physical and spatial abilities as he repeatedly climbed up, over, and down a huge pile of dirt.

Like other activities in High/Scope programs, field trips provide children with concrete experiences and opportunities for active involvement and are geared to children's interests and developmental levels. Well-planned field trips are also smoothly integrated with the rest of the program.

Thus, even though the children all go together to the same place, each child's experience is different. When adults are attuned to the many variations in children's responses, the field trip becomes a richer experience for both adults and children.

Primary-Grade
Field Trips That Work

By Diana Jo Johnston

• •

Like preschool field trips, those in elementary school provide direct, active experiences that enhance classroom learning. Here are some ideas:

All the Senses

It is important to plan field trips that involve children in touching, listening, feeling, smelling, manipulating, using language—in other words, learning in the most active way possible. **Restructure your outings to traditional destinations to allow for more direct experiences.** For example, field trips to view musical performances are common, but many children are unaccustomed to sitting still and listening to music. You can make such outings more active and developmentally appropriate (and avoid many discipline problems) by arranging for children to first become acquainted with the musicians and instruments. If children can come up to the stage before the performance, talk to individual musicians, touch and even try several instruments, and see how it feels to be on stage or in the orchestra pit, it adds to their enjoyment of the performance. If possible, let the children sit on stage as the musicians perform.

A nature walk is another example of a field trip that lends itself to direct sensory experience. Giving children a paper bag, so they can collect things to bring back, will make the experience even more concrete for children. In planning such activities, also **think about giving children opportunities to use their senses in new ways**—take them on a night walk in the mountains, for example, and focus on heightened opportunities for listening and smelling and for seeing things differently. Have children also take a day walk in the same location; once back in the classroom, encourage them to compare these experiences and to relate them to what they are learning in science and social studies.

Field Trip
Family Helpers

Parents

Parents are a necessary presence at most field trips. To use your parent volunteers in the best way possible, prepare them beforehand. Parents may think they are there only to supervise disputes and get children across the street safely. Instead, help them think of themselves as facilitators of what children are learning. Encourage parents to talk with children about what they are seeing and experiencing, to entertain and help children find answers to questions. Request that parents leave younger siblings with another caregiver, so they are free to focus on the older children.

Family "Insiders"

When older siblings, cousins, and other relatives have special knowledge about your field trip destination, involving them in the outing can often make the experience seem more concrete to young children and thereby add to their interest. If a student's relative works at the police station, it may be better for the group to talk with that person rather than with the regular guide. Such family "insiders" often share behind-the-scenes information and can provide access to experiences that make a topic more exciting. The fact that your guide has close ties to someone in the group will help all the children connect what they are learning to their own lives.

Behind the Scenes

Understanding how something works often means taking it apart and putting it back together. Similarly, field trips that help children mentally assemble a process or attraction are often the most engaging. For example, instead of just viewing the exhibits in a museum, ask for a tour behind the scenes, so you can see how the artifacts and bones are sorted, cleaned, and labeled; how the miniature people, animals, and grasses for the dioramas are made; how exhibits are repaired or updated. Similarly, at a puppet show, ask the puppeteers to take children behind the stage afterwards to show them how the puppets are made and operated.

Last Things First

Teachers often plan a field trip as the culmination of several weeks' study of a particular topic. For example, at the end of a unit on slavery and the Civil War, a class might visit some local buildings that were once on the Underground Railroad. What sometimes happens with such outings, however, is that the topic doesn't become understandable and exciting to children until *after* the field trip. Then, children are excited and primed to learn more—but the class is scheduled to start another unit. If this has been your experience, next time, turn it around: Do the trip first, then follow the outing with related classroom activities. For most young children, starting with a concrete, direct experience (the field trip) and then moving to more abstract activities such as writing, reading, or discussion will result in a deeper understanding of the topic.

Chapter Seven

Child Observation, Team Planning, Assessment

*I*n the High/Scope approach, the teamwork process is built around *observation of children's behaviors. While interacting with children throughout the day, staff of child care and preschool programs observe and jot down anecdotal notes on the developmentally significant behaviors that occur. The teaching or care-giving team meets daily to discuss these observations, which are then used in developing strategies for working with individual children and in planning for the next day's activities. The daily anecdotal notes that staff record also become part of a collection of* information that is used at regular intervals to complete High/Scope's child assessment instrument, the High/Scope Child Observation Record (COR) for Ages 2½ to 6. The results of COR assessment are used in making further plans for individual children and for the program as a whole. The results are also useful for describing children's progress to parents and other audiences.

This chapter's articles deal with the team process of child observation, documentation, planning, and communication. The first article, a panel discussion involving present and past High/Scope Demonstration Preschool teachers, deals with building a new teaching team. Early childhood teams change membership frequently, and the insights shared by the panel should be helpful to early childhood programs that are launching a new teaching team or simply getting started for another year's session. As the panel participants point out, open communication is an essential ingredient of the team-building process. In the second article, "Saying What You Mean," Mary Hohmann offers hints for recognizing barriers to team communication and guidelines for promoting an open exchange of ideas.

In the next article, "An Effective Tool for Developmentally Appropriate Assessment," Lawrence J. Schweinhart discusses the need for a developmentally appropriate observational assessment measure such as the COR and briefly explains how the COR is used. In the succeeding article, "Saving Time With the COR–PC or the COR–Mac," Charles Hohmann introduces the two computer versions of the COR.

The next selection, "Anecdotes: Focusing in on Children," explores the anecdotal note-taking process that is the basis for COR assessment and daily team planning in programs using the High/Scope approach. Beth Marshall discusses how to take anecdotal notes on children's developmentally important behaviors and explains why such notes are a powerful teaching tool. In a follow-up article, "Anecdote-Writing Hints," Marshall gives several practical suggestions for efficient note-taking.

The chapter's last article, "Rethinking the IEP Process," discusses the use of COR assessment in programs serving children with special needs. Sandy Slack explains that assessment with the COR can help special educators who are moving away from directive teaching practices, because it offers assessment procedures compatible with new curriculum approaches.

Building a Teaching Team

By Sam Hannibal, Michelle Graves, Carol Beardmore,
Barbara Carmody, and Mary Hohmann

. . . .

Creating cohesive teaching teams when new staff join the agency is a common issue in most early childhood programs. New staff assignments are particularly frequent in the fall, when many programs begin a new session.

In the following panel discussion, the authors of this article (all past or present High/Scope Demonstration Preschool teachers) discuss issues that arise when a new person joins the early childhood team and suggest ways to strengthen teamwork during such transitions.

Sam: The issues of adding a new team member are particularly relevant to us at the Demonstration Preschool because Carol Beardmore has recently joined Michelle Graves on the teaching team. (Carol previously worked in the High/Scope Research Department.) Carol and Michelle, could you share some of the things you've done to come together as an effective team at the start of a new school year?

Michelle: Carol started just before school opened this fall. At the time, we didn't know each other at all, and the first day of the session was just a few days away. So we jumped right in, focusing one by one on the things that had to be ready for the children. To get to know each other better, we did each job as a team, even though there were some tasks that one person might have done more efficiently by herself. For example, we went through the classroom, area by area, talking about what materials were there now, what should stay and what should go, and what new things we could add. As we looked at each area, we kept our focus on the children who were coming. I shared some of the things I knew about the children and about the materials they liked to use, and Carol told me what materials had worked well with children in her other teaching experiences. We went about organizing the materials, making the labels, and planning the details of the daily routine in much the same way. As we went along, we also ended up sharing personal information as well.

Sam: So, talking about your personal lives was important.

Michelle: Yes, but the primary focus was on the children and the job to be done. There was a mutual feeling that all these things had to be done and that we could do them together.

Another thing that was important was to keep each other upbeat. A new school session always brings unexpected problems. For example, this year, we had more children than we have had in the past. Our attitude was "Okay, what are we going to do to make this work?" This process of taking concrete problems and finding solutions one by one is what bonds you together as a team.

Sam: Carol, implementing the High/Scope approach is a new experience for you. Was this difficult? How did you prepare yourself?

Carol: Before I came to High/Scope, I had nine years' experience teaching in a similar approach, but I hadn't actually implemented the High/Scope Curriculum. Since joining the Foundation staff, however, I've become more familiar with the High/Scope approach. When I accepted this teaching position, I did more reading and watched videotapes about the Curriculum. So, when I arrived in the classroom the first morning, I had a sense of some things that had to be ready, and I started making lists on my own.

Michelle: When I came to the classroom that first day and found Carol already making lists, I knew we would work well as a team.

Sam: I think one of the things Carol's experience suggests is that a teacher who is new to the curriculum needs some additional training. Yet, it's just not realistic to expect the co-teacher to take on the full responsibility of training a new staff member in addition to all the other things she or he must do to carry on the program. It helps if a newcomer like Carol is willing to do outside reading, watch curriculum videos, and attend training workshops. And it's the job of the program administrator to make provisions for the new staff members to participate in ongoing curriculum training sessions.

Michelle, Barbara: Yes.

Sam: Yet, even though the more experienced member of the team shouldn't have to see herself as *the* trainer for a new team member, the senior team member still has important information and teaching strategies to share with her teammate. What are some ways she or he can do this?

Michelle: I see this as a two-way exchange. Instead of simply telling the new staff member "We handle discipline this way. . .," I might start by asking "How was discipline handled in the last program you worked in?" Then I would share what we do here.

Make a List!

A basic aspect of teamwork is first analyzing all the big jobs that have to get done in the program and then breaking each of them down into a list of smaller tasks to be done daily, weekly, monthly, and so on. Then team members decide who will do each smaller job and when. For example, if the job is preparing for field trips, the subtasks might be the following:

- Planning arrival and departure times

- Contacting your hosts to plan activities at the site

- Arranging transportation

- Preparing things to take

- Contacting families and keeping track of which family members are coming

- Arranging children's meals or refreshments

Below are two lists of the *big jobs* involved in typical teamwork situations—jobs to do before the session starts, and jobs to do throughout the session. How would you break these tasks into *smaller tasks* to make them more manageable for the team?

Before the session:	Throughout the session:
Arrange the classroom for the new session.	Act on issues that arise daily in the classroom.
Finalize the daily routine.	Refresh, replenish, and replace materials in the interest areas.
Group the children for small-group activities, planning time, and recall time.	Add or eliminate interest areas.
Make sure that information forms on each family are complete.	Record and compile information on each child.
Set up a system for documenting child observations.	Communicate with parents about their children.
Organize and schedule the first parent-teacher conferences.	Get the room ready for children daily.
Get outdoor play equipment ready.	Order supplies and equipment.
Prepare name-tag symbols.	Care for pets, plants, etc.
Plan for field trips.	

Doing teaching tasks together that are ordinarily done separately is another way for team members to communicate about their teaching practices. In the first two days of the year, for example, we decided to do planning and recall times together in one group instead of breaking into two small groups. This worked well, because the number of children was small (we had one half of the group come in on the first day, and the other half on the second day). Because Carol and I were teaching side by side at these times, we

Doing teaching tasks together that are ordinarily done separately, as in leading this group movement activity, is another way for team members to communicate about their teaching practices.

could observe and support each other. After the first two days, we formed separate small groups, as is usual for planning and recall.

Barbara: It's important that Michelle is stressing having an *exchange of ideas*, rather than one person being the expert. Experienced teachers can become territorial about "their" classrooms and "their" ways of doing things—there is sometimes an unwillingness to change things when a new person comes in. One of the keys to forming a successful team, however, is to recognize that any new team member brings in new strengths and ideas. Most new team members have had valuable experiences with children and can share these with the team. The new person's personal interests and talents—for example, in gardening or woodworking—are another important resource for the program. It's up to the rest of the team to take advantage of these strengths.

Sam: Each team member needs to have an equal voice on the team, even though one teacher may have greater administrative responsibilities. Regardless of their official titles, teaching team members in High/Scope programs are co-teachers: They share all the major teaching tasks on an equal basis. This means all team members conduct planning and review times with children, interact with children at work time, lead group activities, document child observations, participate in team planning, talk to parents, and so forth.

Mary: To me, this is important not just because it is the High/Scope philosophy—it's a matter of basic survival. When you're faced with the

How Can I Encourage Co-teaching?

In High/Scope classrooms, teammates are expected to function as co-teachers, but I've found that some teacher-aides are reluctant to take an equal role in making decisions and interacting with children. The aide may prefer to take a supportive role: doing housekeeping chores, passing out materials, taking children to the bathroom, etc. How can I encourage my teacher-aides to take on more responsibility for teaching?
—A head teacher in a Head Start program

To help your aide function effectively as a co-teacher, start by building this expectation into your hiring process. Explain to candidates that professional development is part of the job, and choose an aide who is willing to function as a co-teacher.

You'll also need administrative support for this policy. Ask the administrator to arrange training experiences for the aide, and if possible, find a way to give the aide appropriate degree credit or certification for the development of teaching skills on the job. The administrator should also arrange for the aide to participate in team planning sessions and to be paid for the time this requires.

In the classroom, model appropriate teaching practices, and help the aide take on more responsibility gradually. For example, to help the aide lead a small-group time, the two of you could prepare together an outline of the small-group session, discussing what might happen in each part of small-group time. On an interim basis, you might also try doing planning, recall time, or small-group time in large groups, so both of you can teach side-by-side until the aide becomes comfortable interacting in a teaching role.

daily issues involved in managing a classroom full of children, you and your teammate have to share the teaching responsibilities equally. Even if your titles are "aide" and "head teacher," the children won't understand this distinction; they will expect all the adults to support them and interact with them. If one person is always "in charge," the other team member will hold back and won't work effectively with the children.

Sam: Once the new team is established, what are some things to keep in mind to keep the team functioning well?

Barbara: Again, keep the focus on the children, rather than on the adults.

Michelle: Yes, and the other thing to remember is to *communicate, communicate, communicate.* You have to be open enough with each other to face issues directly. For example, maybe you're uncomfortable because you feel as if you're taking the major responsibility for dealing with parents' concerns. You have to tell your team member what's bothering you, and then, together, you can discuss what to do about the problem.

Each team member needs to have an equal voice on the team, even though one teacher may have greater administrative responsibilities. Regardless of their official titles, teaching team members in High/Scope programs are co-teachers. They share all the major teaching tasks on an equal basis.

People also have to be open about things they really don't want to do. Last year, my co-teacher wanted to add hermit crabs to the classroom, but I told her I really didn't want to have anything to do with those animals. She was interested enough to volunteer to take care of them on her own. It's okay to acknowledge people's strengths and let them do what they enjoy.

Carol: It's also important to be flexible and willing to help out. If one person has car trouble and is late coming in, the other person should be willing to take over her before-school tasks. Because there will always be unexpected events, no plan should be followed rigidly. Sometimes the roles you've planned need to be switched at a moment's notice to respond to what is going on in the classroom. If it's one teacher's turn to start large-group time, but she is busy with a parent, the other teacher should keep the ball rolling.

Sam: The things to remember when building a new team are the same fundamentals that are important in ongoing teamwork: breaking large tasks into smaller tasks; sharing responsibilities equally; keeping the focus on the children and the curriculum; taking advantage of each team-member's strengths; being flexible, supportive, and open to change; and above all, communicating regularly. And of course, **daily planning sessions are a necessity** to make all this happen.

Michelle, Barbara, Mary: Yes, absolutely!

Saying
What You Mean

By Mary Hohmann and David P. Weikart

• •

Effective teamwork depends on open communication. But an honest exchange of ideas is not always easy to achieve. Psychologist Virginia Satir (1988) has identified four crippling patterns of communication that often hamper the productiveness of working teams:

• **Placating:** "No matter what I think or feel, I'll agree with whatever she wants."

• **Blaming:** "I'll find fault with her idea, so she'll know that I'm not someone she can push around."

• **Computing:** "I'll use a lot of jargon, so she'll really be impressed by how much I know."

• **Distracting:** "I'll change the subject, so we don't have to deal with this uncomfortable issue."

The alternative to these negative communication patterns is what Satir calls *leveling:* saying what you mean. In a team situation, leveling means openly and specifically identifying issues of concern and discussing how to deal with them.

Let's look at how these common patterns of communication might come into play in a typical team session:

Teaching team members Shawna, Melany, and Sue are planning to make pancakes with the children tomorrow. Shawna is concerned that the pancake activity won't include the **ingredients of active learning (choice, materials, manipulation, child language, adult support).** Here are four different ways Shawna might communicate her concerns:

• **Placating:** "I'm really sorry to ask such a dumb question. Promise you won't get mad at me. Making pancakes with kids is great. They each get a chance to stir the batter. Maybe I don't understand. Is this active learning?"

- **Blaming:** "What's the matter with you? Don't you remember anything about active learning? You've missed the boat with this pancake activity."

- **Computing:** "The ingredients of active learning should provide the parameters of any developmentally appropriate process we engage in with preoperational children."

- **Distracting:** "Pancakes. Grandad used to make them at our house. I'll look in the kitchen to see if we have everything we need. [Calls from the kitchen.] We're out of juice and napkins. I'll stop at the store on my way home."

Though Shawna could choose to avoid communication in one of the above ways, she instead decides to level with her teammates. She gets right to the point: "So far the only action we have children doing is stirring the pancake batter. How can we give them materials to manipulate, choices to make, and opportunities to talk about what they are doing?"

Shawna's willingness to take a risk and share her concerns leads to a discussion in which team members pool their individual strengths to solve the problem. Sue is an experienced cook, Melany is an engaging storyteller, and Shawna is well-versed in the ingredients of active learning. Together they come up with a sure-fire plan for the activity that includes an easy pancake recipe; materials and ingredients, so each child can make and fry his or her own batter; and plans for the group to eat the pancakes and listen to an Indian folk tale about runaway batter. Thus, Shawna's decision to communicate honestly becomes the catalyst for creative problem solving.

This article is adapted from High/Scope's preschool manual entitled *Educating Young Children: Active Learning Practices for Preschool and Child Care Providers,* by Mary Hohmann and David P. Weikart, Ypsilanti, MI: High/Scope Press, 1995.

For more information on the patterns of communication identified by Virginia Satir, see Satir's book *The New People Making,* Mountain View, CA: Science and Behavior Books, 1988.

An Effective Tool for Developmentally Appropriate Assessment

By Lawrence J. Schweinhart

· ·

In the early 1990s, after two years of development and field testing, a new assessment tool—the High/Scope Child Observation Record (COR) for Ages 2½–6—became available for widespread use by staff of early childhood programs. The tool is suitable for use in preschools, child care programs, home-based programs, Head Start programs, and programs for children with special needs. This article describes the COR and explains its usefulness.

Early versions of the High/Scope COR had been developed in the 1980s by Foundation staff, but the COR at that time was aimed specifically at programs using the High/Scope Curriculum. The current instrument stands out from its predecessors because it can be used to meet assessment needs in *any* developmentally appropriate program of early childhood care or education.

The current COR and accompanying materials were developed by High/Scope researchers in a project funded by the U.S. Department of Health and Human Services. In the COR study, 64 teams of Head Start teachers in the Detroit metropolitan area field-tested the materials. (About 40 percent of the teachers and aides in the COR study were familiar with some aspects of the High/Scope Curriculum.)

The field test provided research staff with many insights on the practicality and usefulness of the instrument in actual early childhood programs. The aim of the COR study was to develop an assessment system that teaching staff could comfortably use, providing they had administrative support and training in the use of the instrument.

The Need for Observational Measures of Child Development

The COR provides an alternative to test-based systems of assessment. It is an *observational* instrument, designed to be used by early childhood program staff—teachers, aides, caregivers, administrators—during regular program activities. Staff complete the COR by using observations they have gathered during the normal activities of preschool and child care programs—as children are playing, building, exploring, pretending, drawing, moving to music, planning, solving problems, conversing, negotiating, and making friends.

Because of the urgent need that so many early childhood programs have for such a meaningful assessment tool, High/Scope decided to tailor the current version of the COR to a broad spectrum of programs. Good measures of child development can be helpful in many ways in early childhood programs: They can help teachers, caregivers, and administrators monitor each child's developmental progress, pinpoint the strengths and weaknesses of the program, and communicate effectively with parents and other important decision-makers about children's attainments. If assessment is a program requirement (as it is in many Head Start and public school early childhood programs), good assessment tools are a necessity.

It is important that an observational instrument be widely available to early childhood educators. Dissatisfied with the test-based assessment systems that have long been available, teachers and caregivers find that such systems assess narrow, selected skills rather than the broad range of cognitive, social-emotional, and physical abilities that are the focus of developmentally appropriate programs. For example, many tests measure children's performance on specific mathematical or logical tasks, but few measure children's creative representation, planning, initiative, and social problem-solving—which are aspects of growth that developmentally oriented educators consider to be crucial for young children. The mismatch between some tests of development and the curriculum goals most educators consider important can make assessment seem like busywork to the hard-pressed teacher or caregiver.

Do Children Have to "Fit" the COR Sequence?

I've noticed that some children don't always do things in the developmental sequences given on the COR. For example, the other day, I noticed that Jenny could use some distance words like *closer* and *farther away* correctly (COR item—Describing spatial relations, Level 5), but she still often mixes up some of her position words like *behind* and *in front of* (Describing spatial relations, Level 3). How would I score Jenny on this COR item?
—*A Head Start teacher*

The COR items are intended to describe general patterns of child development, but these are not lock-step sequences—there will always be individual children who do not do things in the expected sequence. If a child apparently reaches a higher level on a COR item without attaining one or more intermediate steps, do not give the child the higher score until he has achieved all the intermediate steps. Score Jenny at Level 3, but use the note space provided below the item to comment that you did observe Jenny doing a Level-5 activity. No assessment measure can ever provide a complete picture of a child's abilities—that's why the extra note space is provided. Also, teachers using the High/Scope Curriculum generally collect much more information on individual children's development than is recorded on the COR.

Another problem with most tests is that testing itself may be intrinsically inappropriate for young children. Testing procedures usually require that children be taken out of normal program activities to perform a set of standardized tasks. For many children this is a totally foreign situation, and they often react by freezing up or acting up.

Because of these and other problems with the use of formal tests in early childhood programs, the National Association for the Education of Young Children (NAEYC) and the National Association of Early Childhood Specialists in State Departments of Education have issued guidelines recommending observational assessment over artificial test procedures that disrupt children's activities. The guidelines, published in the March 1991 issue of *Young Children*, state that teachers should be the primary assessors of children and that assessment should be based on observation of children, anecdotal records of children's performance, and work samples.

The High/Scope COR and its accompanying materials aim to provide such a broad-based, observational assessment system. COR evaluation relies on real-life data rather than on performance on narrow, "set-up" tasks. Unlike a narrowly focused, one-shot test-procedure, the COR summarizes observations made over the course of several months during a wide range of activities. This offers a well-rounded and accurate picture of children's abilities.

The COR assesses child development in six broad areas: *initiative, social relations, creative representation, music and movement, language and literacy, logic and mathematics*. Teachers and caregivers take daily anecdotal notes on children's progress in these key areas, making notes on a few children each day. When it comes time to score the COR, program staff

Sample COR Items

In each of these sample items from the High/Scope COR, there are five levels of behavior. Based on their anecdotal notes and other documentation of children's behavior, adults decide which level of behavior is most characteristic of the child.

From the *Initiative* Section:

B. Solving Problems

1. Child does not yet identify problems.

2. Child identifies problems, but does not try to solve them, turning instead to another activity.

3. Child uses one method to try to solve a problem, but if unsuccessful, gives up after one or two tries.

4. Child shows some persistence, trying several alternative methods to solve a problem.

5. Child tries alternative methods to solve a problem and is highly involved and persistent.

From the *Language and Literacy* Section:

S. Showing interest in reading activities

1. Child does not yet show interest in reading activities.

2. Child shows interest when stories are read.

3. Child asks people to read stories, signs, or notes.

4. Child answers questions about a story that has been read or repeats part of the story.

5. Child often reads a book or tells the story while turning the pages.

Observer's name: SHARON SMITH

Child's name: LA TANYA PHILLIPS

High/Scope
Child Observation
Record (COR) for
Ages 2½ – 6

Music and Movement	Language and Literacy	Logic and Mathematics
(9/16) HOPS ON ONE FOOT, SKIPS, JUMPS FROM SMALL PLATFORM, BOUNCES BALL DURING GYM	(9/16) TELLS ABOUT LAST NIGHT'S OUTING: "LAST NIGHT I WENT TO MC DONALD'S AND I GOT A HAPPY MEAL AND I GOT A TOY"	(9/16) HELPS SORT BOTTLE CAPS, CORKS, AND BUTTONS INTO CANISTERS AT CLEAN-UP TIME
(10/2) CUTS PAPER W/SCISSORS W/OUT HELP	(10/2) CHOOSES BOOK AND TURNS PAGES; LOOKS AT EACH PAGE	(10/2) TELLS MEGAN AT SNACK TIME THAT THE APPLES ARE RIGHT IN FRONT OF HER
(11/4) MANIPULATES SMALL PUZZLE PIECES WITH THUMB AND FOREFINGER	(10/17) LOOKS AT BOOKS WITH ME, POINTS TO SOME PICTURES, NAMES THEM	(10/17) SAYS, "FROGS ARE GREEN"
(11/17) WRITES WITH PENCIL, ROLLS PLAYDOH INTO TINY BALLS	(11/4) SAYS, "I WANT TO PLAY IN THE BLOCK AREA AND MAKE A TRAIN STATION"	(11/4) WHEN I ASK IF THERE ARE ENOUGH MARKERS FOR SIX KIDS, LA TANYA COUNTS THEM CORRECTLY, TOUCHING EACH AS SHE DOES SO
(12/6) DANCES TO A STEADY BEAT AT GROUP TIME	(11/18) WRITES THE "L" IN LA TANYA	(12/6) L-TELLS A SHORT STORY AND SAYS, "NEXT TIME I'LL TELL A LONGER STORY"
	(12/6) READS "K MART" FROM NEWSPAPER; RECOGNIZES "THE END" IN A STORY	

Program staff may use the COR Anecdotal Notecard to record observational notes used for team planning and COR assessment. In addition to the three categories on this side of the card, there are three more on the reverse side—initiative, social relations, and creative expression.

decide how to score each item by referring to their anecdotal notes, children's work samples, and other documentation.

The COR contains 30 items, each representing a key dimension of child development. Within each item are five levels of behavior, representing a sequence of developmental progress for that item. Teachers choose the level of behavior that best characterizes the child. (See sample items, p. 279.)

The COR and the High/Scope Curriculum

How does the COR—an instrument that can be used with a wide range of curricula—fit within High/Scope Curriculum programs? Readers who are already using High/Scope Curriculum procedures know that in the High/Scope approach, carefully observing children's activities and taking daily anecdotal notes are central to planning and teaching throughout the program year. Thus the COR assessment process can be viewed as a natural extension of the observation and note-taking that many adults in High/Scope programs are already doing.

Finding efficient ways to take accurate daily notes on children's development is one of the critical parts of this observation/planning/assessment process. During training workshops for the COR, teachers

Staff of High/Scope programs may prefer to use the Key Experience Note Form to record daily anecdotal notes. To see how the High/Scope key experiences relate to the COR child development categories, copy the notes from the sample COR Notecard on the previous page onto this form, classifying them by key experience category.

learn how to capture the most important aspects of their observations in brief, objective notes. We recommend that program staff record their daily notes on **COR Anecdotal Notecards** or **High/Scope Key Experience Note Forms** (see the samples on p. 280 and above).

The COR Anecdotal Notecards were developed during the COR field tests with Head Start teachers. Staff of High/Scope Curriculum programs, who are used to interpreting their observations in terms of the High/Scope key experiences, may prefer to use the Key Experience Note Form to record the notes they will later use in scoring the COR. This form is divided into nine key experience categories (instead of the six categories shown on the COR form). These two forms represent different ways of organizing similar developmental information. The major difference between the COR categories and the key experience categories is that on the Key Experience Note Form, the COR category *Logic and Mathematics* is broken into five categories—*Classification, Seriation, Number, Space,* and *Time*. Another difference is that on the Key Experience Note Form, the COR *Social Relations* and *Initiative* categories are consolidated.

High/Scope Child Observation Record for Ages 2½–6: Available Materials

COR Assessment Booklet—The COR form; sold in sets of 25

COR *Manual*—Detailed instructions for COR assessment; report on COR validation study

COR Anecdotal Notecards—Cards for recording notes on children's developmental progress; sold in sets of 25

COR Poster—A wall chart to be hung in the classroom or center

COR Parent Report Form—Form to be used in reporting on children's abilities to parents; Spanish-language version also available

COR Kit—Everything needed for COR evaluation of a group of 25 children over one school year: 25 Assessment Booklets, COR *Manual,* 4 sets COR Anecdotal Notecards, 50 Parent Report Forms, Poster

COR–PC or COR–Mac Kit—Contents similar to the regular COR Kit except that features corresponding to the COR Assessment Booklet (the COR instrument) and Parent Report Forms are included in a software program (see next article).

The above materials are all available from the High/Scope Press, 600 N. River Street, Ypsilanti, MI 48198-2898. Phone 800-40-PRESS, FAX 800-442-4FAX. To sign up for a COR training workshop, contact the Training Coordinator at the address above or phone 313/485-2000; FAX 313/485-0704.

Though some form of anecdotal note-taking is a necessity for those conducting COR assessment, program staff are not bound to either of the two forms we've discussed here. They may devise any system for documenting observations that works well for them. More important than the particular observation system that is chosen are the *responsive planning and teaching* that result from careful observation of children and from daily discussion of these observations by the teaching team.

As early childhood providers try out the COR, we are eager to hear about *their* experiences. Serving children more effectively, of course, should be the ultimate goal of any assessment system. We hope you'll let us know how the COR contributes to this goal for you.

Saving Time With the COR–PC or the COR–Mac

By Charles Hohmann

• •

Classroom adults in early childhood pro-grams can document children's actions in many ways: Anecdotal notes are the primary means, but snapshots of children's creations, samples of children's "writing" and artwork, tape recordings, and so forth, can also yield useful information. These authentic forms of documentation are excellent sources of information on children's developmental progress. And such observational records—unlike traditional, test-based systems of assessment—complement children's learning experiences and support appropriate teaching methods.

But anecdotal note-taking and other such methods of gathering information on children's learning have one disadvantage: They can yield mountains of data that may be difficult and time-consuming for educators to summarize, interpret, and communicate to others.

For some years now, the *High/Scope COR for Ages 2½ to 6* has offered a solution to this problem. **The COR is an observational system of child assessment that teachers can use to organize and interpret data they have collected on children's everyday actions and language.** The anecdotal note-taking process described on pp. 279–282 is a necessity for classroom adults using the COR, but once they are comfortable with note-taking, they can conduct COR assessment with just a little additional effort. Now, computer versions of the COR—the **COR–PC**

Planning With the COR–PC

At the High/Scope Demonstration Preschool, teachers have streamlined the process of collecting and recording anecdotal notes by using the COR–PC software in their daily planning sessions.

The process goes like this: Teachers plan in the classroom computer center after children have left for the day. With one teacher sitting at a computer, they discuss each segment of the daily routine, recording and discussing anecdotes as they go along.

For example, as they are discussing planning time, they first talk about how planning went in that day's session, using the COR–PC to enter and score any anecdotes they have on children's actions at planning. After typing in this information on the computer, they discuss strategies for the next day's planning time. Then they go through the same process for work time and the other segments of the daily routine.

Note: COR training, available through High/Scope, is necessary for effective use of the COR–PC, COR–Mac, and other versions of the COR.

for DOS/Windows machines and the **COR–Mac**—are available to make the COR assessment process even more efficient and useful.

High/Scope's COR assessment system provides standardized measures and procedures for collecting, organizing, and scoring observations of children and their work. The COR—in both print and software versions— produces profiles of children's developmental progress in six key areas: **creative representation, language and literacy, initiative, social relations, music and movement, logic and mathematics.**

The computer versions of the COR simplify the labor of collecting, sorting, and rating child observation data. The teacher uses the COR software to type in anecdotes, then assigns COR categories and developmental levels to each anecdote with a few clicks of the mouse. All anecdotes are kept on-line and can be easily reviewed. The software automatically tallies the anecdotes in each category for each child, helping to prevent any child from being overlooked. In addition, the teacher can use the COR software to generate, in seconds, profiles of individual children's developmental progress and narrative parent reports. The software can also provide summaries and profiles for the developmental progress of the class as a whole. And, for teachers in larger centers, the software can accommodate multiple classes and allow records to be easily moved from one class to another.

The COR–PC runs on IBM and compatible computers with a hard disk, 640K of RAM, DOS 3.3 or above, and a black-and-white or color monitor. The COR–Mac runs on color Macintosh computers with a hard disk, 2MB RAM (System 6.0.8) or 4MB RAM (System 7). The Macintosh version of the program, in addition to having all the same useful features as the COR–PC, provides improved print output, scoring shortcuts (for oft-repeated observations and familiar COR items), and audio recording of anecdotes.

Anecdotes:
Focusing in on Children

By Beth Marshall

• •

It's the beginning of work time, and preschoolers Alex, Donald, Kayla, and Frances are working at the sand table, now filled with dried beans. Holding up a cup filled with beans, Donald says, "There's rocks in here. This is my coffee." Alex fills a scoop with beans, some of which have been painted red or blue. "Magic beans," he says, picking out the blue-painted beans and setting them aside. Leaving the bean table, Donald goes to the toy area, and brings back a large rubber dinosaur. "T-Rex eats rocks," he explains, putting the beans in the dino-saur's open mouth and making munching sounds: "Myum, myum, myum."

Kayla and Frances fill and empty containers of various sizes with beans. While doing so, they talk intently about the kinds of cereal they like to eat: "I like that kind with the holes in it," Kayla says. "Cheerios?" Frances asks. "No, not Cheerios, it's different holes," Kayla replies.

Nearby, Megan is painting at the easel. She covers her paper with layer upon layer of different-colored paints, covering the whole paper with one color, then an-other. When she's finished, she takes her paper off the easel, hangs it on the drying rack, and then hangs up her smock.

Meanwhile, Daniel picks up a cowbell in the music and movement area. Striking it with a mallet, he giggles. In the same area, Steven picks up a small xylophone and makes a cascade of sound by running a mallet over the bars. Then Daniel and Steven, still playing their instruments, begin marching around the room. Seeing them, Mark picks up a tambourine, Victor grabs a set of bells, and both join the line of marchers. The band marches through the block area, snakes through the house area, and circles back around the toy area, where the marchers carefully step over Carleen and Saraya, who are lying on the floor, putting pegs into pegboards. Counting "1, 2, 3, 4, 5, 6, 7, 8, 9, 10," Carleen points at a differ-ent pegless hole as she says each number. Saraya lies next to her and makes a tower out of pegs (the pegs are the stacking kind). Neither girl gives the marchers more than a brief look.

At a glance, you might sum up this scene as "just another work time." However, we invite you to take a closer look—with the aid of an in-

Writing anecdotes may take some practice. Why go to all this trouble? Because teachers who try this system become firm believers in it. They report that the process of writing and using anecdotes yields a wealth of information on their children, their classrooms, and their teaching practices.

formation-gathering system used by many experienced High/Scope teachers. Like these teachers, you can bring the world of children into sharper focus by discovering the power of **anecdotes.**

In High/Scope programs, anecdotes—short written records of classroom incidents—are written every day by teaching adults. Rather than set aside a specific time to observe children (an impossible or impractical task in a busy early childhood setting), adults integrate note-taking into their normal teaching activities and record anecdotes throughout the daily routine. For example, an adult might pause to jot down a quick anecdote while pretending to eat birthday cake with children in the house area or just after kicking the ball with children outdoors.

If you are new to writing anecdotes, here are some basic guidelines. First, begin your anecdote with some background information to set the scene. For example, most anecdotes start with the date, the time, and the place of the incident, and the names of children involved. The opening of an anecdote about Donald's activities at the bean table might, for example, read something like this: *10-23, Work time at the bean table, Donald. . . .*

For the middle of your anecdote, jot down brief, specific, factual information about what the child did or said (if possible, write down the child's actual words enclosed in quotation marks). Adding to Donald's anecdote, then, we now have this: *10-23, Work time at the bean table, Donald filled a cup with beans and said, "There's rocks in here. This is my coffee."* Note that this anecdote now tells us not only what Donald *did* but also what he *said.*

Finally, to complete your anecdote, consider whether the incident has an ending, or an outcome. For example, if Sherry tries several different ways to get her block tower to stand up and is finally successful, it is important for the adult to record that outcome. In the anecdote about Donald, however, there really wasn't an outcome to his activities, so the anecdote is complete as originally written. We could, however, make our task easier by using abbreviations to stand for some of the words. *Work time* then becomes *WT, bean table* becomes *BT.* The result is a shortened anecdote: *10-23, WT at BT, D filled cup w/beans, said, "There's rocks in here. This is my coffee."* Of course, you may prefer to use another system of abbreviating; teaching teams can work together to come up with their own High/Scope shorthand! (For additional examples of anecdotes written about the children in our opening scenario, and for some High/Scope shorthand ideas, see "Sample Anecdotes.")

Writing anecdotes like these is a precise process that may take some practice. Why go to all this trouble? Because teachers who try this system become firm believers in it. They report that the process of writing and using anecdotes yields a wealth of information on their children, their classrooms, and their teaching practices. Following are some of the ways anecdotes are useful for adults working with young children:

• Anecdotes can help us identify **key experiences** and thus document the learning that is taking place in our classrooms. (For those who are unfamiliar with them, the High/Scope key experiences identify developmentally important behaviors in key areas of growth and learning.) As Donald and Alex worked with the beans, for example, they were pretending, which is a key experience in the *representation* category. As

---

Sample Anecdotes

Here's how teachers used anecdotal notes to record the incidents in the opening scenario on page 285:

10-16 WT at BT, Donald filled a cup with beans and said, "There's rocks in here. This is my coffee."

10-26 WT at BT, Alex picked out the blue beans from the white and red beans and said "Magic beans."

10-26 WT at BT, Donald put beans into the large dino's mouth and said, "T-Rex eats rocks. Myum, myum, myum."

10-26 WT at BT, Kayla talked with Frances about cereal. Said, "I like that kind with the holes in it" and "No, not Cheerios, it's different holes."

10-26 WT at easel, Megan covered her paper with layers of paint, first painting the whole page blue, then red, then brown.

10-26 WT Daniel and Steven played instruments and marched around the room. Mark and Victor joined in and they continued playing and marching for about 10 minutes.

10-26 WT, TA Carleen put pegs in the pegboard and then counted holes with no pegs in them: "1, 2, 3, 4, 5, 6, 7, 8, 9, 10."

Using Anecdotes
With Parents

Teachers who write anecdotes regularly in their classrooms find that the practice helps to strengthen **teacher-parent relationships**. When sharing information with parents about their child's day, the teacher can often use anecdotes as a springboard for conversation.

Parents are often eager to hear specifics about how their child's day was spent, and teachers have this information at their fingertips when they have been collecting anecdotes regularly. Because Kayla's teacher, Carol, had recorded an anecdote on Kayla's conversation with Frances about cereal (see "Sample Anecdotes"), Carol was able to recall this incident when she talked with Kayla's mother at the end of preschool. For Kayla's mother, this was far more informative than a vague "She had a good day" would have been.

When teachers are in the habit of sharing such anecdotes with parents, parents often reciprocate by sharing stories about what the child has done at home. When discussing the cereal incident with Kayla's mother, Carol found out the name of the favorite cereal Kayla had probably been talking about. Kayla's mother agreed to save the box for this cereal when it was empty, so it could be added to the house area in the preschool.

Kayla and Frances discussed their favorite cereals, they were talking about personally meaningful experiences *(language and literacy)*. When Alex picked out the blue beans, he was sorting *(classification)*. By making adults aware of the key experiences children are engaging in, anecdotes strengthen the classroom adult's understanding of both **child development** and **the educational philosophy of the High/Scope approach**. Watching and documenting Megan's painting activities *(representation)* reinforced her teachers' knowledge of the developmental stages of painting. In reviewing Megan's anecdote, they reaffirmed their belief that children first need to explore the paint before they are ready to paint representations of objects. They realized that Megan's explorations with paint were just as significant for her as painting detailed representations might be for another child.

• Focusing in this way on what children are specifically doing inevitably helps classroom adults become more **child-oriented**. As the teacher pauses to write an anecdote, he or she must observe the child closely. The result is valuable information that can guide the teacher's subsequent decisions about how to support the child. For example, the teacher who has just recorded the "marching band" incident might decide to pick up an instrument and join the marchers.

• Anecdotes such as these help us see the children's *strengths*. By contrast, many common approaches to child observation focus on whether children have reached a particular learning goal. Such approaches tend to focus the adult's attention on what the child can't yet do or didn't do. But observational notes that simply describe what children are saying and doing help the observer discover what is important and significant for *the child*. Thus, the anecdote on Megan, instead of pointing out the fact that she didn't paint a recognizable object, helps us see how she explored the paints, put away her smock, and hung up her own painting. Similarly, the anecdote on Carleen helps us note that she counted 10 holes that didn't have pegs in them; it doesn't mention what she didn't do (interact with the other child). In a similar vein, the anecdote on the marchers tells us that they continued with their band for about 10 minutes—the fact that they didn't play quietly doesn't enter into the picture! Such insights on children's strengths are useful not only to classroom adults but also to parents (see "Using Anecdotes with Parents," facing page).

• Looking at a body of anecdotes gives the team new insights about the **classroom experiences and materials** they are providing. One teaching team found that they had few anecdotes in the *movement* category of key experiences. This lack of anecdotes made them realize there were few movement opportunities for the children in their program, something they hadn't really thought about before. In discussing the lack of move-

By making adults aware of the key experiences children are engaging in, anecdotes strengthen the teacher's understanding of both child development and the educational philosophy of the High/Scope approach. This adult is focusing on children who are playing "hospital," (a creative representation key experience: pretending and role playing).

ment anecdotes, the teachers decided to include movement experiences in their large-group times; they also decided to add to the classroom shelves some simple movement props and sound-making materials: carpet squares, scarves, beanbags, a tape recorder, and tapes. Once the team had made these changes, they found that children included more movement ideas in their plans, and team members found themselves recording many more movement anecdotes.

Thus, in so many ways, **anecdotes enable us to see children and the classroom environment objectively.** Regularly recording child observations helps teachers answer questions like these: What are children's interests? What are the strengths of the program? Are we neglecting any child development areas? Are there materials to support all of the key experience categories? What materials and experiences can we add? Are our routines comfortable for children? Anecdotes help teachers put everything in perspective—the *child's* perspective. In child-centered High/Scope programs, that's right where the focus belongs!

Anecdote-Writing Hints

By Beth Marshall

• •

"There's so much happening in my classroom. Sometimes I feel like there's so much I'm not getting down in my anecdotes."

The above is a familiar lament for many early childhood educators who are just beginning to write anecdotes. If this is a concern of yours, first of all, don't worry. There will always be some things missed! Even experienced note-takers can't get everything down. Keep in mind that as classroom adults, our first priority is to be there for the children, supporting them and interacting with them as co-players. Nevertheless, with some practice, you can take good notes while interacting with children. The key is to integrate taking notes into your normal daily routine. Here are some of our favorite ideas for efficient note-gathering:

• First, **keep plenty of note-taking materials handy** in the classroom. Everyone has a favorite way to record anecdotes (see "Note-Taking Equipment: Some Suggestions"). Find something that works for you, and stock up on what you need.

• Second, if you are just starting to record anecdotes, **set a realistic goal for the total number you wish to record.** An initial goal of perhaps four or five anecdotes daily can help you be successful. Gradually, the anecdote-writing process will become just another part of what you do as a classroom teacher. You'll soon find yourself going beyond your original goal (at least on most days).

Note-Taking "Equipment": Some Suggestions

• Write anecdotes on sticky notes or mailing labels. Simply peel the notes off at the end of the day's session and stick them on the note form for that child.

• Wear a **necklace pen** (available at most office supply stores). This way, you'll never have to hunt for something to write with.

• Talk into a **voice-activated tape recorder.**

• Wear a **shop-type apron** with pockets that will hold a small note pad (or index cards) and a pencil.

• As you discuss them with your teaching team, type your anecdotes, using one of High/Scope's **computer programs,** the **COR–PC** or **COR–Mac.** (For more on these computer programs, see the article "Saving Time With the COR–PC or COR–Mac" on p. 283).

• Another way to simplify the recording process is to realize that **the same anecdote can be used in more than one key experience category.** For example, perhaps a child planned to make a barn out of blocks and then did so. We could record this anecdote under either of two key experience categories: **initiative and social relations** or **creative representation.** *Cross-referencing,* that is, recording the anecdote under one category and making a reference to another, expedites this process. Usually, teachers number the key experience categories to help them with cross-referencing. For example, we could record our anecdote under **creative representation** and write a "3" after it to indicate that it also belongs under **initiative and social relations.**

• Another strategy that eases the task of writing anecdotes is to **share the work.** Don't assume that only classroom adults who are officially "teachers" can write anecdotes. If foster grandparents or parent volunteers have a regular role in your classroom or center, include them in your anecdote-writing process. You might ask your helpers, for example, to take anecdotes for the whole class on one item. In one class, the teachers wanted to know which children were *acting on movement directions,* a **movement** key experience. They gave a parent volunteer a class list with these simple directions: "During large-group time, watch what the children do, and put a check by the names of children who are following our movement directions." At the end of large-group time, the teachers easily wrote up 12 anecdotes for those 12 children the parent had observed.

• Additionally, don't be afraid to **use anecdotes created after the fact from photos, tape recordings, and actual samples** of children's creations. One idea is to use your **instant camera** to help you capture children's art, models, and play structures as they create them. A snapshot of a block structure or a pillow cave provides a quick record of an incident that you can return to later when you produce a written anecdote. Other teachers find it helpful to use a **tape recorder** to capture children's planning and recalling statements. Replaying this tape later may help you collect information on children's use of language and their ability to plan and recall in detail. Another thing you can do is to save the actual item that is the source of an anecdote. Put the child's drawing, writing sample, or painting in his or her portfolio.

ও

In sum, remember that anecdotes are a record of what is happening in the classroom. As you take notes, look for the High/Scope key experiences. In doing so, you'll find yourself recording many typical behaviors as well as those that are new or unique for children.

Rethinking the
IEP Process

By Sandy Slack

• •

It's frustrating when you have to write objectives that don't reflect what you're doing in the classroom. Here I was, trying to support children's active learning and provide developmentally appropriate activities, yet I was still writing objectives that were based on skills—like copying a vertical line or repeating two-digit sequences. It seemed ridiculous! I also felt foolish telling parents that their child hadn't reached this age or that age in a particular skill—specified right down to the month—when I knew that you just can't say exactly when a skill should develop. After an IEP conference with a parent, I would walk away feeling that I'd undermined all my other work in conveying the developmental approach to the family.

The special education teacher quoted above voices a typical concern that teachers have about writing skill-based objectives for children. As a member of an early childhood special education team, I find one of the most exciting developments in my field to be the move toward forming objectives that reflect *developmentally appropriate practices.* This move is due to the fact that many special educators who work with young children are moving away from highly directive teaching. Instead of spending most of their time drilling children on narrow skill sequences, they are providing learning experiences in which children can use the full range of their developing abilities in real-life contexts. In this newer approach, adults focus on children's abilities rather than disabilities and encourage children to initiate their own activities and solve problems.

Support for these developmentally appropriate teaching methods has come from many sources, including professional associations like NAEYC, state departments of education, and institutions that, like High/Scope, offer curriculum training and materials.

However, as more and more of us in the field of early childhood special education have made changes in the ways we work with children, a new problem has arisen: We've become increasingly dissatisfied with the traditional ways of assessing children and developing IEPs (Individualized Educational Plans). Since state and federal law require special educators to do regular assessments and develop IEPs for each child with special needs, this is not an issue we can avoid or minimize.

At Project REACH, our early childhood special education program in Lynchburg, Virginia, we've had firsthand experience with this issue. In 1991, we initiated a staff-training program in the High/Scope Curriculum. Since that time, our special educators have been moving toward full implementation of the High/Scope approach. As we changed our classroom environments, routines, and interaction styles, we realized that we had to make a corresponding shift in our methods of assessing children and developing IEPs. Our assessment and IEP procedures, developed during an era when direct teaching was the prevailing approach, seemed "out of sync" with what was going on in classrooms.

We resolved this problem by reorganizing procedures for child observation, assessment, and IEP development around High/Scope's child assessment instrument—the High/Scope COR (Child Observation Record for Ages 2½–6). In this article, we describe the experience that project REACH has had with COR-based assessment and IEP development, and we offer practical suggestions to other special educators who may want to make a similar transition.

Project REACH is staffed by eight early childhood special educators housed at the Hutcherson Early Learning Center in Lynchburg. Six of these educators are classroom-based, serving 68 young children with special needs, and two work out in the community in various settings. Children who are 2 to 5 years old and at least 25% delayed in one or more areas of development are served.

Although Project REACH classrooms have always been considered "developmentally appropriate," until a few years ago we were actually using a skill-based program. Teachers selected specific skills in children's deficit areas and then artificially taught these skills through teacher-directed activities. This began to change with the decision to implement the High/Scope approach.

What Is an IEP?

Education programs serving children who have special needs are required by federal and state law to develop an Individualized Educational Plan (IEP) for each child who qualifies for special services. The IEP is developed by a team that includes the child's teachers, the parents, and the other professionals who work with the child (occupational, physical, and speech therapists, etc.).

The heart of the IEP is a list of objectives—statements of the educational goals for the child in the upcoming year. Included with each objective is a statement of the criterion to be used to assess whether the objective has been reached.

Each child's IEP is reviewed and updated at regular intervals. In Virginia, for example, state regulations require the IEP team to develop a new IEP each year and to review and update the plan with parents three times a year.

The High/Scope COR is an observational assessment tool. The adult gathers the data for assessment not by administering tests or conducting artificial exercises with children, but by making daily anecdotal notes on children's behavior as they go about their normal activities in the early childhood setting.

As staff worked with our in-house High/Scope certified trainer, they made a huge leap toward practices that truly met the definition of "developmentally appropriate" as put forth in NAEYC guidelines. But our outmoded IEP process was causing frustration for teachers.

Seen in terms of our new understanding of teaching and child development, the IEP objectives we were writing often seemed fragmented, arbitrary, and unrelated to the broad abilities that we knew were important. For example, a typical objective for a 4-year-old might read, "By 6/93, the child will cut a strip of paper ¼-inch wide and 5-inches long."

Our procedures for writing IEPs were closely tied to the assessment instruments we were using, which tended to focus on small, isolated developmental steps involving very specific skills. These instruments usually attached a chronological age to each skill without regard for the wide age-span of normal development in any skill. At age 48 months, for example, one instrument asked us to demonstrate for the child how to fold an 8½-inch x 11-inch paper in half horizontally, then vertically, and then diagonally. To receive credit, the child would be given three trials to imitate the demonstration. In addition, with our old instruments, skills were assessed out of context rather than in real-life situations. For example, we might ask children to repeat digit sequences, instead of noting the same skill when it occurred naturally as children learned fingerplays and songs. Or, we might interrupt a child's play to ask "How do you drink milk? . . . Where do you drink milk?" instead of noting the child's use of similar language in a normal conversation at snack time.

We also noticed major gaps in the content of the old instruments. In our classrooms, we were now encouraging children to make choices and initiate activities on their own. Yet decision-making and initiative were not even included on the assessment tools that were the basis for our IEP goals.

We knew we had to move away from our old ways of assessing children's progress and doing IEPs, but we weren't sure how to proceed. The release of the new High/Scope COR early in 1992 was the catalyst we needed to rethink the IEP process.

Using the High/Scope COR

The High/Scope COR is an *observational* assessment tool. The adult gathers the data for assessment not by administering tests or conducting artificial exercises with children, but by making daily anecdotal notes on children's behavior as they go about their normal activities in the early childhood setting. Six categories of development are covered in the COR: initiative, social relations, creative representation, music and movement, language and literacy, and logic and mathematics. (For more information on the COR, see the articles by Lawrence J. Schweinhart, Charles Hohmann, and Beth Marshall in this chapter.)

By last spring, the Project REACH staff had decided to try to use the new COR as the basis for writing IEP objectives. The certified High/Scope trainer on our staff developed a series of workshops to help us make the transition to the COR.

One of the first steps in our COR training was to learn how to take anecdotal notes and then how to complete the COR. Most of us were accustomed to collecting child-assessment data based on number of trials or time required to complete a task. For each IEP objective, the state requires us to specify a criterion for assessing whether the objective has been reached. For example, the criteria portion of the IEP often had statements like this: "Randomly present to the child, one at a time for five seconds, three flash cards with the numerals 1–3. Child must name each of the three numerals in one try." We would make charts of such statements and check off the objective when the child had satisfied the criterion.

By contrast, the High/Scope COR required us to write short, factual, descriptive anecdotes describing what children did during their everyday

The COR-based assessment offers special educators the tool they need to write educational objectives that are measurable yet broad enough to be achievable through developmentally appropriate practices. They now have a tool available that can facilitate, not hinder, the transition to active learning classrooms.

activities: "During planning, J. pointed to the block area, where he wanted to play, and then pointed to the picture of the block area on the planning cards."

Learning how to take these anecdotal notes took practice. During our training workshops, we practiced taking notes as we observed role-play situations and video footage. Gradually, we got the knack of taking brief, objective notes. We noticed immediately that the "can-do" examples we captured in our anecdotal notes enhanced our ability to see children positively and to communicate children's abilities to parents.

Writing IEP Objectives

The next step for us was to tackle the process of writing IEP objectives that reflected our new approach to teaching and assessment. Because some teachers were apprehensive about making this change, we started cautiously. We went through several rounds of field-testing sample IEPs; teachers worked in pairs and consulted parents as they drafted new IEP objectives.

The IEPs that are developed through a COR-based process are very different from the kind we developed in the past. Our new IEP objectives often reflect such High/Scope Curriculum elements as the **plan-do-review sequence** and children's **active learning, problem solving,** and **initiative.**

Writing COR-Based IEP Objectives

As described in this article, special education teachers in Project REACH have revamped their procedures for writing an IEP (Individualized Educational Plan) to make it more developmentally appropriate and meaningful. The High/Scope COR assessment instrument provides a framework for the new IEP development process. Below are some sample objectives taken from IEPs written by teachers at Project REACH. Note the contrast between IEPs written the "old way" and IEPs written the "COR way."

As you read the examples, think about the following questions: Which objectives encourage or force teachers to stage demonstrations or tests to assess mastery? Which objectives can be assessed during child-initiated activity? How well does each set of objectives capture developmentally significant goals? How do you think each set of objectives will influence the teaching approach used in the classroom?

"Old Way" IEP Objectives

Annual goal: Improve cognitive skills.

Short-term objectives and criteria for evaluation:

By 10/89 student will be able to build a tower 3–4 blocks high using 1-inch cubes 100% of the time, after demonstration.

By 2/90 student will be able to hand to an adult, on request, objects similar to a familiar sample with 75% accuracy.

By 6/90 student will be able to repeat two digits in correct sequence with 75% accuracy.

* * *

Annual goal: Improve functioning in gross-motor skills.

Short-term objectives and criteria for evaluation:

By 10/89 student will be able to climb into adult seat and turn around to sit 90% of the time.

By 2/90 student will be able to walk with one foot on a 3-inch x 6-foot walking board in 100% of trials.

By 6/90 student will be able to walk backward (when behavior is modeled by teacher) a distance of 6 feet in 75% of attempts.

"COR Way" IEP Objectives

Annual goal: [Child's] ability to use a variety of materials to pretend,

---

Also captured in the objectives we write are such traditional IEP areas as gross- and fine-motor development, language, concepts, self-help, and social-emotional development. In all of these areas, we refer to the COR and our anecdotal notes to assess the child's current level of development and to project the next steps in the child's growth.

The following is the process we now use for writing IEP objectives. In special education, state regulations require teachers to track the child's areas of development that are at least 25% delayed. These "areas of need" are the areas for which IEP objectives must be written. We now look for the relevant COR items in each area and use our anecdotal notes to assess the child's level of development on each item. Then, for each item, we go to the next level on the COR scale and find the "next step" in develop-

make and build, draw and/or paint representations of real objects and events will improve by [annual review date of IEP].

Short-term objectives and criteria for evaluation:

By 11/1/92 [child] will be able to use materials to make a simple representation and say or demonstrate what it is as noted in three anecdotes recorded by the teacher and kept in a log of anecdotal notes.

Evaluation procedures and schedule:

Progress will be evaluated three times (11/1/92, 3/1/93, 6/1/93) through developmental observations on the Child Observation Record (COR) based on anecdotal notes that are kept in a log by teachers, staff, and parents and/or mutually agreed upon as the child's consistent behavior by two observers.

* * *

Annual goal: [Child's] ability to express choices and plans and to solve problems while using materials will improve by [annual review date of IEP].

Short-term objectives and criteria for evaluation:

By 11/1/92 [child] will indicate, with a short sentence, desired activity, place of activity, materials, or playmates, as noted in three anecdotes recorded by the teacher and kept in a log of anecdotal notes.

By 3/1/92 [child] will show some persistence in solving problems during play, trying several alternative methods to solve a problem, as noted in three anecdotes recorded by the teacher and kept in a log of anecdotal notes.

By 6/1/93 [child] will indicate, with a short sentence, how plans will be carried out, as noted in three anecdotes recorded by the teacher and kept in a log of anecdotal notes.

Evaluation procedures and schedule:

Progress will be evaluated three times (11/1/92, 3/1/93/, 6/1/93) through developmental observations on the Child Observation Record (COR), based on anecdotal notes that are kept in a log by teachers, staff, and parents and/or mutually agreed upon as the child's consistent behavior by two observers.

ment for that child. These "next steps" then become the basis for the IEP objectives. For example, if our notes indicate that Dean now participates in program routines but does so inconsistently, we would assess him as being at Level 2 of Item D in Section I of the COR ("Child sometimes follows program routines"). We would then look to the COR for the next step in development (Level 3 of Item D: "Child participates in program routines when directed to do so"). That step would then become the basis for the following IEP objective: "By 2/15/93 Dean will participate in program routines when directed to do so, as assessed by the COR." The last phrase, "as assessed by the COR," is included to meet the state requirement that each objective specify an assessment criterion. (For more examples, see "Writing COR-Based IEP Objectives.")

One of the exciting benefits of writing IEPs using the High/Scope COR, as described here, is that the parent's knowledge of their child becomes more important. Since the COR gives both teachers and parents awareness of the next step expected in a child's development, parents are primed to report changes to us. For example, the parents of one child, Jennifer, told us in September, "Jennifer is putting two words together at home, although some words are still hard to understand." This helped us successfully project that by January, Jennifer would probably be doing the same thing at nursery school.

We've found that with the COR as a frame of reference, teachers are less likely to write IEP objectives before they've had a chance to confer with parents, because they have so many anecdotal notes to share with the parent and because they want information on the child's home behavior before projecting the child's growth for the next school year. When parents and teachers share and compare observations in this way, the result is a more accurate picture of the child's abilities and expected growth.

Modifying the High/Scope COR for Developmentally Younger Children

Another reason the High/Scope COR has been so useful to us is that as we have used it to formulate IEP objectives, we've gradually found ways to modify it to suit our group of children. Once REACH teachers began their efforts to implement COR-based assessment and planning, they soon found themselves grappling with a common problem: Because many of the children were functioning at a level below age 2½ years and were progressing slowly, the teachers needed to fine-tune the instrument so it would more accurately reflect the range of the children's abilities.

With the support of a High/Scope staff member who had helped to produce the COR, we developed some additional COR items that would capture some of the earlier stages of development and that would measure the smaller changes typical of developmentally delayed children.

At Project REACH we do not use the statements indicating the first level on most COR items, which typically start with the phrase, "Child does not yet . . . ." When children have special needs, statements like this are not specific enough to describe the range of behaviors that fall within this level. In addition, because these are statements of what children cannot do, they cannot be used as the basis for IEP objectives, which are stated in terms of what a child *will do*.

During a weekly staff meeting, we decided to work in teams to look at each COR category and develop items that would occur before the beginning COR age of 2½ years. Teams met weekly for a month. The physical, occupational, and speech therapists were included on the teams. Each team drafted possible additions to the COR, and the drafts were exchanged, commented on, and revised. We tried to keep our additions to a minimum, our wording as much like the COR as possible, and our examples as specific as the COR's examples. We also decided to stay with the COR format of five levels for each item. Instead of adding to the number of levels, which would have changed the scoring of every item, we assigned decimal values to the new items.

At the right, we give an excerpt from a modified COR that reflects the kinds of additions we have made to the instrument. In the example, the Level .5 statement is a new one, added to accommodate developmentally younger children, and the Level 1 statement has been rephrased to make it specific and positive.

We've also found that it's sometimes necessary to modify a specific child's COR by adding smaller steps between existing COR items. For example, in the excerpt, the Level 2.5 statement is new—this was a half-step added to one child's COR to capture the slow but definite progress she was making. When we make modifications like this for particular children, we note them on the child's COR booklet as we're writing the IEP. With modifications such as this, the new High/Scope COR provides an even more useful picture of children's developing abilities.

We feel that this new process of COR-based assessment offers us, as special edu-

Excerpt From Modified COR

Section I: Initiative
A. Expressing choices

.5 Child indicates interest with visual attention to object or activities. *[New item]*

1 Child indicates a choice by reaching, picking up, or manipulating objects. *[New item: replaces "Child does not yet express choices to others."]*

2 Child indicates a desired activity or place of activity by saying a word, pointing, or some other action.

2.5 Child indicates a desired activity, place of activity, materials, or playmates with a two- or three-word phrase, such as "Me ride" or "Play Carol." *[New item.]*

3 Child indicates with a short sentence the desired activity, place of activity, materials, or playmates.

4 Child indicates with a short sentence how plans will be carried out ("I want to drive the truck on the road").

5 Child gives detailed description of intended actions ("I want to make a road out of blocks with Sara and drive the truck on it").

Note: High/Scope does not recommend using the decimal items to compute a total COR score, since they have not been scaled with the rest of the COR. The revised items are intended to be used as descriptors rather than as quantitative indicators of development.

cators, the tool we need to write educational objectives that are measurable yet broad enough to be achievable through developmentally appropriate practices. We now have a tool available that can facilitate, not hinder, our transition to active learning classrooms.

Other special educators may want to use a similar COR-based process to make their assessment and IEP procedures more useful and meaningful. Each program, however, will need to adapt our procedures to accommodate their state's legal guidelines and the specific needs of the children served.

Appendix:
Related High/Scope Press Materials

Early Childhood Curriculum

Print Materials

Educating Young Children: Active Learning Practices in Preschool and Child Care Programs, M. Hohmann and D. P. Weikart, 1995

High/Scope Extensions—Newsletter of the High/Scope Curriculum, N. Brickman, Ed., 6 issues/year

Supporting Young Learners, N. Brickman, Ed., 1991

High/Scope Buyer's Guide to Children's Software, 11th Ed., C. Hohmann, B. Carmody, and C. McCabe-Branz, 1995

Program Implementation Profile: Administration Manual, 1989

A School Administrator's Guide to Early Childhood Programs, L. J. Schweinhart, 1988

High/Scope Child Observation Record (COR) for Ages 2^1/$_2$–6 (kit), 1995

The Early Childhood Playground: An Outdoor Classroom, S. Esbensen, 1987

Head Start Program Manager's Guide, D. McClelland and B. McDonald, 1984

Movement in Steady Beat, P. S. Weikart, 1990

Movement Plus Music: Activities for Children Ages 3 to 7, 2nd Ed., P. S. Weikart, 1989

Movement Plus Rhymes, Songs, & Singing Games, P. S. Weikart, 1988

Round the Circle: Key Experiences in Movement for Children, P. S. Weikart, 1987

The Teacher's Idea Book: Daily Planning Around the Key Experiences, M. Graves, 1989

The Teacher's Idea Book 2: Planning Around Children's Interests, M. Graves, in press

Young Children & Computers, C. Hohmann, 1990

Other Media

High/Scope COR-PC kit (software package), 1994

High/Scope COR-Mac kit (software package), 1995

Computer Learning for Young Children (video), 1989

Bilingual Media for Teachers Series (videos):

    1. *Naturalistic Language Learning*
    2. *Using the Community as a Classroom*
    3. *Supporting Cultural Awareness in Young Children*

Experiencing and Representing Series (videos):

    1. *A Way Children Learn*
    2. *Starting With Direct Experience*
    3. *From Direct Experience to Representation*
    4. *Strategies for Supporting Representational Activity*

Guidelines for Evaluating Activities Series (videos):

    1. *Contrasting Teaching Styles: Small-Group Time*

2. *Contrasting Teaching Styles: Work Time, The Art Area*
3. *Contrasting Teaching Styles: Circle Time*

Helping Children Make Choices and Decisions Series (videos):
1. *A Good Classroom Is a Classroom Full of Choices*
2. *Questions That Help Children Develop Their Ideas*
3. *Exploring the Possibilities of the Room*
4. *Acknowledging Children's Choices and Decisions*
5. *Planning Activities That Include Choices*

Adult-Child Interactions: Forming Partnerships With Children (video), in press
The High/Scope Curriculum: Its Implementation in Family Childcare Homes (video), 1989
Setting Up the Learning Environment (video), 1992
The High/Scope Curriculum: The Daily Routine (video), 1990
The High/Scope Curriculum: The Plan-Do-Review Process (video), 1989
Learning About Time in the Preschool Years (video)

Small-Group Time Media Package (videos), 1988:
1. *Counting With Bears*
2. *Plan-Do-Review With Found Materials*
3. *Working With Staplers*
4. *Representing With Sticks & Balls*
5. *Exploring With Paint & Corks*

Spatial Learning in the Preschool Years (video)
Supporting Children's Active Learning: Teaching Strategies for Diverse Settings (video), 1989
Supporting Communication Among Preschoolers (3 videos)
Thinking and Reasoning in Preschool Children (video)

Elementary Curriculum

Print Materials

Elementary Curriculum Guides:

Foundations in Elementary Education: Overview, C. Hohmann, 1996
Foundations in Elementary Education: Movement, P. S. Weikart and E. B. Carlton, 1995
Foundations in Elementary Education: Music, E. B. Carlton and P. S. Weikart, 1994
Learning Environment, C. Hohmann and W. Buckleitner, 1992
Language and Literacy, J. Maehr, 1991
Mathematics, C. Hohmann, 1991
Science, F. Blackwell and C. Hohmann, 1991

Learning Through Sewing and Pattern Design, S. Mainwaring, 1976
Learning Through Construction, S. Mainwaring and C. Shouse, 1983

Elementary Science Activity Series:

Life and Environment, F. F. Blackwell, 1996
Energy and Change, F. F. Blackwell, in press
Structure and Form, F. F. BLackwell, in press

Teaching Movement & Dance: A Sequential Approach to Rhythmic Movement,
    3rd Ed., P. S. Weikart, 1989

Dance Notations—Teaching Movement & Dance, 3rd Ed., P. S. Weikart, 1989

Guide to Rhythmically Moving 1, E. B. Carlton and P. S. Weikart, 1996

Guide to Rhythmically Moving 2, E. B. Carlton and P. S. Weikart, in press

Other Media

Elementary Curriculum Video Series:
    Active Learning, 1991
    Classroom Environment, 1991
    Language & Literacy, 1990
    Mathematics, 1990

Foundations in Elementary Education: Music, Recordings, E. B. Carlton and
    P. S. Weikart, Coproducers, 1995

Rhythmically Moving 1–9 (records, cassettes, CDS), P. S. Weikart, Creative Director

Changing Directions 1–6 (records, cassettes, CDS), P. S. Weikart, Creative Director

Beginning Folk Dances Illustrated 1–5 (5 videos), P. S. Weikart, 1988, 1989, 1991, 1996

Adolescent Education

Print Materials

Learning Comes to Life: An Active Learning Program for Teens, E. M. Ilfeld, 1996

Program Guidebook Series, S. Oden and D. Weikart, et al., 1994:
    1. *Introduction*
    2. *Workshops*
    3. *Work Projects*
    4. *Evening Programs*
    5. *Room Groups*

For and About Parents

Print Materials

*Designing, Leading, and Evaluating Workshops for Teachers and Parents: A Manual
    for Trainers and Leadership Personnel in Early Childhood Education,*
    J. Diamondstone, 1989

A Guide to Developing Community-Based Family Support Programs, A. Epstein,
    M. Larner, and R. Halpern, 1995

Generation to Generation: Realizing the Promise of Family Literacy, J. S. Brizius and
    S. E. Foster, 1993

Community Self-Help: The Parent-to-Parent Program, 1983

Involving Parents: A Handbook for Participation in Schools, P. Lyons, A. Robbins,
    and A. Smith, 1984

Involving Parents in Nursery and Infant Schools, B. Tizard, J. Mortimore,
    and B. Burchell, 1983

Supporting the Changing Family: A Guide to the Parent-to-Parent Model, B. Reschly, 1979
Activities for Parent-Child Interaction, J. Evans, 1982
Getting Involved: Workshops for Parents, E. Frede, 1984
Good Beginnings: Parenting in the Early Years, J. Evans and E. Ilfeld, 1982

Other Media

Troubles and Triumphs at Home Series (videos):
1. *When "I've Told You a Thousand Times" Isn't Enough*
2. *Converting Conflict to Calm*
3. *Let Them Do It*
4. *Let Them Say It*

Public Policy & Research

Print Materials

High/Scope Monographs:

Longitudinal Results of the Ypsilanti Perry Preschool Project, D. P. Weikart, D. J. Deloria, S. A. Lawser, and R. Wiegerink, 1970 (reprint 1993)

The Ypsilanti Perry Preschool Project: Preschool Years and Longitudinal Results Through Fourth Grade, D. P. Weikart, J. T. Bond, and J. T. McNeil, 1978

An Economic Analysis of the Ypsilanti Perry Preschool Project, C. U. Weber, P. W. Foster, and D. P. Weikart, 1978

Young Children Grow Up: The Effects of the Perry Preschool Program on Youths Through Age 15, L. J. Schweinhart and D. P. Weikart, 1980

Changed Lives: The Effects of the Perry Preschool Program on Youths Through Age 19, J. Berrueta-Clement, L. J. Schweinhart, W. S. Barnett, A. S. Epstein, and D. P. Weikart, 1984

Significant Benefits: The High/Scope Perry Preschool Study Through Age 27, L. J. Schweinhart, H. V. Barnes, and D. P. Weikart, with W. S. Barnett and A. S. Epstein, 1993

Lives in the Balance: Age-27 Benefit-Cost Analysis of the High/Scope Perry Preschool Program, W. S. Barnett, in press

The Ypsilanti Preschool Curriculum Demonstration Project: Preschool Years and Longitudinal Results, D. P. Weikart, A. S. Epstein, L. J. Schweinhart, and J. T. Bond, 1978

Consequences of Three Preschool Curriculum Models Through Age 15, L. J. Schweinhart, D. P. Weikart, and M. B. Larner, 1986

Lasting Differences: The High/Scope Preschool Curriculum Comparison Study Through Age 23, L. J. Schweinhart and D. P. Weikart, (in press)

Training for Quality: Improving Early Childhood Programs Though Systematic Inservice Training, A. S. Epstein, 1993

Home Teaching with Mothers and Infants: The Ypsilanti-Carnegie Infant Education Project, An Experiment, D. A. Lambie, J. T. Bond, and D. P. Weikart, 1974

The Longitudinal Follow-Up of the Ypsilanti-Carnegie Infant Education Project, A. S. Epstein and D. P. Weikart, 1979

IEA Preprimary Project Series:

How Nations Serve Young Children: Profiles of Child Care and Education in 14 Countries, P. Olmsted and D. P Weikart, Eds., 1989

Families Speak: Early Childhood Care and Education in 11 Countries, P. Olmsted and D. P. Weikart, Eds., 1994

Challenging the Potential: Programs for Talented Disadvantaged Youth, S. Oden, M. Kelly, Z. Ma, and D. P. Weikart, 1992

Models of Early Childhood Education, A. S. Epstein, L. J. Schweinhart, and L. McAdoo, 1996.

The Twelve Who Survive, 2nd Ed., R. Myers, 1995

Improving Life Chances for Young Children, R. Egbert (Ed.), 1989

Jerome Bruner Preschool Series, 1980:

1. *Under Five in Britain,* J. Bruner
2. *Childwatching at Playgroup and Nursery School,* K. Sylva, C. Roy, and M. Painter
3. *Children and Minders,* B. Bryant, M. Harris, and D. Newton
4. *Children and Day Nurseries,* C. Garland and S. White
5. *Working With Under Fives,* D. Wood, L. McMahon, and Y. Cranstoun
6. *Parents and Preschool,* T. Smith

Compensatory Education in the Preschool: A Canadian Approach, M. Wright, 1983

When Churches Mind the Children, E. W. Lindner, M. C. Mattis, and J. R. Rogers, 1983

Other Media

High/Scope International Videotape Series—Sights and Sounds of Children:

(15 videos–*Belgium, China, Finland, Greece, Hong Kong, Indonesia, Italy, Nigeria, Poland, Romania, Slovenia, South Korea, Spain, Thailand, United States),* 1994

High/Scope Perry Preschool Study Through Age 27 (video), 1993

This is the Way We Go to School (video)

TO ORDER ANY OF THESE HIGH/SCOPE PUBLICATIONS,
PLEASE CONTACT

HIGH/SCOPE PRESS
600 NORTH RIVER STREET
YPSILANTI, MI 48198-2898
800-40-PRESS
FAX 800-442-4FAX

Index

About the Authors

Carol Beardmore is a High/Scope educational consultant and Demonstration Preschool teacher. She first joined High/Scope as a member of the Research Division, working on a 15-nation international preprimary study. Prior to that she had several years of preschool teaching experience.

Frank Blackwell has been a classroom teacher and headmaster at the early childhood, primary, and secondary levels. He was involved in developing children's science curricula during the 1960s as a Nuffield Foundation Research Fellow in Science Education. His contributions to science education extend to radio and television, where he has served as a scriptwriter, consultant, and researcher for science programming. Now a senior advisor to the president of the High/Scope Educational Research Foundation, he is a consultant for High/Scope's elementary curriculum series and coauthor of *Science* in that series. His most recent publication, in press, is the three-volume *Elementary Science Activity Series.*

Barbara Carmody, a former High/Scope teacher-trainer and Demonstration Preschool teacher, is Director of the Head Start and State Preschool of the Hemet Unified School District in California. While at High/Scope, she assisted elementary school teachers in integrating computer technology into their classroom programs and coauthored the *High/Scope Buyer's Guide to Children's Software*, 11th Edition. Before coming to High/Scope, she taught both preschool and elementary school and was also employed as an associate editor for CTB McGraw-Hill.

Betsy Evans, Director and Head Teacher at Giving Tree School in Gill, Massachusetts, has been teaching young children since 1974. Also a High/Scope adjunct trainer, she conducts Lead Teacher Training Programs throughout the United States and has been instrumental in developing High/Scope training materials on conflict resolution.

Michelle Graves, who has teaching experience in early childhood special education, preschool, and elementary school programs, is a High/Scope consultant. She formerly directed the child care program for employees of the Veterans Administration Medical Center, Ann Arbor. At High/Scope Graves conducts a variety of training projects for early childhood educators. She developed High/Scope's *Small-Group Time* video series and authored *The Teacher's Idea Book: Daily Planning Around the Key Experiences.* She is currently writing *The Teacher's Idea Book 2: Planning Around Children's Interests.*

Sam Hannibal is a High/Scope educational consultant who has taught in the Demonstration Preschool and worked with preschool and elementary educators throughout the United States. He currently directs the High/Scope Visitor Program and helps to coordinate the Annual High/Scope Registry Conference.

Vincent Harris, now retired, is a former High/Scope educational consultant. While at High/Scope, he conducted training workshops on playground safety and design for early childhood educators and directed High/Scope workshop programs for talented disadvantaged teenagers.

Charles Hohmann has been a leader in the development of the High/Scope approach to elementary education from 1972 to the present. During this time, he has been deeply involved in elementary staff development through such projects as National Follow Through, Native American School Improvement through the Bureau of Indian Affairs, the High/Scope IBM Technology Demonstration Partnerships, and various High/Scope teacher education programs. He is the author of the *Overview* and *Mathematics* volumes in High/Scope's elementary curriculum series and coauthor of the *Learning Environment* and *Science* volumes. He also wrote *Young Children and Computers* and coauthored the *High/Scope Buyer's Guide to Children's Software,* 11th Edition.

Mary Hohmann, a High/Scope educational consultant and former Demonstration Preschool teacher, has conducted a variety of training projects for preschool educators throughout the United States and overseas. She is coauthor of the High/Scope preschool manual *Educating Young Children: Active Learning Practices for Preschool and Child Care Programs* and is currently developing a study guide for use with the manual.

Diana Jo Johnston is a High/Scope educational consultant. A former elementary teacher and administrator, she conducts High/Scope training projects for both preschool and elementary teachers and for administrators throughout the United States. She also develops materials for the Training of Trainers projects.

Beth Marshall, a teacher and trainer in the early childhood field for over 12 years, has been a High/Scope educational consultant since 1991. She has also taught in the High/Scope Demonstration Preschool.

Becki Perrett is a former High/Scope educational consultant and Demonstration Preschool teacher. She now directs Partners in Parenting, a company that specializes in parent-involvement workshops and training materials.

Jackie Post is a High/Scope adjunct trainer who specializes in providing workshops for infant and toddler caregivers. She is currently developing High/Scope's manual for adults who work with infants and toddlers.

Lawrence J. Schweinhart, Chair of High/Scope's Research Division, is a policy consultant who addresses policymakers, educators, and early childhood advocates throughout the United States. He is also a nationally recognized author and researcher instrumental in the High/Scope Perry Preschool Project, the High/Scope Preschool Curriculum Comparison Study, and other studies that reveal the lasting human and economic value of good early childhood programs. He has taught early childhood courses at High/Scope, the University of Missouri at Columbia, and Indiana University at Bloomington.

Sandy Slack, a High/Scope adjunct trainer, is an early childhood special educator and trainer for the Lynchburg City Schools in Virginia. She has used the High/Scope approach since 1981 with children in preschool through fifth grade.

Ruth Strubank, a former High/Scope educational consultant and lead teacher in the Demonstration Preschool, is now employed as an education specialist for the City of Phoenix Human Services Head Start Program. As an advocate for children and families at risk, she does teacher training for programs serving children at risk.

Susan M. Terdan, a High/Scope educational consultant, trains and works with educators both nationally and internationally. Prior to joining the High/Scope staff, she used the High/Scope approach for eight years in the Walker, Minnesota, school system in an early education classroom serving handicapped children 3 to 6 years old.

Mark Tompkins is an elementary school principal in East Grand Rapids, Michigan. Formerly, he was a High/Scope educational consultant who conducted introductory curriculum awareness workshops and Training of Trainers projects for educators in the United States and overseas.

David P. Weikart, founder and President of High/Scope Educational Research Foundation, instituted the High/Scope Preschool Curriculum in the 1960s, when he initiated two longitudinal preschool research studies, the High/Scope Perry Preschool Project and the High/Scope Preschool Curriculum Comparison Study. Dr. Weikart also established the High/Scope Institute for IDEAS, a program for talented disadvantaged adolescents. In addition to speaking frequently to a variety of audiences on the long-term benefits of high-quality early childhood education, he has written numerous books and journal articles in the fields of education and psychology.

One of Dr. Weikart's recent publications is the High/Scope preschool manual *Educating Young Children*, which he coauthored with Mary Hohmann.

*L*inda Weikel, a former preschool teacher and "quality improvement" trainer, has been a High/Scope educational consultant since 1994. She conducts training projects for preschool teachers in the United States and overseas and works on the development and improvement of High/Scope training materials.